The Past, Present, and Future
of Evangelical Mission

Evangelical Missiological Society Monograph Series

Anthony Casey, Allen Yeh, Mark Kreitzer, and Edward L. Smither
SERIES EDITORS

———————————

A Project of the Evangelical Missiological Society
www.emsweb.org

The Past, Present, and Future of Evangelical Mission

Academy, Agency, Assembly, and Agora
Perspectives from Canada

EDITED BY
Narry F. Santos
AND
Xenia Ling-Yee Chan

FOREWORD BY
Gary V. Nelson

☙PICKWICK *Publications* · Eugene, Oregon

THE PAST, PRESENT, AND FUTURE OF EVANGELICAL MISSION
Academy, Agency, Assembly, and Agora Perspectives from Canada

Evangelical Missiological Society Monograph Series 15

Copyright © 2022 Wipf and Stock Publishers. All rights reserved. Except for brief quotations in critical publications or reviews, no part of this book may be reproduced in any manner without prior written permission from the publisher. Write: Permissions, Wipf and Stock Publishers, 199 W. 8th Ave., Suite 3, Eugene, OR 97401.

Pickwick Publications
An Imprint of Wipf and Stock Publishers
199 W. 8th Ave., Suite 3
Eugene, OR 97401

www.wipfandstock.com

PAPERBACK ISBN: 978-1-6667-3096-8
HARDCOVER ISBN: 978-1-6667-2296-3
EBOOK ISBN: 978-1-6667-2297-0

Cataloguing-in-Publication data:

Names: Santos, Narry F., editor. | Chan, Xenia Ling-Yee, editor. | Nelson, Gary V., foreword.

Title: The past, present, and future of evangelical mission : academy, agency, assembly, and agora perspectives from Canada / edited by Narry F. Santos and Xenia Ling-Yee Chan ; foreword by Gary V. Nelson.

Description: Eugene, OR: Pickwick Publications, 2022 | Evangelical Missiological Society Monograph Series 15 | Includes bibliographical references.

Identifiers: ISBN 978-1-6667-3096-8 (paperback) | ISBN 978-1-6667-2296-3 (hardcover) | ISBN 978-1-6667-2297-0 (ebook)

Subjects: LCSH: Missions, Canadian

Classification: BV2121 P378 2022 (print) | BV2121 (ebook)

04/20/23

All Scripture quotations, unless otherwise indicates, are taken from the Holy Bible, New International Version®, NIV® Copyright ©1973, 1978, 1984, 2011 by Biblica, Inc.™ Used by permission of Zondervan. All rights reserved worldwide. www.zondervan.com. The "NIV" and "New international Version" are trademarks registered in the United States Patent and Trademark Office by Biblica, Inc.™

Scripture references marked NASB are taken from the NEW AMERICAN STANDARD BIBLE, copyright © 1960, 1962, 1963, 1968, 1971, 1972, 1973, 1975, 1977, 1995 by The Lockman Foundation. All rights reserved. Used by permission. http://www.Lockman.org.

Scripture references marked NRSV are taken from New Revised Standard Version Bible, copyright © 1989 National Council of the Churches of Christ in the United States of America. Used by permission. All rights reserved worldwide.

Scripture references marked NLT are taken from New Living Translation, copyright © 1996, 2004, 2015 by Tyndale House Foundation. Used by permission of Tyndale House Publishers Inc., Carol Stream, Illinois 60188. All rights reserved.

Scripture references marked ERV are taken from the Holy Bible: Easy-to-Read (ERV), International Edition © 2013, 2016 by Bible League International and used by permission.

Contents

List of Figures | x

Foreword | xi
   GARY V. NELSON

Preface | xv
   NARRY F. SANTOS

Introduction: The Prophetic Past and New Imagination for the Present and Future: Clarifying Evangelical Mission in Canada | xix
   XENIA LING-YEE CHAN

Part 1: Mission in Retrospect and Prospect

1. The Past, Present, and Future of Evangelical Missology | 3
   SAM GEORGE

Response to "The Past, Present, and Future of Evangelical Missology" | 15
   SHU-LING LEE

2. Mission Then and Future: Uncreating the Past and Disengaging from Empire | 19
   TERRY LEBLANC

Response to "Mission Then and Future: Uncreating the Past and Disengaging from Empire" | 33
   CLAUDIA ROSSETTO

Part 2: Past Christian Mission and its Relevance to Present Mission

3. Ancient–Future Mission: Clement of Alexandria and Contextual Mission in Late Antiquity | 41
   MATTHEW FRIEDMAN

4. Striking a Hopeful Pose: Extending Ralph Winter's Ten Epochs of Redemptive History | 54
   GLENN MARTIN

5. The Proper Place for a Woman: Submitting to the Original Ideals of the Chinese and Korean Church | 68
   LISA HAMNI PAK AND XENIA LING-YEE CHAN

Part 3: Present Evangelical Mission and its Relevance to Future Mission

6. "Diversity Is a Fact; Inclusion Is a Choice": Is Multiculturalism "Bad" for the Church in Canada? | 85
   SHERMAN LAU

7. Churches Together: Mission-Engaged Differentiated Unity as a Hermeneutic of the Gospel | 98
   DAVE WITT

8. Healing of Memories: Reconciling the Church for the Reconciliation of Community | 112
   MANUEL BÖHM

9. Power and Participation in Evangelical Mission | 125
   MARILYN DRAPER

CONTENTS

Part 4: Present and Future of Workplace Mission

10. The Business of Mission: An *Imago Dei* Model for
    Workplace as Mission | 139
    LAURIE GEORGE BUSUTTIL AND SUSAN J. VAN WEELDEN

11. Renewing the Role of the Church in Cross-Cultural
    Marketplace Ministry | 152
    JONATHAN FULLER

Conclusion: Surfacing Significant Changes in our Understanding,
    Attitudes, and Actions toward Evangelical Mission | 171
    NARRY F. SANTOS

List of Contributors | 181

List of Figures

Figure 1   Openness to Pastors in Sending Marketplace Workers | 158
Figure 2   Churches that Have Sent Cross-Cultural Marketplace Workers | 159
Figure 3   Location Where Marketplace Workers Have Been Sent | 160
Figure 4   List of Cross-Cultural Marketplace Roles | 161
Figure 5   Church Engagement with Marketplace Workers | 162
Figure 6   Church Support for Marketplace Mission Thinking | 163
Figure 7   Issues Affecting Marketplace Workers' Effectiveness | 165

Foreword

GARY V. NELSON

IN 2000, JAMES ENGEL and William Dyrness published a book entitled *Changing the Mind of Missions: Where Have We Gone Wrong?* The authors' intent was to offer a courageous analysis of the challenges facing North American and the Western Christian idea of missions at the turn of the century. The book explored the broad global and societal shifts that were shaping and impacting mission around the world. Their observations appear almost simplistic today. One particular observation was the reality that the challenge of missions was no longer an "over there" reality. This theme weaves its way through the book as they muse on a desire to recapture the vitality and comprehensiveness of the Gospel for the complex plight of today's world.

At the time, this book elicited great conversations. In 2000, I had just arrived in the city of Toronto to direct an established denominational mission organization in need of a serious rethink. Toronto was a hotbed of God's work of bringing the diaspora from around the world to what was quickly becoming the most multicultural city in that world. Engels and Dyrness' conclusion of mission no longer being 'over there' was amusingly simplistic within the context of Toronto. This was obvious and we did need a rethink, but we also needed something much more than a "change of mind."

I had come to this established mission organization from having served as a pastor involved in the renewing of an old downtown church. We had undergone a significant transformation both in a missional and global mindset. To be "missional" had not yet become popularized even in its watered-down version at the turn of the century. The "p" word—postmodernism—was an unexplored buzz word for change. We were both (missional and postmodern), but we had few hooks on which to hang our hats as we grappled with the new society taking shape around us. Still, we did have a nagging feeling that old assumptions and measurements of effectiveness needed to be challenged. They were no longer adequate for the day.

Engel and Dyrness were dealing with the same "not yet" aspects of change that are being explored in their book. They too were grappling with something that had not yet taken shape. They did not have the luxury of hindsight. My guess is that they were simply grappling with the distressing doubts that the world which at one time shaped all of our thinking was being deeply interrupted. They were aware that it would never return to the way it was but were still stuck in the binary idea that if it did not look like "this" then it would look like "that."

Ten years later in 2010, I became President of Tyndale University, the home of Tyndale Seminary, the largest graduate school of theology in Canada. With over 60 people groups represented in its student body and about the same number of denominations, we were tasked to form the next generation of leaders who would become the leaders of the church, mission organizations, and professors.

All this is to say that I have served in all three settings—the Academy, Agency, and Assembly. If I have learned anything in these last years, it is certainly the conviction that the shifts which were once nagging instinctual doubts, are now clearly taking root. In these years, I have also learned, that any book that points to the future—no matter how confidently written, are not written in stone and are not necessarily accurate in their prognostications. A humble sensibility is required. A multitude of perspectives are necessary. It is for this reason that I celebrate the work of Narry Santos and Xenia Ling-Yee Chan. They have compiled the voices of varied writers, the perspectives of many cultural frames and the richness of several personal stories in order to provide possible directions and opportunities.

I highly recommend this book. It is a compendium around a thematic thread in the context of four influencing forces—the Assembly, Agency, Academy, and Agora. These types of compendiums are what is needed to consider future needs and trends. They bring various observers and practitioners together with all of their varied experiences and backgrounds into a conversation about the present and the future. These times demand a rediscovery of dialogue and a skill set of profound listening for different perspectives that give us a more fulsome understanding of future possibilities and directions.

You will notice that the book is as diverse as the writers who presented at the consultation. Women, men, Indigenous/First Nations, people of vastly different cultural and racial backgrounds. In a time where the greatest body of writing in Christian thought is still too white and male, this book is refreshing. Still, these presenters struggle with having been shaped by a western theological framework that formed them. They are kicking against the walls of containment and restriction that influenced them deeply so as to be free to consider strategies for our time.

At a conference I attended a few years ago, I listened to a Turkish Christian academic present his theological paper. I do not remember the content of his paper, but I do remember his introduction to the presentation. He posed a question that has haunted me since that day. "How come, when I do theology," he mused, "it is placed in the framework of contextual theology and when N.T. Wright does theology, it is simply theology? Is not all theology contextual?" For this and this alone, you need to hear from a multitude of voices of theology and praxis. Through them, through these contributors, our worlds can be expanded, and our assumptions challenged.

This book can be a launching pad for you. It is more descriptive than prescriptive. At no point do any of the contributors prescribe "10 steps to a better missiological strategy." Instead, they offer their thoughts and questions about what they are personally experiencing. The book offers a buffet of ideas and reflections focused on a way to address the new forces shaping culture and society. They offer a way forward in which the timelessness of the Gospel's good news of Jesus Christ can be made flesh in a complex and utterly uncontainable world. They are like all theological reflections, contextual in their nature and revolutionary in their impact.

This is a book that must be read not simply because it acknowledges the changes taking place but because it understands that it is in the listening and comprehending that the influencing forces of academy, assembly, agency, and agora will rediscover their synergistic roles. It is written from the assumption that we need a better collaborative model that allows each of these institutions to play their unique role in influencing missional and ministry responses. So, feast at the table of these reflections and ponder how they might shape the places from which you lead and the context for which you are responsible. Come to the table and do not just change your mind but let them shape your attitudes, responses, and heart.

Preface

NARRY F. SANTOS

THIS EDITED VOLUME, *The Past and Future of Evangelical Mission: Academy, Agency, Assembly, and Agora Perspectives from Canada*, is a result of the Evangelical Missiological Society (EMS) Canada Regional Meeting in March 2020. The theme of the annual regional meeting in Canada, along with the other seven regional events in the US, is captured in the main title of this volume. The EMS Canada 2020 conference had 24 papers, six tracks, and three plenary presentations with responses from four centers (Tyndale University in Toronto, Ontario; Canada Institute of Linguistics in Langley, British Columbia; Ambrose University in Calgary, Alberta; and Steinbach Bible College in Steinbach, Manitoba). The Ontario and British Columbia centers were able to conduct their simultaneous events in person, while the Alberta and Manitoba centers could not because of the COVID-19 lockdown protocols. Instead of their in-person sessions, the latter centers received the video recordings of the three plenary presentations and responses, along with the copies of paper presentations in their province.

What is unique in this year's compendium is the inclusion of insights from the agora Christian sector in society. In the first two EMS Canada volumes (*Mission and Evangelism in a Secularizing World* and *Mission Amid Global Crises*), we were able to hear significant voices from the Canadian academy (seminary/university/Bible college), agency (mission group/denomination/parachurch), and assembly (local church). In this current volume, we can finally hear major voices from the agora (marketplace/business/tentmaking)—voices that are usually missing in missiological conversations. Along with the academy, agency, and assembly, the agora voices need to be heard fully, especially as we consider the future of evangelical mission in

Canada. In the last chapter of this volume, Fuller issues the following clarion call on the crucial role of church in marketplace mission:

> Theological and cross-cultural knowledge and experience is available through the agency and the academy, but traditional delivery methods do not work well for marketplace workers. Churches need to coordinate better with agency and academy leaders to provide accessible training opportunities, including in-service and on-line models that fit well with marketplace realities.

The book is divided into four major parts. The first part ("Mission in Retrospect and Prospect") comprises two plenary presentations that present thought-provoking perspectives on mission—a sobering look at the past and an optimistic outlook about the future of North American evangelical missiology from an immigrant mindset, and a prophetic challenge in viewing Western mission through indigenous eyes. Since this edition seeks to showcase various voices, the plenary presentation from the agency (chapter 1) is followed by a response from the assembly, while the plenary presentation from the academy (chapter 2) is followed by a response from the agency. The second major part ("Past Christian Mission and its Relevance to Present Mission") highlights three papers that handle how Christian writings in late antiquity relate to contemporary contextual mission, how reflections in the past several decades on epochs in redemptive mission bring hope for future mission, and how a historical-theological exposition of the proper place of women in ministry from immigrant cultural contexts can invite current churches to welcome emerging young women leaders.

The third major part ("Present Evangelical Mission and its Relevance to Future Mission") contain four papers that reflect on relevant Canadian realities—discussing how to view multiculturalism differently can positively influence mission and church, how city engagement by a network of churches can yield differentiated unity, and social and spiritual transformation, how churches in conflict can take part in reconciliation of community for the healing of memories, and how a fresh look at power and participation can revitalize evangelical mission. The fourth and final part ("Present and Future of Workplace Mission") presents two papers on the value of God's mission in the workplace—one paper offering a theology of workplace mission through the *imago Dei* (or image of God), and the other paper emphasizing the integral role of the church in cross-cultural marketplace ministry.

In addition to the plurality of Canadian voices coming from the academy, agency, assembly, and agora, this volume offers more diverse perspectives and backgrounds (from women and men; from indigenous, immigrant, and Euro-Canadians; from coast to coast to coast; from first-generation and second-generation leaders)—all reflecting on the lessons and relevance of evangelical mission's past and future. As coeditors, Xenia Chan and I come from different backgrounds and contexts but have the shared desire to gather diverse Canadian voices that reflect on evangelical mission through EMS Canada.

Xenia and I would like to thank all the paper, plenary, and response presenters at the EMS Canada 2020 regional meeting, the chapter contributors who revised their papers, the center coordinators (Ike Agawin, Sherman Lau, Carl Loewen, Charlie Cook, Lauren Goldbeck, and Timothy Tang), and Gary Nelson (former president of Tyndale University) for writing the foreword. We also extend our gratitude to Anthony Casey (EMS VP of Publications) for accepting this volume under the Evangelical Missiological Society Monograph Series, and to Chris Spinks (Pickwick editor) in working with us in the process of publication. Moreover, we express our grateful acknowledgement for the granting of permission to include in this edited volume a revised and condensed version of "The Proper Place for a Woman" by Xenia L. Chan and Lisa H. Pak in *Advancing Models of Mission: Evaluating the Past and Looking to the Future*, Kenneth Nehrbass, Aminta Arrington, and Narry Santos, eds., (Littleton, CO: William Carey, 2021), chapter 5, 65–78. Used with permission.

Finally, the COVID and post-COVID realities, along with the relevant social justice, gender, and anti-racism issues of our day surely impact the present and future evangelical mission in Canada. May this volume help trigger fresh insights and help catalyze decisive action that can prompt the academy, agency, assembly, and agora to join hands more often in seeking to help fulfill God's mission for us in Canada and beyond.

Introduction
The Prophetic Past and New Imagination for the Present and Future: Clarifying Evangelical Mission in Canada

XENIA LING-YEE CHAN

"WHAT DOES IT MEAN to be Canadian?"

Ask this of any Canadian, and it is likely the response will be a rueful chuckle and, "Well, we're not American." The wryness with which this answer is offered belies a fierce Canadian pride, and indeed, Canada is its own entity, however we might like to identify ourselves by negation. As the late historian Richard Gwyn suggests, Canada may very well be the first "postmodern state."[1] Here, identities are under negotiation, and the unique conciliatory character that forms the foundation of this nation-state creates a national identity that is ever inclusive of new identities and ideas.[2] Pluralism is the ideal, and it may very well be that, with each subsequent wave of immigration, secularism has merely become one of the "plurals." Our sense of the collective is negotiated into being out of common individualities and Canadian pragmatism, and it is here that this convergence and negotiation of global narratives have arrived. Indeed, it has become the very air we breathe. As such, it is necessary to think theologically in the Canadian context. Canadian theology is concerned with interpreting essential Christian faith in language that Canadians can understand so that we might begin to engage in genuine dialogue between Christian faith and Canadian culture(s), and to clarify the calling of the Canadian church in mission at this time.

---

1. Gwyn, *Nationalism*, 243.
2. Gwyn, *Nationalism*, 249; Saul, *Fair* Country, 2–3.

Where once the church was tempted by American evangelical narratives of triumphalism, this gift of renewed pluralism has brought with it the awareness that the center of evangelicalism is no longer centered in the West but is increasingly shifting to the Majority World. And the stories of evangelicals from Latin America, Africa, the Middle East and North Africa, and Asia—they bring forth a richness which dislodges the dominance of Enlightenment rationality and re-enchants our understanding of our faith, creating a more robust articulation and praxis of our faith, as well as sharpening the sense of our (collective) invitation into the mission of God. Indeed, this re-enchantment has infected secularity, and those who have been inoculated against the Gospel in years previous have begun to express openness to "spiritual" conversations. The COVID-19 pandemic has brought into focus other changes, too. Writing now a few months into the pandemic, stories of neighboring have begun to emerge, and our conversations have been redirected to relocating the church's mission to our respective neighborhoods. Beautiful stories have emerged of people learning to love interculturally within their own geographical contexts. In essence, this pandemic has revealed a way in which we can live a little more humanly, and to begin to see how we might overcome difference with mustard seeds of compassion and goodness.

The pandemic has unveiled horrific ugliness as well, and amidst this pause, it is clear the ways in which the least of these have suffered most in this time. If we were unaware before, there is no excuse now to ignore the plight of the Black, Asian, and Indigenous communities, just as there is no excuse not to own up to the ways in which we mistreat our migrant workers. And, unavoidably, we cannot point out these injustices without also pointing out that our elderly, our low-income neighbors, and those who experience homelessness have been most at risk. It might be fair to say that we have never been more aware of our own need for the Gospel and our neighbors' hunger for good news. The church needs a way forward, even as we need a guide to identify where we have fallen short—or worse—in the past.

Therefore, this volume of essays is critical for this time. We are invited to prophetic evaluation of the past, but also to new imagination for the current uncertain present and the brave new future. My prayer is that as you read these chapters, the Spirit will bring both conviction as well as new hope for how the Lord is at work in our contexts.

Overview of Chapters

So how do these chapters contribute to our ongoing conversation about the state of evangelical mission in Canada? The first section is composed of chapters reflecting mission retrospectively and offering vision for prospective mission.

Sam George (chapter 1) opens this volume with an overview of evangelical missiology in the context of the United States and Canada. Carefully, he re-treads the past of evangelical mission, recalling the almost mythical stories of the evangelizing efforts alongside the ills brought by the colonial enterprise and from the triumphalist sending from the West to a more solemn reflection to the turning to empowering indigenous, contextualized movements of the Gospel. Acknowledging that the Evangelical church's current witness is in trouble due to the tangling up with materialism, consumerism, and individualism, George nonetheless remains optimistic about the state of mission, trusting that the margins are becoming the new "center," and that Christianity, rather than being dependent on the Western hegemonic frame, is revealing the inadequacies of that system and is also becoming more diverse and globalized in character. George concludes by suggesting that the future for evangelical mission will be found in the willingness to be sojourners in the *motus Dei* as located in the *missio Dei*, and that Christianity's growth will be dependent on international migrants, diffusing the Gospel wherever they go.

In response, Shu-Ling Lee affirms the key points that George makes. Lee brings to the conversation the work of Andrew Root—who draws upon the work of Canadian philosopher Charles Taylor—which reminds the Western church that it operates out of a disenchanted paradigm and has fallen prey to pragmatism and methods of control. Lee also nuances George's use of the *motus Dei* and proposes that the church's mission must be both rooted and displaced: a creeping vine (à la John 15) that is a community of centripetally-oriented love, sharing that same love centrifugally. Lee also suggests that this understanding of mission must necessarily be understood in light of the *patienta Dei*. Finally, Lee provides context for where he has observed the migration pattern George has suggested in spreading the Gospel: his own community of Chinese diaspora in the Greater Toronto Area, which is the result of Hong Kong migrant-missionaries.

Terry Leblanc (chapter 2) provides much needed rebuke for the church. Leblanc calls us to participate in un-creating the past, by which he means we must take a second look at the driving myths of Christendom and come to terms with the horrific consequences of the entanglement of Christianity and empire. This is vital for our mission because of the ways in which this enterprise 'othered' non-European peoples around the globe. This is not an invitation to guilt or to shame, but instead, Leblanc offers the wisdom of his grandfather: always look over your shoulder at where you have been twice as much as you look ahead to where you are going on a new trail. That way, the landmarks behind you will be fixed in your mind the way they will appear to you on the return; you will be able to find your way home. This reflection on the past is to prevent us from becoming disoriented on the trail: creating false landmarks or becoming lost altogether. What, then, is the alternative to Christendom? Our missiology, Leblanc urges, must be focused on right relationship. First, right relationship with God and with other powers; God must be God, and nothing else. Second, right relationship with other human beings, where the Great Commission is understood to be at peace with and do good to all people. And lastly, right relatedness to the rest of the creation of which we are a part. In such a way mission is understood holistically to be the participation with the Creator in the restoration of the cosmos.

Claudia Rossetto heartily echoes Leblanc's exhortation, encouraging in her response a more critical examination of power. She offers a biblical exposition of Israel and the early church's struggle to "keep faithful in [their] love for God alone." Through specific focus on Jesus' interaction with the Samaritan woman, Rossetto highlights that this demand to worship God alone is coupled with Jesus' desire to make her holy and to reflect the image of God. It is then that she is prompted to proclaim the good news of Jesus, desiring the same for others. Rossetto concludes with offering the church some practical application for how this might be enacted: Sabbath, truth telling and conciliation processes, stewarding our finances to protect the vulnerable, and lastly, to proclaim the good news of the gospel, as the church is freed and made whole, just as the Samaritan woman was.

The second section examines past examples of mission and delves into their current relevance to the present. Matthew Friedman (chapter 3) explores how Clement of Alexandria might be classified as an early missiologist, via an examination of his life and works. A convert to the faith, Clement was unafraid of Alexandria's reputation as a major center of philosophy, and saw his part in serving God's mission to help the church "overcome its fear of philosophy and literature," seeing that much of Greek philosophy could be redeemed, and that God "was using to draw the Greeks to himself" and by means of his grace. Clement's writings were also evangelistic in nature, and he actively engaged with Hellenistic philosophers and the Gnostics. Finally, Friedman describes some of the ways in which Clement's principles of indigenization has influenced missiologists all over the world but specifically adds that while Clement may have been a cultural insider, his work included a significant element of *polemic* so to add the necessary "degree of cultural alienation" that occurs in the coming to faith process—that is, the *pilgrim* principle that acknowledges that one is never really at home in this world.

Glenn Martin (chapter 4) suggests that the central global conflict is between a secularization, encouraged and abetted by globalization and technological advance, and fundamentalisms, which is the fundamentalist backlash to these phenomena. Framed by Ralph Winter's ten epochs of redemptive history, Martin explores what faithful witness might look like in the tension between secularization and fundamentalisms, and how pluralism might actually be an opportunity for the church. Martin proposes the acronym H.O.P.E.—hospitality, openness, practical presence, and eternal perspective—as guideposts for the church in navigating this new world.

Lisa Hanmi Pak and I (Xenia Ling-Yee Chan) (chapter 5) offer a historical-theological exposition for the proper place of women in the Chinese and Korean churches: serving as full partners in the Gospel for the sake of the Kingdom of God. Pak and Chan present a history of the Korean and Chinese churches through the lens of their foremothers. Indeed, women played a vital role in the proliferation of the Gospel in early Protestant missions, and that the subsequent relegation of women to the domestic sphere is largely due to Confucian and Victorian English norms, and not due to the liberating, empowering norms of the Gospel. Tracing forward to the present, Pak and Chan detail the plight of modern Chinese and Korean— and their diaspora in North America—women in ministry, who continue to be faithful despite the obstacles in front of them. Finally, Pak and Chan conclude by inviting the church to affirm women and their callings to ministry, even as God has called and affirmed them.

The third section examines the current state of affairs and how the Evangelical church may consider change as she looks towards a future of mission in a post-COVID, post-Christendom Canadian context. Sherman Lau (chapter 6) opens this section with an investigation of whether multiculturalism ought to be a value of the church. In this chapter, Lau argues that Canadian multiculturalism has created a false solidarity that obscures the fact that tolerance has become the norm, rather than full inclusion. This includes the church, where "little [has been] done to overcome barriers to integration in homily or ecclesial leadership." Lau retraces Canadian history to establish how multiculturalism came to be, followed by a section on immigration and the increasing diversity of religious Canada as a result. Finally, Lau proposes why he sees inclusion as *the* reality, establishing the need for an intercultural ecclesiology, becoming able to "speak each other's language by intentionally seeking to increase our intercultural awareness, repent of our prejudice, and start integrating voices who are missing from our churches." Lau concludes this is the only way a Kingdom community will be made possible.

Dave Witt (chapter 7) offers the story of the TrueCity network of churches in Hamilton, Ontario. Spurred on by the Missional Conversation, this network emerged out of a desire to be "churches together for the good of the city." Witt notes that this network is defined by differentiated unity grounded in the catholicity of the historic creeds. This is not merely an abstract idea, and Witt also brings to the table the various methodologies that facilitated the making of this idea into reality. Witt has brought the gift of the TrueCity network as a paradigm for other missional church networks, demonstrating that not only is collective mission possible cross-denominations, but when differentiated unity is desired and lived out, witness is amplified such that the contexts we live become more "acutely aware of how God is at work in [our] midst."

Manuel Böhm (chapter 8), centers reconciliation as the heart of the mission of God, where God's desire is for people to be reconciled to him, and the church is invited into that same ministry. Key to this reconciliation for Böhm is the Healing of Memories methodology that first emerged in post-apartheid South Africa in conversation with the concept of reconciliation as described in Pauline theology. In such a way, the church might be able to reckon with her own conflicted past and not excuse it, but "through confession of sin a clear step of forgiveness is possible," make space for God's vision to become the base for peace and a common future together. As the church takes ownership and pursues a path of healing, this might prompt curiosity in others to become part of the healing, reconciling work of Jesus Christ.

Marilyn Draper (chapter 9) offers a prophetic critique of current evangelical mission via Jacques Ellul, and where evangelical adoption of *technique* may have led to a "human-powered enterprise characterized by human misuses of power and methodologies." Draper proposes that this understanding of doing mission "for God" might be reframed to understanding mission as being fundamentally *participatory*, connecting with "God's greater purposes in the *missio Dei*" in worshipful engagement and cruciform weakness, and in which we as participants seek to discern where God's Spirit is already at work within the particular contexts we inhabit. In this manner, the church might be able to truly witness and bear witness to who God is and his mission in the world.

Lastly, the final section offers a vision for present and future mission in the workplace. Laurie George Busuttil and Susan J. Van Weelden (chapter 10) presents a theology of workplace missions grounded in the *imago Dei*, that is, "workplace as missions is founded on being and acting as image bearers of God and recognizing that others are also made in his image." Busuttil and Van Weelden provide three theological perspectives of *imago Dei*, before turning to how this might be lived out in the workplace, and how Christians can live out of the security knowing their own status of image bearers and offering that same dignity to those around them, thereby being salt and light in their workplaces. Finally, they offer what future generations will need to be prepared for this mission field.

Jon Fuller (chapter 11) brings to the fore the false divide between mission and vocation that has left the church without a vision for supporting missionaries who practice their vocations in different parts of the world—marketplace workers. Briefly going through biblical models of mission, Fuller points out that "tentmaking" is a viable model for mission, and indeed, may be the model going forward in a post-Christendom reality, and more "accurately reflect[ing] the ways in which the Gospel spread historically prior to the development of the Western mission agency." Fuller argues that the church is vital to the marketplace workers' ministry. In examining the Canadian Evangelical Mission Survey, Fuller notes that the responses seem to be encouraging in terms of the development of cross-cultural marketplace mission in the Canadian context and concludes by suggesting further ways in which the church can come alongside marketplace workers.

Conclusion

Each contributor has offered thoughtful critique as well as a way forward for the church to become who we were created to be, and to become full participants in the mission of God as God intends. As we look to the hurting, hungry world around us, may we be able to see with the fullness of God's abundance, and to participate with all hope and joy, knowing that just as he has reconciled us to himself, he so desires the same for others and all of creation. So, would we embrace the call to reckon with our pasts, tracing our landmarks, confessing our sins, and knowing with full joy that the God who redeems sends us out to be about his redemptive work in partnership with and empowered by the Spirit?

Bibliography

Gwyn, Richard. *Nationalism Without Walls: The Unbearable Lightness of Being Canadian.* Toronto: McClelland & Stewart, 1995.

Saul, John Ralston. *A Fair Country: Telling Truths About Canada.* Toronto: Penguin Canada, 2008.

Part 1
Mission in Retrospect and Prospect

I

The Past, Present, and Future of Evangelical Missiology

Sam George

I dread at the prospect of having to predict the future of evangelical missiology accurately, knowing very well of others who attempted to forecast the future and how wrong they turned out to be. When computers first came out, an IBM economist claimed that automation would reduce work to 20 hours a week and people spend the rest in leisure! Or a Norwegian missiologist in 1900 developed a mathematical formula of the growth of Christianity over prior two centuries and predicted that the entire human race will be won to the Christian faith by 1990. Someone said, "A good forecaster is not smarter than everyone else; he merely has his ignorance better organized." At the risk of being called a false prophet and derided in the future, I sincerely undertake the task entrusted to me with much fear and trembling.

In this chapter, I survey the development and issues related to the past, present, and future of the evangelical missiology in the context of North America at large. My attempt to forecast the evangelical missiology comes with my distinctive vantage point and socio-cultural location. I am of Asian Indian origin, have lived in five countries and currently make home in the suburbs of Chicago, USA. My heritage comes from the ancient apostolic St. Thomas Christians of India and has been influenced substantially by Reformed, Evangelical, and Pentecostal traditions. My research interests are in global migration, diaspora missiology, and World Christianity, and I teach at six institutions in Asia, Africa, UK, and USA. I direct the Global Diaspora Institute at Wheaton College and serve as a Catalyst for Diasporas for the Lausanne Movement.

PART 1: MISSION IN RETROSPECT AND PROSPECT

The Well-Trodden Paths of Evangelical Missiology

Before looking into the future, I want to briefly reflect on where we have been as evangelical missiologists and highlight some select milestones in the history of the missionary movement. Though many important lessons can be drawn from the Bible and foundations for mission laid by the Reformers, Moravians, Puritans, Pietists, and Wesleyans, I begin with the Modern Missionary Movement. William Carey, the father of the movement before setting out to British India in 1792, did extensive studies and made a compelling case for overseas mission to use means for the conversion of heathens[1] but was ridiculed by his senior Baptist ministers, "Young man, sit down! .... When God pleases to convert the heathen, he'll do it without consulting you or me."[2] However, he went on to establish a mission society, penned his treatise listing countries, land size, population, and religious preference of peoples of the world along with detailed tabulations and maps, went to India on colonial ships, translated the Bible into several Indian languages, sought social reforms, and established a college and publishing venture in India.

Ever since, well-documented research, education, social development, Bible translation, mission societies, charismatic pioneering spirit, and personal sacrifices have been characteristic features of the mission enterprise worldwide. The subsequent generations of British missionaries to Africa (David Livingstone) and China (Hudson Taylor) inspired thousands of Christians to pursue missionary careers, and numerous mission societies were established in Europe and North America. As a result, the nineteenth century became the greatest century of Christian expansion. A Christian historian claimed that never before in a period of equal length had Christianity or any other religion penetrated for the first time as large an area as it had in the nineteenth century.[3] However, it made Christianity look European worldwide and Western theology, and ecclesial practices became normative to the faith. Christianity was coupled along with colonialism, trade exploitation, slavery, racism, and the civilizing agenda of the West. Mission was viewed in terms of expansion, occupation of fields, conquest of other religions, and imperial motives. It depended on wealth, power, infrastructure, organizational models, and

---

1. Carey, *Enquiry*.
2. Attributed to Rev. John Collett Ryland in William Carey's biographies.
3. See Latourette, *History of Expansion of Christianity*.

training of the Western nations and resulted in much abuse, subjugation, inequity, corruption, and dependencies.

When the British conquered the seas and ruled the world (remember the claim, "The Sun never sets on the British Empire"), one of the landmark mission events of the twentieth century was held in Edinburgh, Scotland known as the World Missionary Conference of 1910, and it is best known for its clarion call: evangelization of the world in this generation.[4] More eager for Christ's return when all the world has heard the gospel and to see a world where all people have been evangelized, the challenge posed at the conference continued to inspire generations of Western Christians in the ensuing decades. Though the two world wars and the Great Depression impacted the missionary undertaking of the West in a significant manner, Christianity grew in unexpected ways in the postcolonial lands through indigenous methods and leadership in the second half of the twentieth century.[5] The collapse of the colonial enterprise and associated rationale and economic structures for foreign mission caused much soul searching among Western Christians. As the dominance of the Western Christians declined and the Global South Christians are no longer subservient to their Euro-American masters, transformation of power relations and interpersonal dynamics of the missionary enterprise occurred dramatically. The native missionaries, new levels of partnerships, voluntarism, resource sharing, and new mission-sending nations surfaced. Several new mission initiatives emerged, such as church growth, unreached people group, 10/40 windows, AD2000, cities, and business as mission (BAM) to redirect the meager mission resources, personnel, and training toward new focus areas. Many new strategies and tools were developed to pray, mobilize, deploy, govern, and serve in mission in the late twentieth century.

The unprecedented scientific progress of the twentieth century was heralded by the Western evangelicals as the advent of the Kingdom of God. More spiritual and other-worldly views gave way to rampant materialism and consumerism as well as resulted in a greater disparity between haves and have-nots. The social gospel arose in response and the cry for justice, equity, and reconciliation entered mission work. The dichotomized view of mission as "home" and "foreign," as well as sectarian ecclesiastic structures and theological disciplinary silos, remained as major challenges to the

---

4. See Stanley, *World Missionary Conference Edinburgh 1910*.

5. For an assessment of mission in the twentieth century, see Sunquist, *Unexpected Christian Century*.

widespread acceptance of missionary undertaking. A romantic notion of distant peoples and cultures, as well as enchantment with others, has been associated with mission for a long time. The notions of manifest destiny and military metaphors (e.g., army; crusade; conquest; advance; marching order) came alongside of mission. This era was also marked by sustained bondage to missiological training and intellectual traditions of the West.

Undoubtedly, a major missiological concept that emerged in the middle of the twentieth century was *missio Dei* (mission of God), providing a theological impetus by making a decisive shift in our understanding of mission. Mission, henceforth, was believed to be derived from the very nature of God and put in the context of the doctrine of Trinity, not of ecclesiology, or soteriology. It is not perceived as an activity of the church but as an attribute of God. The God of the Bible is a missionary God and the focus shifted from the biblical foundation for mission to missional hermeneutics of the Bible.[6] The liberation theologies of Latin Americans brought reflection among evangelicals to include integral mission into missiological conversations.[7]

Missionary anthropologists emphasized the importance of cultural realities for the spread of the Gospel and developed models of contextualization.[8] Yet, missionary imposition and lack of appropriation abound in mission history. Mission advocates were blind to their own ethnocentrism and confused Western ideals with Christianity. Elitism, territorialism, and triumphalism have been a bane to the evangelicals over the last few centuries. Pragmatism, competition, and reliance on strategies have impeded the missionary task. Numerous divisions among Christians and the denominational spirit have created much confusion and disdain among non-Christians and have been a hurdle to meaningful missionary engagements. Radical individualism and personality cults have been ill-suited for people in communitarian societies of the world. Western evangelical ignorance and derision over supernatural realms, healing, spiritual powers, demons, and visions have compromised the witness of the Christians.

The theology of mission was charted by David Bosch along thirteen interrelated paradigms.[9] The Gospel and Culture movement of the late

6. Wright, *Mission of God's People*.
7. Padilla, *Mission between Times*.
8. Hiebert, *Gospel in Human Contexts*.
9. Bosch, *Transforming Mission*; cf. Kirk, *What is Mission?*; Wrogemann, *Theologies of Mission*.

twentieth century got the Western churches to realize its missionary mandate as the core reason for its existence and development of missional ecclesiology.[10] In recent decades, there have been many attempts to include the voices of the theologies of mission from the Global South, even as they are engaging in reverse mission (or the re-evangelization of the West). The progressive indigenization and national consciousness of new churches in the Majority World played a vital role in the development of multiple streams within World Christianity.

The Current State of Evangelical Missiology

The secularization of Western culture has undermined the influence and strength of the evangelical church. The ostentatious lifestyle of Christian leaders and shallow morality has permanently tarnished the image, and the falling from grace of many televangelists and evangelical church leaders in recent years have exposed the bankruptcy of evangelicals. The exodus of younger generations and the issue of homosexuality have emptied the pews of many churches in the US and Canada. A tectonic shift has occurred in the demographic centre of Christianity over the twentieth century, while the greying of the churches, dwindling financial resources, and lack of interest in overseas missions continue to plague the North American evangelical churches. A new generation born in the twenty-first century is posing a serious challenge to current ecclesial thinking and practices, foraging opportunities with their gifts in compassion and justice. Race relationships, economic inequity, psychological disorders, and ecological crises remain problematic issues among evangelicals.

Currently, the term evangelicalism has come under severe strain. In the US, it has been politicized as a voter category with its definition and representation blurred, and they are being manipulated by the popular media. Many are increasingly distancing themselves from such labeling and trying to reinvent themselves. Moreover, evangelicals in Asia, Africa, and Latin America do not identify with such depiction as issues that are very different from the socioeconomic and political realities of the West. The terms "mission" and "missiology" have come under critical review and epistemological makeover as many programs, faculty titles, and department names have been changed from mission studies to world religions to intercultural studies to missiology, depending on various disciplinary dominance. In short,

10. Guder, *Missional Church*.

the term "evangelical" is in trouble; "missiology" is in trouble; and hence, "evangelical missiology" is in big trouble!

Missional ecclesiology brought a renewed thrust on the "sent-ness" of the church based on the Johannine commission (John 20:21) and Trinitarian theological foundation for missionary praxis.[11] However, it also reinforced the critical role of the sender, sending bodies, and resources—an imbalance between senders and receivers which resulted in the reproduction of the sending institutional cultures in foreign lands. As new churches and nations become both mission senders and mission receivers, it has become difficult for former senders to be in the receiving end. As a result, the missionary task is undergoing a fundamental realignment globally. Another recent shift in missiology comes from the Pentecostal missiological formulations, which added a pneumatological perspective[12] and invigorated mission theology in the areas of spirituality, spiritual warfare, supernatural, signs and wonder, principalities and powers, and charismatic renewal. Attempts have been made to salvage the mission enterprise using "witness"[13] and "participation"[14] as primary theological lenses in order to develop a new epistemological reconstruction of mission.

While some missiologists have alarmed us about the contemporary "crisis in mission" and described it in terms of "moratorium" and "euthanasia" of mission.[15] Some others argue that the term "mission" has run its course, and it is time to reinvent language, since we are now in a post-mission era.[16] The argument stems from the fact that we live in a new world that is post-colonial, post-Western, post-Enlightenment and post-Christendom. Mission has many colonial undertones since it was forged as a by-product of colonialism and established upon the foundation of the linkages, wealth, and power of colonial empires. Andrew F. Walls first began to notice the shift in the center of gravity of Christianity and many others have subsequently examined closely the significant growth of Christianity in Africa,

---

11. See Hastings, *Missional God*.

12. E.g., Yong, *Missiological Spirit*; Ma and Ma, *Mission in the Spirit*; and McGree, *Miracles*.

13. Stone, *Evangelism after Christendom*; see chapter 5.

14. Bellini, *Participation*.

15. Stroope, *Transcending Mission*; Reese, "Moratorium on Missionaries," 245–56; Gittins, *Ministry at Margins*; Hanciles, *Euthanasia of Mission*.

16. Yong, *Mission after Pentecost*; Escobar, *New Global Mission*.

Asia, and Latin America.[17] Thus, mission is not "from the West to the rest" anymore and missionary work is not the exclusive prerogative of Western nations anymore, but with the rise of many new mission-sending countries, mission is now from "everywhere to everywhere." The focus, resources, and personnel for missionary task are arising from different parts of the world as much as from former heartlands of Christianity (which is needing to be re-evangelized afresh). Such redirection and flow of missionary personnel, resources, and training are making Christianity polycentric and transforming the margins as the new centers of Christianity.[18]

As we enter the third decade of the twenty-first century, Christianity is more global, more geographically dispersed, and more diverse than it has ever been in its history. Since the Great Commission (Matt 28:19, 20) and the birth of the church (Acts 2), Christianity can now be found in every nation (geopolitical entity) of the world. As a global faith, its beliefs and practices come in many different stripes, colors, languages, and cultures from the world. The Bible has been translated to different languages, and singing and worshiping are conducted every Sunday across different time zones in diverse styles. The number of denominations has grown exponentially, and renewalist groups are a dominant part of this growth especially in the Majority World. The chief representatives of Christianity, at least in terms of size of the church and growth rate of the faith (but not in terms of resources), are now in the Majority World, and we must pay closer attention to that part of the world to discern the emerging trend in theological and missiological developments. The composition of Christianity has changed beyond recognition, making what was a Western religion into principally a non-Western faith.[19] This has broken the dominant Western hegemony in mission and also exposed fissures and fractures among the eclectic evangelical community worldwide.

The Future Trajectories of Evangelical Missiology

In the midst of the unparalleled and precipitous changes of our times, there is a pressing need to reimagine mission and mission theology for the twenty-first century by building upon the foundations and drawing appropriately from the rich resources of scriptural and theological

17. Walls, *Cross Cultural Process*, 45–47.
18. Kalu et al., *Mission after Christendom*; Yeh, *Polycentric Missiology*.
19. Walls, *Crossing Cultural Frontiers*, 259–66.

literature without retrieving the baggage of colonial enterprise. Missiologists must attend to emerging contexts and dramatic societal transformations that we are seeing on account of new technologies, economics, and media, which will force us to reflect afresh and produce new mission literature. The far-reaching repercussion of the latest innovations (such as artificial intelligence, processor power, data storage, cloud computing, 5G smartphones, autonomous vehicles, and robotics) are not fully realized yet. How people think, learn, relate, congregate, practice, and serve, are being fundamentally altered, especially in advanced economies. These repercussions are trickling down to other regions of the world, even as it creates greater division and deterioration among peoples everywhere. Amidst unforeseen transformation of family, culture, work, economy, organization, communication, and education, we must ask, "What does it mean to be a community of followers of Jesus Christ?" This is bound to affect how we practice and propagate our faith.

Christianity is a de facto missionary religion par excellence, not primarily on account of a few random verses of mission mandated at the end of the Gospels. Its tenets and practices are not static or confined to any geography but are dynamic, translatable, and moves unceasingly. It is a translatable faith since no one language is considered exclusive to Christianity. It is never confined to a place, culture, or people as different regions and peoples have been chief representatives of the Christian faith. It possesses an inherent power to diffuse across cultures and geographies. It is ultimately a mobile faith and its mobility brings about the need for fresh translation, which in turn causes cross-cultural diffusion and Jesus to be incarnated among peoples of the world. Mission, mobility, and translatability are closely linked and are salient features of the faith.

Migration, whether voluntary or forced, has played an enormous and determinative role in the development and expansion of Christianity throughout its history. In fact, Christianity is a mobile religion because of its missionary mandate and mobility of its adherents. Christians are more likely to travel beyond places of their birth since they are not bound to any locale and their peripatetic encounter with foreign cultures and languages leads to new endeavors in adapting and translating the tenets of their faith and practices into new contexts. On the contrary, Hinduism is considered as a rooted religion with its prohibition to traverse large expanses of water in its scriptures and remain largely bound within a particular land and culture. Likewise, Islam is a rooted faith on account of its pilgrimage, prayers uttered facing a particular location, and untranslatable scriptures, even as it has primarily spread through conquests.

Allow me to attempt some brushstrokes on the canvas of theology, as I gaze into the future from my vantage point as a diaspora missiologist for our post-mission era. Firstly, *motus Dei* (Latin for the move of God) is akin to the notion of the *missio Dei*. God is on the move all over the world and is moving powerfully among people on the move. God is a living and moving being. Godhead and Trinitarian theology need to be reconceived afresh in motile terms. The doctrine of incarnation is evident in the words "and the Word become flesh" (John 1:14a), which can be rendered as moving into our neighborhood. Likewise, salvation involves our turning toward God and moving closer to God to be transformed from the inside out. It is time to reimagine mission theology kinetically. A maxim for our emerging times can be "I move, therefore I am" (*moveo ergo sum*). Moving is a core essence of our being than stasis, bringing fresh dynamism to our conceptualization of human identity, relationality, fall, salvation, and the mission of God. Our earthly life and eschatological future must be viewed in motile terms. Thus, mission is all Christ-followers synching their steps with a moving God to see him make all things new (Rev 21:5).

Many biblical motifs are helpful in this regard: church as God's pilgrim people, wandering, exodus, exile, diaspora, and sojourner. To be a pilgrim in the world means to intrinsically not belong or tied down to any particular place. It is *ek-klesia* (called out) of the world and *dia-spora* (scattered) for God's mission in the world. Pilgrims need only support for the road. With vision for their anticipated future, they travel through the valleys and seasons in life. Their eschatological hope propels them to live faithfully each day with a divine sense of a greater purpose for their lives. They have no fixed abode on earth; earthly home is *paroikia* (dwelling beside/among), a temporary residence with eyes fixed on their eternal abode.

Secondly, we live in an age of migration and we will see a major surge in human mobility. We will travel more frequently and repeatedly to more places than our ancestors ever dreamt. We will cover more distances, at higher speed and lower cost on surface, subterranean, and in air. We are at the cusp of major technological breakthroughs in transportation, which will transform our societies and economies. More people will move about more incessantly than before and will live in several places over one's lifetime. The movement of people is of utmost importance to Christianity as it is a migratory religion, and the movement of people has advanced and transformed faith throughout its history. There is no fixed geographical or cultural center for Christianity. It is not confined to any people or language or nation, because it is bound to diffuse across cultural lines and different people have been its chief representatives over different eras.

Human beings are *homo mobilis* and nomadism has reached global proportion. Travel and connectivity are prerequisites for nomadism. The uprooting and transplantation are fundamentally disruptive, posing major challenges to our notion of identity, community, and praxis. The access and cost of travel will plummet drastically, and more earthlings will become extra-terrestrial as we set up factories and homes in neighboring planets. As cities become more powerful than nations, the rural to urban migration will continue, but it will create new crises and inequity. The domestic migration will surge and serve as a launching pad for international migration. Many new laws will be written to regulate, and new walls constructed to curtail people moving across national borders. Yet, the movement of people will remain unstoppable.

A metaphor about doing mission in the age of migration is "shooting a moving target." Our theologies and strategies for mission engagement must be completely reinvented in the context of global diasporas. The unreached people groups (UPGs) are no longer bound within a window or geographical region but have moved next door to us. As in archery, strategies to shoot a fixed target and moving target are poles apart, and archers are trained not to shoot where the target is now but where it will be when the arrow reaches there. This requires anticipating where the target is going, creative and quick thinking, mastery over equipment, taking into account the environment and its high failure rates.

Thirdly, the movement of people has many causative factors and always occurs along certain routes. In the first century, when Christianity grew in Jerusalem and the Roman persecution intensified, people were dispersed along the Roman roads. God used the travel routes of their times, developed for the movement of soldiers and maintenance of *Pax Romana*, to establish a widespread Jewish diaspora all across the Mediterranean world. The early churches were established among the dispersed people, and Gospel diffused to Gentiles through Hellenized Jews. Likewise, today's diaspora communities are at the forefront of Gospel movement, cross-cultural diffusion, and transformation of Christianity itself. Major infrastructural projects, like the One Belt–One Road Initiative, will disperse tens of millions of Chinese across the Middle East and Europe. More people are moving within Africa and out of the continent on account of new policies and economic realities. Indians, Brazilians, and Filipinos are scattering in larger volume and more widely than before, leveraging their global network of connections. Just as missionaries were cross-cultural migrants, international migrants serve as missionaries for the diffusion of the gospel.

Conclusion

Evangelical missiology has a seasoned history but currently is at a crucial juncture in its development for relevance in the ensuing decades. I believe we have much work cut out for us: learn lessons from the past, assess contemporary realities of our world, and develop robust evangelical missiology for the future. We must abandon the baggage associated with Christendom and colonialism and stand on the shoulder of the giants who have gone before us, while breaking free of the cultural captivity of past missiological concepts to reinvent missiology for the coming generations. I pray that a new breed of evangelical missiologists will multiply and flourish to develop well-grounded pertinent theologies of mission for a post-mission era.

Reflection Questions

1. What lessons from the past of evangelical missiology are relevant today?
2. What are some major mission challenges facing the evangelical church in North America?
3. How would you compare and contrast the strengths of reconceiving a theology of mission in terms of *motus Dei* for an age of migration?

Bibliography

Bellini, Peter. *Participation: Epistemology and Mission Theology*. Wilmore: Emeth, 2010.
Bosch, David. *Transforming Mission: Paradigm Shifts in Theology of Mission*. 20th anniversary ed. Maryknoll, NY: Orbis, 2011.
Carey, William. *Enquiry into the Obligation of Christians to Use Means for the Conversion of the Heathens*. Leicester, UK: Ann Ireland, 1792. https://www.wmcarey.edu/carey/enquiry/anenquiry.pdf.
Escobar, Samuel. *The New Global Mission: The Gospel from Everywhere to Everyone*. Downers Grove, IL: IVP Academic, 2003.

PART 1: MISSION IN RETROSPECT AND PROSPECT

George, Timothy. *Faithful Witness: The Life and Mission of William Carey*. Christian History Institute, 1998.

Gittins, Anthony. *Ministry at the Margins: Strategy and Spirituality for Mission*. Maryknoll, NY: Orbis, 2002.

Guder, Darrell, ed. *Missional Church: A Vision for the Sending of the Church in North America*. Grand Rapids: Eerdmans, 2009.

Hanciles, Jehu. *The Euthanasia of Mission: African Church Autonomy in a Colonial Context*. Westport: Praeger, 2002.

Hastings, Ross. *Missional God, Missional Church: Hope for Re-evangelizing the West*. Downers Grove, IL: IVP Academic, 2012.

Hiebert, Paul. *Gospel in Human Contexts: Anthropological Issues for Contemporary Missions*. Grand Rapids: Baker Academic, 2009.

Kalu, Ogbu U., et al. *Mission after Christendom: Emergent Themes in Contemporary Mission*. Louisville: Westminster John Knox, 2010.

Kirk, Andrew. *What is Mission? Theological Exploration*. Minneapolis: Fortress, 2000.

Latourette, Kenneth Scott. *A History of Expansion of Christianity: The Great Century, AD 1800–1914, Europe and North America*. New York: Harper & Bros., 1938.

Ma, Wonsuk, and Julie Ma. *Mission in the Spirit: Toward a Pentecostal/Charismatic Missiology*. Oxford: Regnum, 2011.

McGree, Gary. *Miracles, Missions and American Pentecostalism*. Maryknoll, NY: Orbis, 2010.

Padilla, Rene. *Mission between the Times*. Grand Rapids: Eerdmans, 1985.

Reese, Robert. "John Gatu and the Moratorium on Missionaries." *Missiology* 42 (2014) 245–56.

Stanley, Brian. *The World Missionary Conference Edinburgh 1910*. Grand Rapids: Eerdmans, 2009.

Stone, Bryan. *Evangelism after Christendom: The Theology and Practice of Christian Witness*. Grand Rapids: Brazos, 2007.

Stroope, Michael. *Transcending Mission: The Eclipse of a Modern Tradition*. Downers Grove, IL: IVP Academic, 2017.

Sunquist, Scott. *The Unexpected Christian Century: Reversal and Transformation of Global Christianity*. Grand Rapids: Baker Academic, 2015.

Wright, Christopher. *The Mission of God's People: A Biblical Theology of the Church's Mission*. Grand Rapids: Zondervan, 2010.

Wrogemann, Henning. *Theologies of Mission, Intercultural Theology*. Volume 1. Downers Grove, IL: IVP Academic, 2013.

Yeh, Allen. *Polycentric Missiology: Twenty-first Century mission from Everyone to Everywhere*. Downers Grove, IL: IVP Academic, 2016.

Yong, Amos. *The Missiological Spirit: Christian Mission Theology for the Third Millennium Global Context*. Eugene, OR: Cascade, 2014.

———. *Mission after Pentecost: The Witness of the Spirit from Genesis to Revelation*. Grand Rapids: Baker Academic, 2019.

Walls, Andrew F. *The Cross-Cultural Process in Christian History: Studies in the Transmission and Appropriation of Faith*. Maryknoll, NY: Orbis, 2002.

———. *Crossing Cultural Frontiers: Studies in the History of World Christianity*. Maryknoll, NY: Orbis, 2017.

Response to "The Past, Present, and Future of Evangelical Missiology"

Shu-Ling Lee

I would like to thank Sam George for his paper and for humbly taking on this immense task of trying to forecast the future of evangelical missiology. This short response will not be able to do justice to comprehensively engage his work but hopefully will provide a brief engagement with his main points while adding some supplemental thoughts.

Assessing the State of Evangelical Missiology

First, it is clear that George could only quickly skim the surface of evangelical missiological history. One of the main issues that he highlighted was the Euro-centric, white Western theological and church practices, which were spread to other countries and became the norm for many in the Christian faith. One could argue this is still evident in many evangelical churches today. The important philosophical issue that he brings to our attention is the ignorance and disregard of Western evangelicals over the supernatural and how that has compromised the witness of Christians. The works of Charles Taylor and Andrew Root identify the immanent frame that so many Western evangelicals are trapped inside during this secular age. Modern evangelical Christians are immersed in this disenchanted world where the "buffered self" seemingly protects us from all things supernatural through rationality and self-sufficiency, but conversely, it has tended to disengage us from the transcendent or awareness of God.[1] One could argue that instead of Spirit-driven discernment and mission, Western evangelicals today have mostly succumbed to pragmatism and business-oriented methods to try to control the outcome.

Motus Dei + Rootedness

Moving onto the three conceptual ideas that George offered, his first idea is that the *motus Dei* (movement of God) should be situated in our understanding of the *missio Dei*. He illustrated this by pointing to the church as God's wandering pilgrim people—sojourners who are not tied down to any particular place because they know it is only a temporary, non-eternal home.

George is correct in asserting that God's movement models for us the missional movement that we are to join him in, and the pilgrim motif is quite clear, especially in a Scripture passage like Luke 10. However, his point about "not being tied down to any particular place" could use further nuancing. It is clear that Christians should be open to the practice of displacement as a biblical pattern. However, displacement does not always equate to "dislocation."[2] For example, living in suburbia could already be seen by some as being displaced or being part of their pilgriming journey. Mission in the context of the Greater Toronto Area (GTA) and especially in many of its local neighbourhoods is where the nations already gather at the doorstep. As we disciple Christians in the missional church to live as pilgrims and sojourners in this temporary residence, there must also be an embodiment of relational rootedness as part of the mission and for the church to be so close to God and to people that they can wisely discern how and when to move. As George pointed to John 20:21 for the Johannine commission, John 15 and the recent work of Michael Gorman supplementally speaks about Jesus' paradoxical tension in mission: to "abide and go." This tension has to do with resting or staying put in the Lord and in his community, while the latter has to do with moving and acting. The image that Gorman proposes from John 15 is this: the disciples of Jesus must be a mobile, creeping vine, a community of centripetally (spiralling inward) oriented love that shares love centrifugally (spiralling out) as

---

1. Root, *Pastor in a Secular Age*, 64–72.
2. Hsu, *Suburban Christian*, 185.

they move out from themselves, all the while abiding in the vine, the very source of abundant life.[3]

Therefore, I contend that the movement of God needs displacement *and* rootedness, because part of the mission is to tie ourselves down to a particular location with a particular people as the mission of the church includes both movement and abiding. The missional church is this mobile, creeping vine together wherever it stays or goes.

Human Mobility + *patienta Dei*

Secondly, George predicts that in this "age of migration," we will see a major surge in human mobility. First of all, the missiological imagination in connecting human mobility to the point of extra-terrestial colonization and evangelization has much merit for consideration! However, there are also a few questions that need be asked regarding the acceleration of human mobility. Can the missional church demonstrate to the world an alternative way to the frenetic and unsustainable pace that we find ourselves in? What would it look like for the *motus Dei* (movement of God) to be tied to the *patienta Dei* (the patience or longsuffering of God)? In the mission of God, would tethering the movement of God with the patient or longsuffering character of God better prepare our mission-minded people for slow discipleship as Eugene Peterson so eloquently showed us in his seminal work, "A Long Obedience in the Same Direction"? Similarly, can we learn to see mission as "the patient ferment" in the vein of the Alan Kreider work? These are a few questions that could use further reflection in light of this prediction.

Certain Routes + Continuing Routes

Lastly, in relation to George's third point, there is much evidence in terms of diaspora communities being at the forefront of cross-cultural diffusion and Gospel engagement. Personally, growing up as a second-generation Canadian-born Chinese and now ministering in a Hong Kong immigrant-based diaspora church, I am a firsthand witness to the natural diffusion of the Gospel and church practice from the Cantonese-speaking Hong Kong immigrants to the next generation Canadian-born Chinese and also to the

---

3. Gorman, *Abide and Go,* 101–5.

Taiwanese and Mainland Mandarin-speaking immigrants. The route for Chinese immigrants to Canada is an example of one of these routes that George describes. This diffusion even has further evidence of route continuity as my own church recently sent a few of our English-speaking congregation to a neighboring city to plant a church site in an up-and-coming area of the GTA to reimagine newer ways of Gospel engagement. This is the route of Hong Kong immigrant missionaries reaching the diaspora in Canada who are now sending and enabling their next generation to reach their multicultural Canadian neighbors, where "the nations" are already inhabiting.

Conclusion

In conclusion, the words of Pentecostal-evangelical theologian, Amos Yong, help to tie this all together succinctly:

> If the Spirit immigrates into human hearts, so do we, as living epistles, immigrate into the proximity of the lives of strangers, and there seek to take root, not in the sense of making their world our home, but in the sense of enabling the gospel to flourish deep in the hearts and lives of our hosts. Thus, the call of the Spirit is the empowerment to take up and leave our homes and our comfort zones, to be guests of others in strange places, so that the triune God can become home for us all.[4]

May we continue to abide and go as Christ taught us in John 15. Let us move out together in faith, joining the patient movement of our triune God whether he continues to root us for mission where we are presently or be open to his uprooting elsewhere, to extend his very presence here and to the ends of the earth.

Bibliography

Hsu, Albert Y. *The Suburban Christian: Finding Spiritual Vitality in the Land of Plenty.* Downers Grove, IL: InterVarsity, 2006.

Gorman, Michael. *Abide and Go: Missional Theosis in the Gospel of John.* Eugene, OR: Wipf & Stock, 2018.

Root, Andrew. *The Pastor in a Secular Age: Ministry to People who no Longer Need a God.* Grand Rapids: Baker Academic, 2019.

Yong, Amos. *The Future of Evangelical Theology: Soundings from the Asian American Diaspora.* Downers Grove, IL: IVP Academic, 2014.

---

4. Yong, *Future of Evangelical Theology*, 184.

2

Mission Then and Future

Un-creating the Past and Disengaging from Empire

TERRY LeBLANC

The newcomers looked out on the land with disdain. How was it possible that such vast and fertile lands—lands cluttered with bounty—could lie untouched? Sights and sounds of abundance were everywhere. "Why," they asked themselves, "were these savages allowed by God to inhabit such prosperous holdings—holdings rich with resources they were so ill-equipped to utilize?" It seemed inconsistent with all they knew and understood about the use of lands and goods. It must be that God had prepared this bounty, keeping it in trust just for them. Prosperity waited.

Introduction

IN EACH SEASON OF the life of the church of Jesus Christ, the church has struggled to understand itself and its mission—not simply for that time and place, but also across time and space. This may seem obvious to those of us living in the first quarter of the twenty-first century, looking back, but it has not always seemed so to peoples living in and for a given time. Nor, for that matter, have those living in their specific time necessarily understood that they might be prone not simply to recovering their history but repeating it.

In this brief chapter, I would like to raise two questions about the mission of the church and its prosecution in the world—though I will by no means thoroughly discuss or support the contentions of either. That would take a more significant work than this chapter can provide time and space to accomplish.

PART 1: MISSION IN RETROSPECT AND PROSPECT

The first question is asked in an effort to engage our history more thoughtfully and honestly, focusing on the fact that mission was not (and may not yet be) what we thought it was. The second asks a very hard question of the church's allegiance—a question that raises deep concerns of our mission in the past and should of our mission in the present.

Un-creating the Past[1]

There are two clear ways in which we must un-create the past to provide for better engagement in mission in the present and for the future. First, we must cease the incessant drive of the church toward an idyllic, often fictitious articulation of the future, driving us toward an unknown and unknowable eschatological ending. We must, therefore, change the theological framework within which we conceive of the mission of the church from one driven by destination, escape from hell and obtaining heaven, to one that focuses on the journey we have been set on individually and collectively that has spatial, temporal, and directional reality.

When Jesus said, "No man knows the day or the hour," I think he meant it. In fact, he was so emphatic about it that he included himself in the collection of humanity for whom the date and time was unknown. The Scriptures say that the women and men described in the "faith" chapter of Hebrews looked toward the arrival of the promise of God, an unknown event on an unknowable day. When we read their stories, however, they nonetheless lived each day for that day to ensure that should these things be forestalled, they would continue their faith journey in a good way.

With few exceptions, Western church traditions have driven mission—the singular focus on the conversion of human souls—toward the unknown fulfilment of all things. Calls of "fit them for heaven," "prepare them to meet their maker," "turn or die," or the contemporary equivalents, rang out throughout history. While these phrases and others that may be like them may seem only trite statements of some hoped for, yet unrealized future, they nonetheless articulate the sense that today's life is to be lived for tomorrow's future—and it had better be on the right side of conversion.

For Indigenous and other peoples of the world, the implications of this future-focused thinking of the church in mission were clear: the future required a complete suppression of the present to ensure a full eradication

---

1. This section contains some material previously written and published in the Edinburgh 2010 reports, but which is germane to the paper.

of the past. After all, pagan, heathen savages and their ways of life could make no contribution to a future reign of God. Indigenous epistemologies, ontologies, worldviews, and perceptions were neither relevant nor required, since they lacked the necessary means to contribute. Wherever significant historic cultures had thrived for millennia, the trajectory of mission was essentially the same.

While conquest and/or colonization were the most widely employed engines of this eschatologically driven mission during the rise of Christendom, a less physically violent, though still ethnically enervating one, issued from Edinburgh 1910 as a rallying cry to mission: "Civilize and Christianize."[2] Echoing from its halls of meeting, the refrain was: "These heathen must first be civilized before they can become fit receptacles of the gospel."[3]

Eschatologically driven mission made clear that histories of Indigenous and other peoples, in lands occupied for many thousands of years, were completely irrelevant to the Christian God.[4] This, as I have said on many occasions, was tantamount to the theist believing the deist's truth: God had ignored all but the development and flourishing of Europeans.[5]

The second, very connected way in which we must un-create the past is by challenging persistent notions of the idyllic Christian era: church and society uniquely God-focused, emulating the ideals of Christian faith. This attitude had, and still has, very real traction. It reflects the desire for a better time ahead predicated on an idealized memory of the past, all with a view to obtaining an eschatological future.

Whereas one behavioral truism appears to be that human beings tend to evaluate others' experiences by their own, a second is that we tend to view history through the lens of our present understanding—and that they are often rose-colored. When undertaken collectively well, the first can assist us in finding multi-beneficial solutions for common concerns. Such is

---

2. For further discussion of this aspect of the Edinburgh conference, see Stanley, *Edinburgh 1910*, 283–87.

3. Paraphrased from, LeClercq, *New Relations*, 103.

4. Choctaw clergyperson and author Steven Charleston reflects on the lack of any substantive foundation for Indigenous people to embrace the Gospel of Jesus Christ such as that provided for those of European ancestry via the Hebrew Scriptures and post-Constantine Roman Empire *cum* Kingdom of God. *Cf.* Charleston, "Old Testament," 50.

5. Is it any wonder the majority of the historic images of heaven, in the Western church at any rate, depict a Euro-centric view of God, of Jesus, of the Holy Spirit, and of the populations of heaven? In light of this legacy, we should not be surprised that many Christians today still have a significantly distorted view of what heaven will be like.

the case with societal shifts toward socialized medicine or old age pensions. In the latter case, we might desire that images of the past (good or bad) be restored in the present. Such might be the case with the rise of conservative (or liberal) fundamentalist movements.

With respect to Christian mission, these maxims have largely undergirded the notions of a golden Christian era frequently viewed as a time without contemporary sins and a greater openness to the ability of the Christian message to bring total transformation. The unfortunate news is that it did not exist. As scholars in many fields tell us, such a history existed only in movies, selective memory, victors' histories, and mission letters home, if at all.

As far back as 1973, Karl Menninger, quoting Daniel J. Boorstin, director of the National Museum of Science and Technology, noted,

> We have lost our sense of history . . . lost our traditional respect for the wisdom of ancestors and the culture of kindred nations . . . we haunt ourselves with the illusory ideal of some 'whole nation' which had a deep and outspoken 'faith' in its 'values.'[6]

Menninger went on to say that this loss was deeply rooted in the well-established human ability to ignore various behaviors when politically, economically, socially, and/or religiously expedient. Euphemisms replaced more incisive vocabularies, terminology becoming more soothing of individual and collective conscience. Consequence deferred becomes focused through the lens of an unrealistic expectation that "it," whatever "it" is, will get addressed and/or "fixed" in the future.

Rather than the passage of time dealing with the consequences of initial behavior, however, one of two things is more likely to happen: the behavior gradually becomes normative, or it compounds, further complexity accrues to it, and to turn a biblical phrase, "the last estate becomes worse than the first." This, we might suggest, speaks to an essential state of unrepented sin. Not unexpectedly then, the book in which Menninger quotes Boorstin has the telling title: "Whatever Became of Sin?"[7]

Taking up Menninger's cry for a truer connectedness to our past to understand the reality of our present, Gregory Boer, in his 2008 PhD thesis, observes,

---

6. Menninger, *Sin*, 181–83.
7. Menninger, *Sin*, 184–85.

> We must address at least two significant ways of losing our imagining of history. One is . . . that the present becomes a defense against the knowing of the past, and what is past is concretized, placed in a literal framework, rather than critically examined. The other is that we lose history through what has come to be known as biased historical knowledge [whereby] a general written history of Western civilization . . . has excluded significant contributions of people of color.[8]

Applied to the trajectory of European mission, Menninger's and Boer's ideas suggest that mission either drove blindly forward, the past and its consequences to be dealt with in a hoped-for future, or there was an idealizing of the past so that it became something that never was, essentially neutralizing any need to address its errors. In so doing, Euro-centric mission was provided the means and justification to avoid contemporary responsibility, confession, repentance, and accompanying restitution. According to University of British Columbia anthropologist, Wade Davis, "Fluidity of memory and a capacity to forget is perhaps the most haunting trait of our species. As history confirms, it allows us to come to terms with any degree of social, moral, or environmental degradation."[9]

We must be very clear about this glossed history of the Christian era. It included crusade slaughter in the name of Jesus, persecution of infirm and "different" persons, cultural bigotry and hatred, unrestrained greed, attempts to "civilize," Christianize, and subjugate peoples, spiritual, physical and sexual abuse in mission stations, *encomienda*,[10] boarding schools, residential schools and catechetical training centres. In countless ways, it was not "Christian." In many corners of the world, we continue to observe similar efforts, apparently aimed more at converting people into the image and likeness of missioner and missionary than Christ. The "majority report" from Edinburgh 2010, the centenary of the original conference, offers a telling reflection of this historic reality:

> As many of us understand them, had the objectives of the 1910 conference been fully met, most of us in the Indigenous and global Southern contexts would not have been uncomfortable during much of the 2010 conference. An examination of the policies and

8. Boer, "Depression and Melancholia," 41–42.

9. Davis, "Unraveling," 2.

10. *Encomienda* was a system introduced by the Spaniards as a means of rewarding conquistadors and others with the labor of the conquered. They were monopolistic and given in perpetuity for the original recipient and his descendants.

practices that emerged from or, were otherwise sanctioned by the 1910 gathering, either directly or—through inaction—indirectly, would show that the intent of missionary efforts from that point forward was an intensification of the ongoing process of Christianising and civilising those of us in the global Southern and Indigenous communities.[11]

The idyllic Christian era of mission absorbed philosophies, epistemologies, teaching, and practice that placated the masses, secured the support of the wealthy, and enfolded "pagan" and "heathen" ways as it did so.[12] It was this trajectory, which ultimately "othered" non-European people from around the globe. So, let us be clear: looking at where we have come from is of utmost importance to mission engagement. The way in which we do so, however, makes all the difference.

Looking back is Critical

A teaching that I learned from my grandfather might help here. As my grandfather, my father, and I were walking through the woods to go fishing one time in my childhood, my repeated, anxious inquiries about finding our way back were responded to by "Always look over your shoulder at where you have been twice as much as you look ahead to where you are going on a new trail. That way, the landmarks behind you will be fixed in your mind the way they will appear to you on the return; you will be able to find your way back home." It was sound teaching. While I may never have blazed exciting new trails in the wilderness, I have always been able to get back to the starting point—to home.

Without a clear and accurate map of the return trail stored neatly in your head, it is very easy to cover the same ground over and over again, ultimately becoming entirely disoriented. It is easy in such a circumstance to think that you have either seen some spot in the trail or brush pattern before or for the very first time. By the time you sort it out, you can be hopelessly lost. The desired destination is then exchanged for some sort of survival where you find yourself. Sadly, we frequently find ourselves looking at history through the lens of one whom, having become disoriented on the trail, seeks to identify landmarks, in retrospect, and by memory.

---

11. Kim and Anderson, *Today and Tomorrow*, 345–50.
12. For an example, see the documentary work of Viola and Barna, *Pagan Christianity*.

Often, perhaps unwittingly, discussions of the post-Christian era interpret the landmarks of Christian mission as either less or more than they were. It might be more appropriate to ask, "If this is post-Christian, when was it Christian? And what exactly did that mean?" Examining our history is crucial, but it is equally critical that it be apprehended with a clarity that can only come through the lens of theological, missional, and ecclesial truth telling and integrity. Perhaps we have less to trumpet than we might like to think. If the church in mission is of concern, its missiology at times troubling, of equal or greater concern, are the consistent efforts of the church to bed with temporal power to accomplish its assignment.

Disengaging from Empire

The romanticized and largely fictitious Christian era that I posit above, the one that people are often found reminiscing about with deep longing, was also the era of politics—not of Jesus but of power brokering and collusion. If historic mission was branded by ethnocentric idealism, it was further characterized by a continued effort to wield temporal power in the exercise of its oft-distorted mandate.

Just over a century following the resolution of Gentile membership requirements, the tables had turned, and the church had embarked on a deepening posture of anti-Semitism.[13] By "the thirteenth century [while the] attitude toward Jews seemed to hover between severity and tolerance," praxis was not even remotely charitable.[14] Their 1497 forced conversion in Portugal would not be the last effort at expunging Jews from the world religiously and/or physically.[15] Nor would they be the only ethnic, cultural, or racial group to be targeted for such treatment. As the fifteenth century drew to a close, the "press-gang" approach to Christian mission among Jews had now expanded to include most everyone who was "other." The Doctrine of Discovery, Terra Nullius, and the socio-politically ethnocentric notion of Manifest Destiny now philosophically drove this "othering."

From the days of the Hebrew cry, "Give us a king," organized followers of God have struggled to differentiate the Kingdom of God from the kingdom of their monarch. Altogether too often, the Kingdom of God and the kingdoms of this world have been conflated, in both form and function.

13. See the series of essays in Dunn, *Jews and Christians*.
14. Webster, "Achievement," 175.
15. Barrett, *Christian Encyclopedia*, 26.

This phenomenon found its beginnings soon after the death and resurrection of Jesus. Arguably, from Acts 15 onwards, the church has witnessed one group of believers and/or people seeking dominion over another, empire becoming the principal mechanism of this undertaking.

Dvornik, in his study of the early ecumenical councils, described their conflation of church/state leadership this way:

> We can be certain that such gatherings of bishops gradually modelled themselves on the rules under which the sessions of the Roman Senate were held. The presiding bishop assumed the role of the Emperor or of his representative in the Senate. He used the same words for the convocation of the Council as were used in the imperial summons for the meeting of the Senate; and the conduct of debate, the interrogations of the bishops, and their responses also imitated the procedure of the Senate.[16]

Reflecting further on what he terms the church's Constantinian roots, Dvornik describes a syncretic consolidation whereby Roman ecclesial and temporal authority is increasingly woven together with the church's celestial spirituality. He observes,

> Of course, he [Constantine] knew only one political system, that of the autocratic monarchy into which the Roman Republic had been transformed under the influence of the Hellenistic political philosophy. This philosophy had deified the ruler and had given him absolute power over the material and spiritual interests of his subjects. The first Christian political philosophers, especially the Church historian Eusebius of Caesarea, adapted this political system to Christian teaching. The Emperor was thus deprived of his divine character but made to be the representative of God on earth, who had been given by God supreme power in things material and spiritual.[17]

Following this line of reasoning then, it could be said that it was under the pretext of pursuing and obtaining unity of thought, doctrine, and ecclesial action, inasmuch as such was possible, that the Councils were convened. To obtain this unity required a degree of standardization that many continued to militate against, for it required that diversity necessitate

---

16. Dvornik, *Ecumenical*, 10.
17. Dvornik, *Ecumenical*, 11.

homogeneity. Heterodoxy was not welcome; orthodoxy and orthopraxy were the order of the day.[18] Erasure of difference became normative.

By the turn of the fourth century and the convening of the ecumenical councils, church and state had begun to be all but indistinguishable, one from the other.[19] Arguably then, by the time of Chalcedon, the pattern had become firmly set. The sword of state wielded steel, not the sword of the supplicant Spirit, would now increasingly characterize the conversion experience.[20] In many ways, its justification for mission and many of its operational and missional settings would be supplied to the church through ties to empire forged during this same period.

Fanning pushes us to understand that conversion here involved more than simply reciting a creed or saying the sinner's prayer. He argues this way:

> The evolving Roman-Germanic culture became inseparable to the culture of the Church. To become a Christian, you had to become a Roman citizen culturally. Thus, the Christianizing of a nation became the civilizing of a people.[21]

What is more, as the empire continued to be conflated with the church and vice-versa, people's "authentic Christian conversion" was now almost always experienced alongside their concomitant conquest. The resultant faith was not simply anaemic; it actually became a seedbed for the furthering, even intensification, of this pattern. Fanning's question then, is entirely apropos.

> Did these methods generate true "belief" or merely nominal faith? Nominalism will result from "conversions" based on false premises (intimidation, peer pressure, coercion, or an emotional experience), rather than an understanding of the truth of the gospel and a commitment to trust that biblical truth. However, in a day when

---

18. The very exclusion of oppositional positions by censure and/or execution for heresy of the councils and their representatives of empire ensured this would continue to be the chosen means for dealing with diversity of opinion and theology throughout history, further ensuring that the trajectory of mission would inevitably be that which Indigenous peoples of the globe experienced—assimilation and/or social, cultural or physical eradication.

19. See Fanning, "Barbarian Invasions," 10–11, for a reasoned discussion of the formation of this amalgam.

20. See, for example, Fletcher's discussion in *Barbarian Conversion*.

21. Fanning, "Barbarian Invasions," 2.

everyone was obligated to hold to a faith that was the faith of your nobleman or prince, then nominal followers were inevitable.²²

Not only did this collusion in mission produce questionable outcomes in terms of authentic conversion, it also led to a greater likelihood that "state converts" would uphold the continued purpose and function of the state as agent of conversion. By the time we arrive at the more recent colonial eras, we see this phenomenon reflected in legislative doctrines and joint ventures of church and state.²³ In Canada, the Gradual Civilizations Act and the Indian Act are examples of this thinking, each clearly situate in an assimilative mentality, and each fully supported by church leadership.

Still the Same Today

As we have tangentially noted above, enmeshment with temporal power contributed to the church becoming so deeply Euro-centric that it no longer was mission bringing the gospel to all the earth but rather the establishment of a Christo-European kingdom. During the Edinburgh 2010 Mission Conference, Indigenous and majority-world Christian leaders were confronted with this continuing reality, ultimately concluding that the majority church was perceived, implicitly and explicitly, as a lesser version of the now minority church. As a result, the gathered Majority World delegates at Edinburgh 2010 affirmed the following:

> The inescapable reality, had this [Edinburgh 1910] been completely successful, is that we would have become 'Europeanised' and therefore completely comfortable in a Euro-centric setting. Our cultures and languages would have been absorbed into the body politic of the church and its surrounding society—at best tactically assimilated, becoming 'window dressing' to the historic and more 'authentic' culture(s) of the church; at worst our uniqueness's in the Creator's economy would have been eradicated entirely. Sadly, for some of the peoples we represent, the latter became their current reality.

---

22. Fanning, "Barbarian Invasions," 22.

23. The establishment of the United Church in Canada is a clear case in point. See Moriarty, *Manual*, 9.

Toward Change: Taking the Trail Home

Even a cursory reading of Acts 17:24–28a makes clear that people in all times and places have had the same purpose—to seek and find the one who made them so as to have a fully integral worshiping relationship. We believe this when it comes to our evangelism courses ("we have God-shaped vacuums") but struggle with it when there is a difference in the vacuum's cultural shape.

As an Indigenous Jesus-follower, I have seen the results of well-intentioned mission directed at a people of "strange" beliefs and customs. In the aftermath of mission, I have listened to converts lament the loss of identity and culture; though now Christian, they possessed limited ability to have life make sense. I have heard the pain of not belonging. These are people whose cultures and lifestyles have been compared, in their time, to that ideal "Christian era" of the past and found wanting. Are we positioning to do it again? Possibly, but it can, I believe, be staved off. To do so, however, we need a different missiology, one focused through the lens of three critical concerns.

First, right relationship with God and other spiritual powers. Over the centuries, mission had acquired a highly sensitized disposition toward spirits and spiritual powers of the malevolent sort. On more than a few occasions in history, in fact, it produced a witch-hunt disposition. Yet, with few exceptions of note, no similar turning to the spiritual forces of wickedness in high places of which Paul spoke had taken place.[24] Limited ability to recognize spiritual forces of wickedness not simply of the ethereal and demonic, but also those undergirding the use and abuse of temporal power had developed. Whereas demonic, pagan, syncretic, and animistic were used to describe the former, euphemisms like greed, lust for power, loyalty, and politics were used to characterize the latter.

The early church, confronted by this challenge made clear that whereas Romans may have viewed Caesar as "godlike," to early Christians he was certainly not God, so they would neither bow to nor seek to appease him.

Second, right relationship with other human beings. In the human sphere, the pursuit of right relationship in the human community should constitute normatively expressed and experienced Christianity. Admonitions to be at peace with all people, and do good to all people, in short,

---

24. Some will note Luther's theses here as a counter, but they are for another conversation.

the Great Commandment, should unequivocally characterize integral mission. Seeking to walk life's path well with others, even in these most basic ways, would avoid the misleading trail markers of a strictly Eurocentric mission. In so doing, we would be less likely to fixate on culturally circumscribed social and moral manners, or whether someone's attitude, ethnicity, or behavior was precisely the same as ours.

Third, if we were more concerned about right relationship with and right relatedness to the rest of the creation of which we are a part, we would be more inclined to engage life as followers of the Jesus Way, so as to ensure that restoration of the cosmos was as close to our heart as it is to our Creator's.[25] Mission would be seen as participation with our Creator in the renewal of the entirety of creation, not just human beings, and definitely not simply their soul salvation.[26] We would understand that Paul is describing an interdependent salvation, not a contingent one in Romans 8:18–23. If no other biblical text makes it clear, this passage should be seen to do so.

Drawing on biblical as well as Indigenous exegesis, Brett and Zacharias offer an alternate way of understanding human relationship with and relatedness to the rest of creation. They suggest that a classic reading of Genesis 2:15

> reflects a modern agrarian ideology that fits all too comfortably with colonial uses of the biblical discourse. A fresh examination of the Hebrew text through Indigenous eyes leads to the more literal translation "to serve her and conform to her." This rendering presents human obligations in relation to the earth...[27]

If our missiology were more oriented toward the restoration of the entirety of creation, as described in these three emphases, we would be less likely to be idolatrous, ethnocentric, or anthropocentric. We would, instead, be both theocentric and creation-centric without apparent conflict leading to idol worship of any sort.

Looking over our shoulders we should see the past for what it really was, not what we have idealized it to be. What is more, we should both be more honest about the destructiveness of colluding with empire to accomplish its purposes and more circumspect about the manifold ways in which this takes place under our noses. In so doing, we will be able to

---

25. *Cf.* Woodley, "Community of Creation," 92–94.
26. Snyder and Scandrett, *Salvation*, 21–27.
27. Brett and Zacharias, "Intercultural Reading," 1.

navigate home, to the beginning, to Jesus, the Alpha and Omega, to start fresh again, the end becoming the beginning.

Reflection Questions

1. If the two central theses in this chapter even remotely resemble an accurate portrayal of historic and contemporary church-state collusion and colonial mission glossing, what pragmatic steps might be taken to ensure that we begin to curtail each in our own mission endeavors?
2. What, if anything, should the relationship of church and state look like, in regards to the church in pursuit of its mission, "Go into all of the cosmos and make disciples of all nations"?
3. Consider the three spheres of relationship and relatedness that the author considers to be the restorative focus of God in Christ. How might your current mission model be reframed and/or retooled, so as to ensure that each of these three spheres is being addressed, not simply in turn, but integrally?

Bibliography

Barrett, David, ed. *World Christian Encyclopedia*. Oxford: Oxford University Press, 1982.
Boer, Gregory. "Images of Depression: A Theoretical Study of Depression and Melancholia as Expressions of an Absence of Imagining and an Unrequited Unconscious Need for Transformation." PhD diss., Pacifica Graduate Institute, 2008.
Brett, Mark G., and H. Daniel Zacharias. "To Serve Her and Conform to Her: An Intercultural Reading of Gen 2:15." In *FS Fernando Segovia*, edited by Francisco Lozada Jr. and Amy Lindeman Allen (forthcoming).
Davis, Wade. "The Unraveling of America." *Rolling Stone* (August 6, 2020).
Dunn, James D. G. *Jews and Christians: The Parting of the Ways, A.D. 70 to 135: The Second Durham-Tübingen Research Symposium on Earliest Christianity and Judaism*. Wissenschaftliche Untersuchungen Zum Neuen Testament. Tübingen: Mohr, 1992.
Dvornik, F. *The Ecumenical Councils*. Hawthorn, 1961.
Fanning, Don. "The Dark Age Church of Barbarian Invasions." *History of Global Missions* 3 (2009) 1–25. http://digitalcommons.liberty.edu/cgm_hist/3.
Fletcher, R. A. *The Barbarian Conversion: From Paganism to Christianity*. 1st American ed. New York: H. Holt, 1998. http://www.loc.gov/catdir/enhancements/fy0667/97050170-b.html.
Kim, Kirsteen, and Andrew Anderson. *Edinburgh 2010: Mission Today and Tomorrow*. Regnum Edinburgh 2010 Series. Oxford: Regnum, 2011.

PART 1: MISSION IN RETROSPECT AND PROSPECT

Le Clercq, Chrestien, and William F. Ganong. *New Relation of Gaspesia: With the Customs and Religion of the Gaspesian Indians*. Publications of the Champlain Society. Toronto: Champlain Society, 1910.

Menninger, Karl A. *Whatever Became of Sin?* New York: Hawthorn, 1973.

Stanley, Brian. *The World Missionary Conference, Edinburgh 1910*. Studies in the History of Christian Missions. Grand Rapids: Eerdmans, 2009.

Snyder, Howard A., and Joel Scandrett. *Salvation Means Creation Healed: The Ecology of Sin and Grace (Overcoming the Divorce between Earth and Heaven)*. Eugene, OR: Cascade, 2011.

Thistlethwaite, Susan Brooks, and Mary Potter Engel. *Lift Every Voice: Constructing Christian Theologies from the Underside*. Rev. and expanded ed. Maryknoll, NY: Orbis, 1998.

Viola, Frank, and George Barna. *Pagan Christianity: Exploring the Roots of Our Church Practices*. Carol Stream, IL: Barna, 2008.

Webster, D. "The Achievement and the Technique of Missions in the Middle Ages." *The Churchman* 59 (1945). https://churchsociety.org/churchman/page/churchman_vol_059_1945.

Woodley, Randy. *Shalom and the Community of Creation: An Indigenous Vision*. Prophetic Christianity. Grand Rapids: Eerdmans, 2012.

Woodley, Randy. "Early Dialogue in the Community of Creation." In *Buffalo Shout, Salmon Cry: Conversations on Creation, Land Justice, and Life Together*, edited by Steve Heinrichs, 92–108. Harrisonburg: Herald, 2013.

Response to "Mission Then and Future"

Claudia Rossetto

Introduction

Terry LeBlanc notes that Christian individuals and churches continue to struggle in our ability to relate to power well. Nigerian pastor and activist, Zac Niringiye also says, "Discipleship is about how we relate to power . . . if we are afraid of discussing power, we become prisoners of power."[1] Power is the capacity and opportunity of individuals or systems to do their will, sometimes against the resistance of others. God's definition of power is visible on the cross: an all-powerful God giving up ultimate power for the benefit of others. Humans do not know how to relate to God's power nor to the power of others. Our modern structures, enterprises, and the state of nature tragically reflect the damages caused by an anthropocentric culture that misuses power. LeBlanc's paper is an exposition of the ways in which power seemed to have caused memory issues in the church and created misplaced allegiances.

In the first part of this chapter, I will respond to LeBlanc's points, which engage the memory of our church history and allegiance. In the second part, I will pose a question from a missionary discipleship perspective and offer a biblical analogy as a response. In the final part, I will present a hope and a call to action for the church.

---

1. Niringiye, "Christian Witness."

PART 1: MISSION IN RETROSPECT AND PROSPECT

Engaging the Memory of our Church History and Questioning our Allegiances

The wise words of LeBlanc's grandfather ("Always look over your shoulder at where you have been more than you look ahead to where you are going when you are on a new trail") invite us to be mindful of our true past. We need to look even beyond the two thousand years of church history, and even all the way back to after the fall and to the history of Israel. Looking this far back give us a realistic perspective on our present as individuals and churches. The Bible documented how we have misused power to make others into "our own image," rather than welcoming the different image of our neighbor. God had to remind the Israelites regularly to treat those different than them as their own (Lev 19:33–34; 2 Chr 6:32–33; Jer 22:3). The horrors of the Crusades, colonization, the sexual misconduct and abuse in our churches, and even our monocultural churches are examples of God's people using power to alienate and to abuse. As the Uruguayan journalist Eduardo Galeano said: "We live in a culture of isolation, where we see our neighbor as a threat and never as a promise."[2] This is the ultimate expression of the fall.

I echo LeBlanc's second point, which was a call to identify our church allegiances. The ultimate question is: Who do we really worship, individually and collectively? Or what do we hold as the highest value? We prefer a tamed God, rather than a sovereign and mysterious one. So, we become idol manufacturers. We make our own gods and move them according to our will. Our history shows how God's people, starting with Israel and then the church, created systems that aimed to speak and to act on behalf of God but became idolatrous displays of a human quest to dominate others. Many of Israel's oral laws and Christendom religious systems are examples of love of power more than love of God. God often rebuked Israel for their idolatry and warned them against the dangers of it (Exod 20:3–6; Isa 44:9–20; 45:20; Jonah 2:8; Ps 135:16–18). Numerous missionary methods of Christendom mirrored the expectations of the Judaizers of Galatians 2. These Judaizers were Jewish Christians who expected Gentile Christians to live as Jews in accordance with Jewish customs, because this was aligned with their understanding of salvation. Any attempt to make others into our own image elevates ourselves to the place of God and that is a God-defying idolatry.

2. "Interview with Eduardo Galeano."

The reality is that followers of Jesus struggle to keep faithful in our love for God alone. We live in empire-building cultures that accumulate power for the purpose of self-aggrandizement. Our imaginations are tamed by the modern empires of humans, as Brueggemann describes in his "Prophetic Imagination."[3] As in the times of Elijah, individually and collectively, we find ourselves ostentatiously dancing around the altars of power, wealth, honor, pleasure, and endless productivity. We harm ourselves in the process of trying to get our gods to do our will. Yet nothing happens. We cannot manufacture the fire or passion we are seeking. So, we look for it in another idol. Only Yahweh is alive and able to respond with fire. As individuals and as the church, we must be able to ask ourselves (and be mindful to ask each generation): "How long will you waver between two opinions? If the Lord is God, follow him; but if Baal is God, follow him" (1 Kgs 18:21).

A Question and Biblical Analogy as Response

If many of the missionary efforts of the church are a cumulative expression of the misuse of power, what is our hope for the world? How can faith communities with a colonized memory still proclaim hope and be good news for their neighborhoods and beyond?

The hope is that Jesus meets the church and makes her whole, so she can proclaim the gospel despite her past—just as he did for the Samaritan woman in John 4. The story of Jesus and the Samaritan woman is rich in history and symbolism.[4] It offers hope for the church. Like the Samaritan woman, God's people—from Israel to our modern expressions of the church—have gone to bed with many wrong lovers. Throughout our history, we, the church, have loved power, wealth, honor, pleasure, and productivity more than God. We are now on our sixth husband (could it be consumerism?) and are still unfulfilled. Like the Samaritan woman, the church seems to be ashamed of her past, so she avoids public places like the well when everybody is there. Despite that, Jesus goes out of his way to meet us and still thinks that we have something to give. He asks for water.

---

3. Brueggemann, *Prophetic Imagination*.

4. The parable of the Samaritan woman points to a rich symbolic history that makes her a representative of Israel pursuing many "lovers" and leaving her husband Yahweh. The five past husbands of the Samaritan woman could be the five empire systems that Israel lusted after and mixed with: Egypt, Assyria, Babylon, Persia, and Greece. The current empire, Rome, was not her husband either.

Like the Samaritan woman, we seem to avoid deep conversations about our past or our current brokenness. When Jesus is inviting truth-telling and confession, we deflect the conversation:

> Jesus said to her, "You are right when you say you have no husband. The fact is, you have had five husbands, and the man you now have is not your husband. What you have just said is quite true." "Sir," the woman said, "I can see that you are a prophet. Our ancestors worshiped on this mountain, but you Jews claim that the place where we must worship is in Jerusalem." (John 4:17–20)

But Jesus insists. He does not only want an agreement about worship. He wants to speak truth and to make the woman clean—the living waters symbolizing freshness and purification.[5] He wants to make her holy. He wants her to reflect the image of God and to worship him alone in Spirit and truth (John 4:24). After Jesus reveals himself as her Messiah, her response is to proclaim the good news of Jesus with an urgency typical of those who met Christ:

> Then, leaving her water jar, the woman went back to the town and said to the people, "Come, see a man who told me everything I ever did. Could this be the Messiah?" They came out of the town and made their way toward him. (John 4: 28–30)

Hope and a Call to Action

The hope for the church is that Jesus still comes out of his way to engage us in truth-telling and liberating conversations. Jesus tells us the truth of our past. Then, we confess, acknowledge him, and go tell others about him, so that others too, "make their way toward him." (John 4:30). Finally, like Gomer,[6] we come back to our husband, Jesus, our only true love.

Meeting Jesus and being made whole by him realigns our powers to his. What would be some signs of that realignment in the church? What does it look like to "worship him in Spirit and truth" (John 4:24)? First, keeping weekly rhythms of Sabbath centered in the worship of God and

---

5. The "living waters" were a reference to waters that were fresh and used for ritual purification.

6. The Samaritan woman can also represent the Gomer. Her story reflected the relationship between God and Israel. Also, the Hebrew for Jesus and Hosea are very similar in meaning: "God is Salvation" and "God, Save."

sharing in community can be a sign and reminder of our allegiance to God and a resistance to the empires of over-productivity, consumerism, and self-sufficiency, among others. Overly busy calendars do not have room for hospitality. Our calendars, like the land of Boaz, need to have something left for gleaners and strangers like Ruth. Like Boaz, we can take interest and inquire about those gleaners and strangers who are in the margins of our lives and make sure that they are protected and provided for (Ruth 2:5). Second, a deeper engagement in truth-telling and reconciliation processes can correct our memory. Not all of us know enough about the "Missing and Murdered Indigenous Women and Girls" and the "Truth and Reconciliation" processes in Canada. Making time in our individual and collective calendars to inquire and engage the reports would be part of a redeemed missionary discipleship effort to engage with our First Nations brothers and sisters. Third, our churches' budgets can reflect our intention to protect the vulnerable by allocating funds to create safeguarding structures to prevent, report, and respond to any type of abuse. Finally, a church that is freed by the truth and made whole by Christ lives and evangelizes[7] with the good news, despite her colonial memory. It is a church that hears and remembers the "word of the Lord . . . saying: Not with an army, nor by might, but by my spirit" (Zech 4:6, Douay–Rheims Bible).

Bibliography

Brueggemann, Walter. *Biblical Perspectives on Evangelism: Living in a Three-Storied Universe*. Nashville: Abingdon, 1993.
———. *The Prophetic Imagination*. Minneapolis: Fortress, 2001.
Niringiye, Zac. "Christian Witness and the Common Good: Rethinking Christian Mission." Public lecture at Regent College, Vancouver, BC, May 30, 2018.
TeleSUR tv. "Interview with Eduardo Galeano—Un Abrazo de Muchos Brazos." March 1, 2011. https://youtu.be/VLoQgT58aeU.

---

7. Walter Brueggemann defines evangelism as "a task not simply of making outsiders into insiders, but of summoning insiders from amnesia to memory. ... amnesia (which on the surface shows up as illiteracy) causes the church to lack in any serious missional energy." Brueggemann, *Biblical Perspectives on Evangelism*, 90.

Part 2
Past Christian Mission and its Relevance to Present Mission

3

Ancient-Future Mission
Clement of Alexandria and Contextual Mission in Late Antiquity

MATTHEW FRIEDMAN

Introduction

IN HIS SEMINAL ARTICLE on the diversity of expressions of the Gospel across time and culture, "The Gospel as Prisoner and Liberator of Culture," Andrew F. Walls made the startling observation,

> Is there any truth which is not God's truth? Was God not active in the Greek past, not just the Jewish? So Justin Martyr and Clement of Alexandria came up with their own solutions, that there were Christians before Christ, that philosophy was—and is—the schoolmaster to bring the Greeks to Christ, just as was the Law for Jews.[1]

Walls goes on to suggest that even as Justin and Clement were wrestling with the relationship between their philosophical, cultural, and even religious background, even so are many emerging believers in various settings. Walls gives the particular example of Sub-Saharan Africa, but as we shall see, there have been wider applications of the two principles that Walls describes earlier on in this same article: the *indigenizing* principle, in which it is understood that the Gospel can be "at home" in any cultural setting but held in tension with the *pilgrim* principle, in which it is understood that the Gospel is never completely "at home" but always brings a challenge and speaks with a prophetic voice.

---

1. Walls, *Gospel as Prisoner and Liberator*, 14.

Before getting into some of the specific possible applications of this, we will journey back more than eighteen hundred years, and observe the life and writings of Clement of Alexandria, one of the most important thinkers in early Christian faith.

Clement's Birth and Spiritual Search

In all likelihood, Titus Flavius Clemens was not born into a Christian family, and from his name may have been descended from a family that was freed from slavery to a Roman nobleman. Though Epiphanius suggests that he may have been a native of Alexandria, it is likely (or at least possible) that he was actually from Athens.[2]

Clement does not give an account of how he came to faith in Christ; John Ferguson suggests that the process may have been more gradual rather than a sudden crisis of coming to faith.[3] Clement travelled in the midst of, or perhaps subsequent to his conversion, and met what he considered to be a remarkable collection of teachers in his journeys.

> Now this work of mine in writing is not artfully constructed for display; but my memoranda are stored up against old age, as a remedy against forgetfulness, truly an image and outline of those vigorous and animated discourses which I was privileged to hear, and of blessed and truly remarkable men. Of these the one, in Greece, an Ionic; the other in Magna Graecia: the first of these from Coele-Syria, the second from Egypt, and others in the East. The one was born in the land of Assyria, and the other a Hebrew in Palestine.[4]

Ferguson estimates that Clement's arrival and teaming up with Pantaenus in Alexandria would have taken place in about the year 180 CE, where he was to engage in his ministry of teaching and discipleship, as well as writing, for over the following twenty years, leaving only when persecutions broke out and made it difficult to remain.[5] During this season of teaching, he had several students who became well known later on, among whom were Alexander, the future Bishop of Jerusalem, Hippolytus, and Clement's

---

2. Tollington, *Clement*, 2–3.
3. Ferguson, *Clement*, 13.
4. Clement, *Stromata* 1.1.
5. Ferguson, *Clement*, 15–16.

most celebrated (as well as reviled) pupil, Origen, who was to succeed him in leadership of the school in Alexandria.[6]

The Alexandria of the late second century CE was on one hand, a major center of philosophy, but it was at the same time a city of unbridled indulgence in every imaginable manner; indeed, Clement's description of the society in which he is bearing witness sounds remarkably like modern life in many Western cities.[7] After fleeing Alexandria, Clement apparently spent time in Cappadocia as well as Antioch, but by 216 CE, his former pupil Alexander, then Bishop of Jerusalem, refers to him in correspondence with others in the past tense. Clement had gone to be with his Master.[8]

Educational Background and Methodology

Clement was not shy about putting his secular education to work in the service of the Lord's ministry. Though he tends not to give lengthy quotes from various sources, Clement's writings are replete with lines from some 384 different authors,[9] in addition to extensive quotations from Scripture. He both quotes from Philo and is clearly influenced by "Philo's synthesis of Greek and Hebrew thought,"[10] but what we see is that Clement is constantly looking for ways to put the Greek writers to work in the service of what he understands to be his part in serving God's mission. Part of Clement's motivation seemed to be to *help the Church overcome its fear of philosophy and literature*, often infused with a non-Christian worldview. He had a healthily positive view of the good aspects of the culture in which he found himself, and was convinced, even as was Justin, that there was much in Greek philosophy which could be redeemed, indeed, that God was using to draw the Greeks to himself.[11] He makes it clear that he considers all that is good in philosophy to be a *preparatio evangelica* for the Greeks, even as the Law was meant to be for the Jews:

> Accordingly, before the advent of the Lord, philosophy was necessary to the Greeks for righteousness. And now it becomes conducive to piety; being a kind of preparatory training to those who

6. MacCulloch, *Christianity*, 149–50.
7. Kinder, "Christian Woman," 4–5.
8. Ferguson, *Clement*, 16.
9. Ferguson, *Clement*, 17.
10. Ferguson, *Clement*, 18.
11. Chadwick, *Early Church*, 95–96.

> attain to faith through demonstration. "For thy foot," it is said, "will not stumble, if thou refer what is good, whether belonging to the Greeks or to us, to Providence." For God is the cause of all good things; but of some primarily, as of the Old and the New Testament; and of others by consequence, as philosophy. Perchance, too, philosophy was given to the Greeks directly and primarily, till the Lord should call the Greeks. For this was a schoolmaster to bring "the Hellenic mind," as the law, the Hebrews, "to Christ." Philosophy, therefore, was a preparation, paving the way for him who is perfected in Christ.[12]

It is about *communication* of the good news of salvation but in language and in a framework which Clement's target audience could understand.

It becomes, then, abundantly clear that Clement was operating out of a principle of critical contextualization, not only for the sake of pragmatism, but because he saw this being played out in principle in the Scriptures themselves. For example, he remarks on Paul's address in the Areopagus,

> Whence it is evident that the apostle, by availing himself of poetical examples from the Phenomena of Aratus, approves of what had been well spoken by the Greeks; and intimates that, by the unknown God, God the Creator was in a roundabout way worshipped by the Greeks; but that it was necessary by positive knowledge to apprehend and learn Him by the Son.[13]

And then goes on to quote Socrates as well as Scripture in support of his argument,

> We do not, indeed, receive absolutely all philosophy, but that of which Socrates speaks in Plato. "For there are (as they say) in the mysteries many bearers of the thyrsus, but few bacchanals"; meaning, "that many are called, but few chosen."[14]

He concludes the matter by saying, "Whether, then, they say that the Greeks gave forth some utterances of the true philosophy by accident, it is the accident of a divine administration."[15]

What we see here, then is that Clement was very *intentional* in his contextualization to Greek philosophy, not only in terms of forms, but in terms of seeing God's hand of prevenient grace as having been active in

---

12. Clement, *Stromata* 1.5.
13. Clement, *Stromata* 1.19.
14. Clement, *Stromata* 1.19.
15. Clement, *Stromata* 1.19.

the midst of the development of the philosophy to begin with, though he recognized that therein was both "untruth as well as truth."[16] He does not regard this uncritically but enters in with a clearly positive attitude. He could and did engage in polemics as well as apologetics in this context, but *even his polemics were contextualized.*

The above was partly illustrated in the classical work of H. Reinhold Niebuhr, *Christ and Culture*, in which he sought to illustrate the various stances the Christian faith might have vis-à-vis culture, though writing in a setting in which perhaps an understanding of "Christendom" was assumed. In his section on "Christ above culture," Niebuhr used Clement as one of his examples of this point. He sees the approach advocated by Clement as being one of *synthesis* between the Gospel and culture, but one in which the Gospel can and does bring a challenge to the culture where appropriate, but otherwise seeks out cultural bridges, as Clement did with Stoicism.[17] For Clement, Christ is "not against culture, but uses its best products in his work" and by means of his grace.[18] His approach thus described might be something rather like what a later generation of missions scholars would come to call a "fulfillment" approach, perhaps most famously advocated by J. N. Farquhar in the South Asian context through his *The Crown of Hinduism*. It is important to note, too, that even as Arkadi Choufrine (as summarized by Neil Anderson) described Clement's approach, he "was not the syncretistic borrower of Hellenistic and Gnostic ideas that some have thought; rather he synthesized these sources directly with the Christian gospel."[19]

It is worth adding that, as some have noted, not only does Clement synthesize his understanding of the Gospel with an expression of this in Hellenic terms, but he has a predecessor and influence on his way of doing this in the writings of Philo of Alexandria, whose contextual expressions of Jewish thought in this context bears both similarities and contrasts with Clement's own treatment of this. As Choufrine has also noted, Clement demonstrates a familiarity with Philo's thinking but also diverges from it in places, particularly in seeking to move his interpretation of the Scriptures in a Christ-ward direction. Choufrine demonstrates this in his analysis of both Philo and Clement's exegesis of Genesis 15:6, noting both parallels

16. McDermott, *God's Rivals*, 120.
17. Niebuhr, *Christ and Culture*, 123–24.
18. Niebuhr, *Christ and Culture*, 127.
19. Anderson, Review of *Gnosis*, 246–47.

and divergences. The influence of Jewish educational methodology in Clement has been noted by others as well.[20]

Clement's Primary Work: His Writings

Although Clement wrote a number of works, some of which are no longer extant, his writings are the three collections, which make up his famous trilogy. As we have already observed, it is in his writings that we see Clement as both missiologist and mission practitioner, seeking to bring the Gospel in a manner which will communicate to the people of Alexandria and beyond. The three books are the *Protreptikos*, or *Exhortation to the Greeks*; *Paedagogus*, or *The Tutor*; and finally, the unfinished monument of the *Stromata*, or the *Miscellanies*.

Consistently enough, the *Protreptikos* is entitled to evoke a "well-known literary genre" of the era: the "exhortation" to the study of philosophy.[21] The *Protreptikos* is focused more on evangelism, polemics, and wordplay, but it is a polemic coming *from within* the Greek philosophical system, not a foreign voice from without. For the most part, Clement seeks to use terminology which will communicate clearly with his philosophically thinking Hellenic audience, intentionally avoiding specifically *Christian* terminology.[22] Thus, he uses the word *philologos*, ordinarily meaning "with reason" to mean "devoted to the Word," and that those who reject the Word, or *Logos*, are being irrational: *alogos*.[23] Robert Louis Wilken notes that here Clement is "strutting before his readers, brandishing his command of Greek literature to play to the gallery. But it does not take him long to come to the point."[24] Clement is establishing his credibility as a knowledgeable speaker, the legitimacy of which will give him a platform from which to speak into the Greek context. He goes on, exhorting his readers that "raising their eyes, and looking above, let them abandon Helicon and Cithaeron, and take up their abode in 'Sion.' For out of Sion shall go forth the law, and the word of the LORD from Jerusalem."[25] Clement begins the final section of *Protreptikos* with exhortation to reach

20. Aswin-Siejkowski, "Clement," 87.
21. Ferguson, *Clement*, 44.
22. Trigg, "Oikonomia," 33.
23. Ferguson, *Clement*, 45.
24. Wilken, *Spirit*, 55.
25. Clement, *Protreptikos* 1.1.

for salvation in Christ, and yet still using illustrations from the Greek classics. See how he turns the illustration of Odysseus sailing past Charybdis and the Sirens into a metaphor of clinging to Christ:

> Sail past the song; it works death. Exert your will only, and you have overcome ruin; bound to the wood of the cross, thou shalt be freed from destruction: the word of God will be thy pilot, and the Holy Spirit will bring thee to anchor in the haven of heaven. Then shalt thou see my God, and be initiated into the sacred mysteries, and come to the fruition of those things which are laid up in heaven reserved for me, which "ear hath not heard, nor have they entered into the heart of any."[26]

Thus, Jaroslav Pelikan notes that Clement is using "the image of Odysseus at the mast as a foreshadowing of Jesus," and that they could successfully bring them past the disaster and temptation "because of Jesus, the Logos and Word of God, the *Christian* Odysseus."[27]

Clement's next book was the *Paedagogus,* or *The Tutor,* as has been mentioned earlier. *Paedagogus* is designed as a manual of discipleship and ethical living and is perhaps in part a reflection of Clement's own widespread learning that he, "consistently saw himself as a faithful pupil of Jesus, the divine Tutor."[28] The Tutor is described this way:

> [T]he good Instructor, the Wisdom, the Word of the Father, who made man, cares for the whole nature of His creature; the all-sufficient Physician of humanity, the Savior, heals both body and soul. "Rise up," He said to the paralytic; "take the bed on which thou liest, and go away home;" and straightway the infirm man received strength. And to the dead He said, "Lazarus, go forth;" and the dead man issued from his coffin such as he was ere he died, having undergone resurrection. Further, He heals the soul itself by precepts and gifts—by precepts indeed, in course of time, but being liberal in His gifts, He says to us sinners, "Thy sins be forgiven thee."[29]

As a whole, *The Tutor,* focusing now on discipleship issues than on evangelism, is significantly (and appropriately) more focused on quoting from the Scriptures than was the more evangelistic *Exhortation,* though

---

26. Clement, *Protreptikos* 1.12.
27. Pelikan, *Jesus,* 42–43.
28. Pelikan, *Jesus,* 38.
29. Clement, *Paedagogus* 1.2.

with the *Stromata* we will see a return to what seems at times to be a radically contextualized format. At the same time, Ferguson notes that, "he begins ... with two almost blatant references to Aristotle and Apollinides, and ends with two equally obtrusive references to Bacchylides and Homer. He sets his Christian injunctions in a pagan framework."[30]

Finally, we come to the *Stromata*, or *Miscellanies*, in which we see a rather jumbled but at times remarkably insightful effort to contextualize the gospel not only to the philosophers, but to the Gnostics who were, in some measure, seeking God, but in the wrong direction. Hence, the full title of this final collection is *Miscellanies of Gnostic Notes in accordance with True Philosophy*.[31] We have already given some quotations from the *Stromata* containing exegesis supporting Clement's contextualized approach. It is worth giving one more quotation, especially as it is focused on the issue of integrity in the work of cultural and/or religious accommodation:

> ... the noble apostle circumcised Timothy, though loudly declaring and writing that circumcision made with hands profits nothing. But that he might not, by dragging all at once away from the law to the circumcision of the heart through faith those of the Hebrews who were reluctant listeners, compel them to break away from the synagogue, he, "accommodating himself to the Jews, became a Jew that he might gain all." He, then, who submits to accommodate himself merely for the benefit of his neighbors, for the salvation of those for whose sake he accommodates himself, not partaking in any dissimulation . . . . But for the benefit of his neighbors alone, he will do things which would not have been done by him primarily, if he did not do them on their account. Such an one gives himself for the Church, for the disciples whom he has begotten in faith; for an example to those who are capable of receiving the supreme economy of the philanthropic and God loving Instructor, for confirmation of the truth of his words, for the exercise of love to the Lord. Such an one is unenslaved by fear, true in word, enduring in labor, never willing to lie by uttered word, and in it always securing sinlessness; since falsehood, being spoken with a certain deceit, is not an inert word, but operates to mischief.[32]

As the expanded title indicates, Clement was seeking to bring the Gnostics into true fellowship with Christ. In the *Stromata*, we see him

30. Ferguson, *Clement*, 101.
31. Ferguson, *Clement*, 107.
32. Clement, *Stromata* 7.9.

using not only their terminology but their very name, in essence co-opting it in order to help them see that their true goals of *gnosis* will be met and found only in union with Messiah.

> As, then, philosophy has been brought into evil repute by pride and self-conceit, so also gnosis by false gnosis called by the same name; of which the apostle writing says, "Timothy, keep that which is committed to thy trust, avoiding the profane and vain babblings and oppositions of science *(gnosis)* falsely so called; which some professing, have erred concerning the faith".... Well, then, if the Lord is the truth, and wisdom, and power of God, as in truth He is, it is shown that the real Gnostic is he that knows Him, and His Father by Him.[33]

Here again, we see Clement engaging in polemics to some degree, but it is a *contextualized polemic*, engaged in as an *insider*.

Some Modern Missional Applications

As has already been noted via Niebuhr, there has been some application of the life and thought of Clement to situations in modern mission. Indeed, having noted the parallels between Farquhar's approach with that of Clement, it is important to note that he was hardly alone in this. A more recent version of this is that of Bede Griffiths. Robert Fastiggi and Jose Pereira have noted such application in the South Asian Hindu context, too, and that even as

> [i]n the Patristic Age, Christian writers like St. Justin Martyr and Clement of Alexandria manifested a deep respect for pagan wisdom and showed a willingness to explain the Christian mysteries in language borrowed from Stoic and Platonic philosophy.[34]

This was also the case with such Indian theologians and missiologists as A. J. Appasamy, who sought to find positive bridges for the Gospel in the Indian *bhakti* devotional tradition,[35] and the numerous accounts of this approach described in Robin Boyd's classic *An Introduction to Indian Christian Theology*. In addressing how this connects with what Boyd sees

---

33. Clement, *Stromata* 1.10.

34. Fastiggi and Pereira, "Swami," 22.

35. See for example Appasamy, *Temple Bells* and Appasamy, *Gospel and India's Heritage*.

as the need of India, and perhaps contra the assumptions of Christendom in Niebuhr's treatment, he sees the importance of bridge-building and innovation as opposed to the construction of more "systematic theologies" in the Indian context. Boyd writes that,

> India's immediate need is not so much for an Aquinas, a Calvin or a Barth as for men like Clement and Origen, men of adventurous mind and vivid imagination, men like Sundar Singh who can convince people's minds in their own language and win their hearts. It is a working, witnessing, convincing theology that is needed and that is in fact being forged today.[36]

In the context of Sub-Saharan Africa, the late Kwame Bediako, in his *Theology and Identity: The Impact of Culture upon Christian Thought in the Second Century and in Modern Africa* sought to pursue, if one will, the suggestion of Andrew F. Walls concerning the application of Clement's principles to theologizing and mission in his own context. He noted that Clement "understood Christianity as the fulfillment of the divine education of the human mind and personality in the Greek philosophical tradition"[37]—the idea being that God *integrated* what was good in Greek philosophy toward his own ends—and that he could do the same with elements of traditional African traditions, too. Significantly, Bediako reflects on the thinking of John Mbiti, who regarded the African Traditional Religion as the "God-given preparation for the Gospel"—for Mbiti, "Christian Faith" was the universal reality, whereas "Christianity" is the local manifestation of that faith in context.[38] Walls, who was Bediako's doctoral supervisor, noted that this volume was of "quite outstanding importance."[39]

It is important to add that this approach has had its detractors, too. Keith Ferdinando, in an analysis of Bediako's thesis, challenges not only Bediako (and those whom he quotes) but also the very approach from Clement on which Bediako has based his presentation.[40] Ferdinando suggests that while there is a significant application of Walls's "indigenizing" principle, it is crucial to also integrate the "pilgrim" principle—there will necessarily be some "degree of cultural alienation" in the process of coming to faith in Christ. He even notes, with Miroslav Volf, in his

---

36. Boyd, *Indian Christian Theology*, 260.
37. Bediako, *Theology and Identity*, 47.
38. Bediako, *Theology and Identity*, 331.
39. Ferdinando, "Christian Identity," 122.
40. Ferdinando, "Christian Identity."

monumental *Exclusion and Embrace*, that even Abraham had to push back against his own cultural milieu.[41] Yet, as was noted above, Clement's work itself included a significant element of *polemic* concerning the Hellenic cultural setting—but his critique was expressed in the language of a cultural "insider," even appropriating and redefining the term *Gnostic* to express Scriptural truth rather than heresy.

In the context of mission in the Muslim context, this type of appropriation of the birth tradition of those coming to faith could also be utilized not only apologetically in the context of evangelism but perhaps in discipleship as well. A. H. Mathias Zahniser has suggested that the Qur'an itself could be regarded as a kind of *preparatio evangelica* for the Gospel, and that, perhaps with care, its contents could be utilized by those coming to faith in Christ from within such communities.[42] While more recent caution has been published on Christian *misappropriation* of the Qur'an,[43] it has also been suggested that Muslim-background Jesus-followers, like Clement before them, might fruitfully employ the Islamic tradition of figural exegesis in *ta'wil* in reinterpreting their ancestral traditions in a manner that will contribute to and integrate with their present faith in Christ.[44]

Conclusion

We have very briefly examined the life and work of Clement of Alexandria here, in relation to the work of mission. While Clement is not often thought of primarily as a *missionary*, it is my contention that he can properly be classed as an early missiologist in light of his dynamically motivated, lifelong focus on bringing the Gospel to the philosophers and intelligentsia of his generation in a manner that served as an example (albeit an unfortunately, often neglected, even virtually forgotten one) for the centuries afterwards and even for us now. Let us be challenged to consider the application of such strategy in our engagement with our own cultures, as well as any other culture to which our Lord may choose to bring us, recognizing the working of God's prevenient grace in their midst—even as we seek to lovingly share salvation with them.

---

41. Volf, *Exclusion*, 39, quoted in Ferdinando, "Christian Identity," 135.
42. Zahniser, "Doctrine."
43. Accad, *Sacred Misinterpretation*.
44. Friedman, *Union with God*, 243–44.

Reflection Questions

1. In what ways did Clement seek to build bridges of understanding for the Gospel using elements of Greek philosophy?
2. Conversely, in what manner did Clement seek to *challenge* the philosophy and worldview of Hellenism? Of Gnosticism?
3. How might Clement have erred in his approach, either in adapting his message to his context or in not going far enough in such adaptation?

Bibliography

Accad, Martin. *Scriptural Misinterpretation: Reaching Across the Christian-Muslim Divide.* Grand Rapids: Eerdmans, 2019.

Anderson, Neil. Review of *Gnosis, Theophany, Theosis: Studies in Clement of Alexandria's Appropriation of His Background,* by Arkadi Choufrine. *Journal of Early Christian Studies* 12 (2004) 246–48.

Appasamy, A. J. *The Gospel and India's Heritage.* London and Madras: SPCK, 1942.

———. *Temple Bells.* Madras: SPCK, 1930.

Aswin-Siejkowski, Piotr. "Clement of Alexandrea." In *The Wiley-Blackwell Companion to Patristics,* edited by Ken Parry, 84–97. Oxford: Wiley-Blackwell, 2015.

Bediako, Kwame. *Theology and Identity: The Impact of Culture upon Christian Thought in the Second Century and in Modern Africa.* Oxford: Regnum, 1992.

Boyd, Robin. *An Introduction to Indian Christian Theology.* Delhi: SPCK, 1998.

Chadwick, Henry. *The Early Church: The Pelican History of the Church.* Vol. 1. Baltimore: Pelican, 1967.

Choufrine, Arkadi. *Gnosis, Theophany, Theosis: Studies in Clement of Alexandria's Appropriation of His Background.* Patristic Studies. Vol. 5. New York: Peter Lang, 2002.

Clement of Alexandria. *Exhortation to the Greeks (Protreptikos).* Translated by G. W. Butterworth. Loeb Classical Library. New York: Putnam, 1919.

———. *The Instructor (Paedagogus).* Translated by William Wilson. In *Ante-Nicene Fathers.* Vol. 2, edited by A. Roberts and J. Donaldson. Buffalo: Christian Literature, 1885.

———. *Stromata, or Miscellanies.* Translated by William Wilson. In *Ante-Nicene Fathers.* Vol. 2, edited by A. Roberts and J. Donaldson. Buffalo: Christian Literature, 1885.

Farquhar, J. N. *The Crown of Hinduism.* London: Oxford University Press, 1913.

Fastiggi, Robert, and Jose Pereira. "The Swami from Oxford: Bede Griffiths Wants to Integrate Catholicism and Hinduism." *Crisis Magazine* (March 1, 1991).

Ferdinando, Keith. "Christian Identity in the African Context: Reflections on Kwame Bediako's Theology and Identity." *Journal of the Evangelical Theological Society* 50 (2007) 121–43.

Ferguson, John. *Clement of Alexandria.* New York: Twayne, 1974.

Friedman, Matthew. *Union with God in Christ: Early Christian and Wesleyan Spirituality as an Approach to Islamic Mysticism*. ASM Monograph Series. Eugene, OR: Pickwick, 2017.

Kinder, Donald Michael. "The Role of the Christian Woman as Seen by Clement of Alexandria." PhD diss., University of Iowa, 1987.

MacCulloch, Diarmid. *Christianity: The First Three Thousand Years*. New York: Penguin, 2009.

McDermott, Gerald. *God's Rivals: Why Has God Allowed Different Religions? Insights from the Bible and the Early Church*. Downers Grove, IL: IVP Academic, 2007.

Pelikan, Jaroslav. *Jesus Through the Centuries: His Place in the History of Culture*. New York: Perennial, 1985.

Tollington, R. B. *Clement of Alexandria: A Study of Christian Liberalism*. London: Williams and Norgate, 1914.

Trigg, Joseph W. "God's Marvelous Oikonomia: Reflections of Origen's Understanding of Divine and Human Pedagogy in the Address Ascribed to Gregory Thaumaturgus." *Journal of Early Christian Studies* 9 (2001) 27–52.

Volf, Miroslav. *Exclusion and Embrace: A Theological Exploration of Identity, Otherness, and Reconciliation*. Nashville: Abingdon, 1996.

Walls, Andrew F. "The Gospel as Prisoner and Liberator of Culture." In *The Missionary Movement in Christian History: Studies in the Transmission of Faith*, 3–15. Maryknoll, NY: Orbis, 1996.

Wilken, Robert Louis. *The Spirit of Early Christian Thought*. New Haven, CT: Yale University Press, 2003.

Zahniser, A. H. Mathias. "The Doctrine of the Incarnation Supports the Christian Use of the Qur'an 'for Example of Life and the Instruction of Manners': A Proposal." In *Jesus and the Incarnation: Reflections of Christians from Islamic Contexts*, edited by David Emmanuel Singh, 31–45. Oxford: Regnum, 2011.

4

Striking a Hopeful Pose
Extending Ralph Winter's Ten Epochs of Redemptive History

GLENN MARTIN

Introduction

THREE MONTHS IN 1984 at the US Center for World Mission in Pasadena marked me. Mission theory pulsated with life in unforgettable interaction with missiologists like Ralph Winter and Don Richardson. Leaving there for the steamy jungles of Belize, Winter's "The Kingdom Strikes Back: Ten Epochs of Redemptive History" was vital to my sense of place in a cosmic narrative.

The genius of Winter's analysis is in its ability to guide the reader toward a missiological perspective on history. One is left asking, "How does what is being reported in the news today affect the Great Commission's advance?" Or perhaps more pointedly, "How is God at work here to fulfill his promise to bless all nations through the seed of Abraham?"

Winter's last five epochs in "The Kingdom Strikes Back" are all geographical in nature (the first five are not). In each epoch, he juxtaposes the people of God in their own process, largely ambivalent about their mandate to carry the blessing forward and a world reality that catalyzes the fulfillment of the expansive purpose of God. This chapter proposes an extension of that rationale, to consider the global tension today between secularization fuelled by the fast pace of modernization, a reactive fundamentalism, and the implications of that tension for mission. Such polarizing dynamics between progressives and conservatives are not unique to Christianity nor the Western context nor even to our era; we see them in the New Testament narratives. What might that say to us about the appropriate qualitative expression of our mandate?

In our classic understanding, a people group is defined as "the largest group within which the gospel can spread as a church-planting movement without encountering barriers of understanding or acceptance."[1] The greatest barriers to the "reaching of the unreached" might be best understood today not as geographical but as conceptual, relational, or even affective, within a globalized world with a widely shared trade language and popular culture. To be a valid expression in our context, the Gospel's advance must be in the spirit of the incarnational suffering servant—"as sheep among wolves"—not only in order to faithfully represent the Master but also to get a proper hearing.

Winter's ten epochs are broad strokes, intended to mark out the contours of mission history, but are, of course, subject to charges of oversimplification. Winter brushes past developments of huge significance in the Church of the East and in Abyssinian Africa (both of which parallel the celebrated Celtic advances), and only gives cursory mention to qualitative issues of enormous import in the Roman Catholic mission to Latin America.

At risk of oversimplification, the central global conflict today is not so much between East and West or between the West and the rest but rather between a secularizing element and a fundamentalist element within each national, cultural, or religious entity: the former abetted by globalization, and the latter by the conservative reaction to it. At its most basic, the argument of this chapter is that the energy of the secularists and the fundamentalist factions will be spent on wresting power from each other, while in the shadow of that conflict—as the wind shakes the trees—counter-cultural Christ-followers sacrificially serving will winsomely gather their fruit. It is a hopeful perspective, in anticipation of both increased shaking and increased harvest.

To develop this argument, we consider both the secularization thesis and fundamentalism as missiological concerns. First, though, we consider Winter's own comments about developments on the horizon beyond his writing of "The Kingdom Strikes Back."

---

1. Winter and Koch, "Finishing the Task," 524.

PART 2: PAST CHRISTIAN MISSION AND ITS RELEVANCE TO PRESENT MISSION

In Winter's Words

The third edition of *Perspectives: A Reader* was published in 1999, two years before the infamous events of September 11, 2001. Winter's own evaluation of that moment is prescient. "Will the immeasurably strengthened non-Western world invade Europe and America just as the Goths invaded Rome and the Vikings overran Europe? Will the 'Third World' turn on us in a new series of 'Barbarian' invasions?"[2]

Speaking of the period from 1945–1969, Winter notes, "If we compare this period to the collapse of the Western Roman Empire's domination over its conquered provinces of Spain, Gaul and Britain, and to the breakdown of control over non-Frankish Europe under Charlemagne's successors, we might anticipate—at least by the logic of sheer parallelism—that the Western world itself will soon be significantly dominated by non-Westerners."[3] Elsewhere, Winter muses, "If we in the West insist on keeping our blessing instead of sharing it, then we will, like other nations before us, have to lose our blessing for the remaining nations to receive it."[4]

Winter notes four redemptive mechanisms by which God fulfills his covenant to Abraham, making his seed a blessing to the nations in each epoch of mission history. Winter calls these: "1) going voluntarily, 2) involuntarily going without missionary intent, 3) coming voluntarily, and 4) coming involuntarily."[5] Except in the first case, the persons coming and going are not usually aware of doing so in fulfillment of the *missio Dei*. One thinks of international immigrants who by the millions have sought the benefits of studying and living in the West, where the freedom of religion, human rights record, educational opportunity, and economic freedom—though imperfect—are clearly improved because of Christianity.[6] Few immigrants and international students articulate their coming as a pursuit of God, though God may well be said to have arranged it. But what of the West to which they have come? Is Christianity really in a definitive decline, suffering from the mortal wound of secularization?

---

2. Winter, "Kingdom," 199.
3. Winter, "Kingdom," 210.
4. Winter, "Kingdom," 213.
5. Winter, "Kingdom," 197.
6. Mangalwadi, *Book*.

Parsing Secularization and its Variants

If secularization puts people off the message of the Gospel, it matters a great deal to mission. Craig Ott contends, "It can be fairly said that most societies around the world are experiencing the forces of secularization as a movement away from traditional religious ways."[7] He adds that "this does not mean that people are necessarily less religious, but that the role of religion in personal lives and in the public square is changing."[8] As Harold Netland says it, "Modern people are often still religious, but the ways in which they understand and express religious commitments today are different."[9]

Netland further notes that secularization is "the process whereby plausible alternatives to the 'God-reference of fullness' arise."[10] Secularization contributes to the co-existence of multiple plausible alternatives, in other words, pluralism. After decades of widely cited research in secularization theory, Peter Berger in 2014 concludes that "pluralism, the co-existence of different worldviews and value systems in the same society, is the major change brought about by modernity for the place of religion both in the minds of individuals and in the institutional order."[11] As against Charles Taylor's *A Secular Age* in 2007, Berger argues, "We don't live in a secular age; *we live in a pluralist age.*"[12] As against his own earlier work, Berger says, "We thought that modernity invariably means a decline of religion. It took me more than twenty years to conclude that the theory is empirically untenable."[13] He calls the evidence "overwhelming" and goes on to say, "The world today is as religious as it ever was, in places more so than ever."[14] In that assessment, Berger echoes the missiological research of Gina Zurlo and Todd Johnson who contend that "despite increased modernity the world has in fact become *more* religious."[15] Zurlo and Johnson note that the percentage of the global population that self-reports religious affiliation increased between 1970 and 2010, from 80.8

---

7. Ott, "Introduction," ix.
8. Ott, "Introduction," ix.
9. Netland, "Secularization," 4.
10. Netland, "Secularization," 6.
11. Berger, *Many Altars*, ix.
12. Berger, "Good of Religious Pluralism," 39.
13. Berger, "Good of Religious Pluralism," 39.
14. Berger, "Good of Religious Pluralism," 39.
15. Zurlo and Johnson, "Unaffiliated," 50.

percent to 88.1 percent, and that rather than decreasing, this number is expected to rise further to 91.5 percent by 2050.[16]

Speaking then of pluralism as his preferred lens, Berger defines pluralism as "the coexistence, generally peaceful, of different religions, worldviews, and value systems within the same society."[17] Though Berger contends that pluralism has happened before in history, he identifies two things that are unique about pluralism today. First, religious pluralism today is accompanied by secularism as an alternative belief system. Secondly, Berger notes that religious pluralism today is globalized.

How did we get here? Strong connections exist between the advance of technology, globalization, secularization, and pluralism. It is helpful to think of those words in a continuum. We are too far removed from advances like the mariner's astrolabe or the mechanical clock to appreciate the difference that they made when they appeared on the scene, but it is manifestly clear that the edifice of globalization would not exist without technological breakthroughs such as these and those that followed them. Increased technological capacity coupled with imperial will in the early modern era to give us a world connected in unprecedented ways economically, politically, culturally, and religiously.

Technology is to globalization as brain is to the mind. Technology can be said to have made globalization possible, yet globalization is much more than just technology. How did these two beget secularization and pluralism? The early modern intellectual context that lent itself to scientific inquiry and technological advance, in other pursuits, assaulted supernaturalism and undermined biblical Christianity. This is the thread of the secularization thesis about which much has already been said. We might say here in summary that advances in science and technology (especially in transportation and communication) tended on one hand to thrust people of diverse faith constituencies together in the same physical space, even while those advances also lent themselves to the undermining of the understood certainties of faith.[18]

Increased trade and migration have led to increased heterogeneity almost everywhere. This has prompted ongoing reflection about diversity, and the search for appropriate metaphors, such as the contrast between a "melting pot" and a "cultural mosaic"—and Canada's preference for the

---

16. Zurlo and Johnson, "Unaffiliated," 50.
17. Berger, "Good of Religious Pluralism," 40.
18. See Martin, "Technology," 157–58.

term "multiculturalism."[19] Where religious freedom is protected by law, racial and cultural diversity naturally lend themselves to religious pluralism: Western urban communities now commonly have mosques and Buddhist temples alongside Christian houses of worship. This development is a matter of consternation to those Christians who interpret it as the supplanting of a Christian heritage. Other Christians, however, view this as a multi-faceted opportunity—as if cued by awareness of Winter's attractive and expansive forces in the fulfillment of the Abrahamic blessing. Immigrants coming from contexts where public witness of the Gospel is illegal might find greater exposure to Christ in the West. Additionally, Christian immigrants themselves may be key to renewal in the West, as (for example) immigrants to Canada are on the whole less secular than Canadians born in Canada.[20] In terms of how Christians tend to respond to pluralism, Berger notes that Christians "like the idea of house churches in China, but they regret the construction of mosques in the Netherlands."[21]

A more troubling pluralism in the West, however, is not the pluralism that we see when a particular piece of real estate traditionally thought of as Christian is given over to a different religion but rather the de-Christianization of a human population that has traditionally self-identified as Christian. This de-Christianization or apostasy is related to the secularism that Taylor[22] more especially speaks of, and that has been documented extensively by Pew Research in the USA, and more recently again by Rick Hiemstra in Canada.[23] This breakdown of a historic Christian consensus arguably tends toward an increasingly polarized society as neighbors with a common ethnicity and common Christian heritage spread ever farther apart down divergent pathways of sense-making or "alternate plausibility structures"[24] in many ways hostile to one another. Thus, Reginald Bibby[25] identifies polarization as Canada's new religious reality, as people who in generations past might have felt societal pressure to appear Christian no longer feel any need to do so and now move outward from the nominal Christian center to affirm convictions either toward secularism or toward

---

19. Burnet and Driedger, "Multiculturalism."
20. Bibby, "Being Pro-Religious"; Martin, "Africa."
21. Berger, "Good of Religious Pluralism," 40.
22. Taylor, *Secular Age*.
23. Pew, "US Decline"; Hiemstra, "Not Christian."
24. Newbigin, *Gospel*.
25. Bibby, "Religious Polarization."

evangelical faith. Even so, this polarization thesis of Bibby's is also contested.[26] The numbers at the moment in Canada are not encouraging and mostly indicate the decline of Christian faith.[27] Much is in process. It is difficult to estimate the long-term Great Commission impact of the COVID-19 pandemic and the social instability around issues of racial injustice. The hope of spiritual renewal is in the air, but empirical indicators of that are yet hard to come by. Many questions remain. If we take Berger's line of thinking and if pluralism continues on the rise, will pluralism lead to increased polarization? If so, what are the poles to be considered here?

Fundamentalism

To return to our overview, this chapter argues that the central global conflict today is between a secularizing element and a fundamentalist element within each national, cultural, or religious entity, the former abetted by globalization and technological advance, the latter by the conservative or fundamentalist reaction to them.

What then is fundamentalism? Berger suggests that fundamentalism is the attempt to restore or create anew a taken-for-granted body of beliefs and values. In other words, fundamentalism is always *reactive*, and what it reacts against is precisely the aforementioned relativization process."[28] Scott Appleby calls fundamentalisms as:

> increasingly sophisticated reactions against secular modernity that seek to fight back against the enemies of traditional religion by constructing religiously inspired and quintessentially modern alternatives to 'godless', idolatrous governments, institutions and political and cultural elites.[29]

The breakdown in communication between polarized elements of society has been particularly noteworthy in American politics and public discourse; social media may well have exacerbated the matter.[30] Ezra Klein notes,

---

26. Reimer, "Conservative Protestants."
27. Hiemstra, "Not Christian."
28. Berger, "Between Relativism," 13.
29. Appleby, "Fundamentalisms," 403.
30. Bail et al., "Exposure."

> The political media is biased, but not toward the left or right so much as toward loud, outrageous, colorful, inspirational, confrontational. It is biased toward the political stories and figures who activate our identities, because it is biased toward and dependent on the fraction of the country with the most intense political identities.[31]

We are still coming to understand how our increasing plurality of news sources, and our tendency to choose to listen to what reinforces what we already believe, interacting with one another either to facilitate our polarization or to arrest it.[32]

Academic sources confirm what we know in our guts to be true: conservative reactions to secularization's relentless impact on culture are evident on every continent and in every major population and religious block. This tension manifests on occasion as violence, or as shouting matches in houses of government but perhaps more commonly and significantly, as silence between old friends unable to get past a difference of opinion. Where do we go from here?

The Best Posture: H.O.P.E.

In the spirit of Winter's "The Empire Strikes Back," what might we call the church to in this epoch? If we understand the unique mark of this age to be *the tension* between secularism and fundamentalism, what does that say about the qualitative nature of our witness? What kind of witness disarms the contentious nature of the current conversation? In what way might we agree with Berger[33] that pluralism is an opportunity for the church?

In proposing a strategy for ministry into an increasingly secularized context, W. Jay Moon identifies six complexities with their corresponding opportunities for the church. The complexities that he identifies are secularism, pluralism, individualism, relativism, identity, and technology.[34] Of note, Moon's words form the acronym "spirit" and instruct us to see these complexities as opportunities, because every challenging cultural trait has a vulnerability to the grace of the Gospel. A secular public may be hungry for the transcendent. Pluralism may mean that a Hindu

---

31. Klein, "Why the Media."
32. Eady et al., "How Many People"; Hameleers and van der Meer, "Misinformation."
33. Berger, "Good of Religious Pluralism."
34. Moon, "Evangelism," 55–60.

feels comfortable going to church with you. Individualism usually means that people carry around an unmet longing for community. Inspired by Moon's acronym and Winter's text, I suggest four words to characterize our witness in this epoch, to spell H.O.P.E.

Hospitality

In the face of narcissistic, atomic individualism and the fortress mentality of collectivist authoritarianism, the church must resist the temptation to withdraw from the world. Hospitality, then, is fitting, as commanded of leaders in Scripture, and as catalyst to so much more. Rosaria Butterfield illustrates what hospitality can do within highly polarized American civil society.[35] Hospitality is also essential in outreach to international newcomers, to leverage the advantage offered us by our physical proximity to one another. How many international students or other newcomers to the USA and Canada ever get to share a meal in a host home? Ed Stetzer estimates that "three out of four international students never set foot in a North American home during their time in school."[36] When we consider that North America is now host to an estimated 1.8 million international students,[37] we are at risk of missing an extraordinary opportunity.

Openness

If we think of polarization as something of the spirit of the age, openness can be understood as its antidote. Openness does not mean that one has no moral convictions or refuses to stand for anything doctrinally. The openness commended here requires an unbending focus on our greater mission-building bridges for the Gospel to the unreached—in spite of the cultural storms that would distract us. Secondly, the openness commended here is a willingness to engage friendships with those who are different, to be "Celtic" in creating community, welcoming people into belonging before requiring "believing and behaving."[38] This might be especially noteworthy in the face of fundamentalism's insistence that behavior

---

35. Butterfield, *Gospel*.
36. Stetzer, "Ministering."
37. Stetzer, "Ministering."
38. Hunter, *Celtic Way*.

is what defines the community.[39] As against secularism, newcomers can belong while they sort out what they believe. As against fundamentalism, behaving is not prerequisite to belonging.

This openness must be willing to engage real friendship with non-Christians. Johnson and others indicated in 2015 that the "most important missions statistic of our day" is that 86 percent of the world's Muslims, Buddhists, and Hindus do not personally know a Christian.[40] Even in the face of unprecedented migration and interaction of diverse peoples around the globe, the troubling statistic is not expected to drop below 80 percent in the next 30 years. How can this be? The crux of the challenge is our extreme ethnocentrism and polarization, augmented by individualism, such that we do not engage meaningful contact with those different from ourselves, whether they live overseas or share an office cubicle with us.

The openness that I commend here might be best understood as the posture of a student of mission attempting to exercise at home what is expected on the field. Our task has always been to adapt to the context without compromising the message. We are ever challenged to be full of grace and truth as Jesus was.

Practical Presence

Rodney Stark provides vivid analysis of how the early church won the Roman Empire, significantly by being present and active in crises such as the devastating epidemics of 165 and 251 CE, when others who had the power to do so fled the cities to the countryside.[41] It is imperative to be present and to serve the physical needs of the hurting around the church. The emphasis here is on local impact, relationally based. One thinks of Gregory in 600 CE marshalling the church in Rome in the face of a catastrophic collapse of basic services. Our government-funded "safety net" in the West is so strong that it might seem a distant possibility that local volunteerism could be vital to our collective survival. The hard times of 2020 may open our eyes to how a locally engaged church can be a lifeline in chaos.

In our prosperous but atomized society, individuals fall unnoticed through the cracks. Rising substance addiction and homelessness baffle civil authorities, and the church's practical help is appreciated. In the West, where

---

39. Denmark, "Fundamentalisms," 577.
40. Johnson et al., "Christianity 2015," 29.
41. Stark, *Rise of Christianity*, 73–94.

the church has been largely dismissed as irrelevant, practical presence may be a prerequisite to a revitalized proclamation of the Gospel.

Eternal Perspective

Hebrews 12:3 says that it was for the joy set before him that Jesus endured the cross. An eternal perspective is a wellspring of courage, longsuffering, and forbearance in both East and West. Witness for Christ in the face of fundamentalist opposition often calls for great courage, as seen of late in sub-Saharan Africa where Christians suffer severe persecution. Loyalty and longsuffering are tested; global leadership will come from such a church. But it is not only in the face of fundamentalism that forbearance is required. Forbearance is also required in the post-Christian West, in the face of a pendulum swing against a Christian moral consensus. We find an interesting parallel in early Christendom. Christianity's endorsement by Roman imperial power in the fourth century made Gospel witness beyond the empire more difficult. Winter notes, however, that in the time of Emperor Julian, the Apostate, the Gospel advance outside the empire encountered less resistance.[42] Though Julian's reign was seen as a cultural setback for Christianity within the empire, outside the empire it had redemptive mission value. Forbearance for us in the post-Christian West is necessary, and an eternal perspective helps us see the silver lining in our cultural crisis. We need forbearance to put up with "pushback," to really hear, without defensiveness, the perspective of those who recount injustices committed by nominally Christian leaders and by explicitly evangelical institutions. An eternal perspective helps us avoid unnecessarily conflating the crisis of our civilization with the end of the world.

An eternal perspective also serves as antidote to materialistic secularism; living for the eternal is a countercultural exercise. Just as it takes an eternal focus to bear persecution and martyrdom that come uninvited, it will take an equally clear eternal focus to willingly deny ourselves what everyone around us understands to be their natural right—to give up our plans for a life of ease and to instead live out our years in daily service to him who said "unless a grain of wheat falls into the earth and dies, it remains alone; but if it dies, it bears much fruit" (John 12:24, NASB). We have in Scripture and in other epochs of mission history bountiful examples to follow in this regard.

42. Winter, "Kingdom," 202.

Conclusion

Winter's ten epochs of history are so neat as to resist easy modification or addendum. How much cleaner can it get than what he came up with—a four-thousand-year continuum from Abraham to the completion of the Great Commission and the Messiah's (anticipated) Second Advent, with the First Advent placed squarely in the center of the timeline? That his final epoch is called "To the Ends of the Earth" has left some to wonder if the only available option to extend Winter's paradigm is the evangelization of the galaxy.[43] Though that would fit the title's Star Wars imagery, it is not the direction we take here. Rather, we extend the paradigm not in terms of physical geography but in terms of relational geography, penetrating barriers of comprehension or acceptance. What new relational territory is the missional church of our epoch to cross our Jordan into?

Reflection Questions

1. In what way does this chapter's argument resonate with you?
2. Where have you seen hospitality open doors for the Gospel?
3. On a personal level, which of the four letters of the acrostic H.O.P.E. stood out to you and why?

Bibliography

Appleby, R. Scott. "Fundamentalisms." In *A Companion to Contemporary Political Philosophy*, edited by Robert E. Goodin, et al., 403–13. Malden, MA: Blackwell, 2017.

Bail, Christopher A., et al. "Exposure to Opposing Views on Social Media Can Increase Political Polarization." *Proceedings of the National Academy of Sciences* 115 (2018) 9216–21.

Berger, Peter L. "Between Relativism and Fundamentalism." *The American Interest* 2 (2006) 9–17. https://www.the-american-interest.com/2006/09/01/between-relativism-and-fundamentalism/.

———. "The Good of Religious Pluralism: Peter L. Berger Outlines Four Benefits of Pluralism." *First Things: A Monthly Journal of Religion and Public Life* 262 (2016) 39–43. https://www.firstthings.com/article/2016/04/the-good-of-religious-pluralism.

———. *The Many Altars of Modernity: Toward a Paradigm for Religion in a Pluralist Age*. Boston: de Gruyter, 2014.

---

43. Todd Johnson, email conversation, January 21, 2020.

Bibby, Reginald W. "Being Pro-Religious, Low Religious, and No Religious in Montreal: A Mirror of Canada and the World." Paper presented to the Catholic Archdiocese of Montreal, November 2017. http://reginaldbibby.com/images/MONTREAL_ ARCHDIOCESE_Thurs_Nov_30_FINAL.pdf.

———. "Religious Polarization in Canada: A Major Empirical Update." Paper presented at the Annual Meeting of the Society for the Scientific Study of Religion, Newport Beach, CA, 2015.

Burnet, Jean, and Leo Driedger. "Multiculturalism." In *The Canadian Encyclopedia*. Historica Canada. Article published June 27, 2011; last modified May 21, 2019. https://www.thecanadianencyclopedia.ca/en/article/multiculturalism.

Butterfield, Rosaria. *The Gospel Comes with a House Key: Practicing Radically Ordinary Hospitality in our Post-Christian World*. Wheaton: Crossway, 2018.

Denmark, Robert. "Fundamentalisms as Global Social Movements." *Globalizations* 5 (2008) 571–82.

Eady, Gregory, et al. "How Many People Live in Political Bubbles on Social Media? Evidence from Linked Survey and Twitter Data." *SAGE Open* 9 (2019) 1–21.

Hameleers, Michael, and Toni G. L. A. van der Meer. "Misinformation and Polarization in a High-Choice Media Environment: How Effective Are Political Fact-checkers?" *Communication Research* 47 (2020) 227–50.

Hiemstra, Rick. "Not Christian Anymore." *Faith Today* 38 (2020) 28–31.

Hunter, George G., III. *The Celtic Way of Evangelism: How Christianity Can Reach the West Again*. Nashville: Abingdon, 2011.

Johnson, Todd M., et al. "Christianity 2015: Religious Diversity and Personal Contact." *International Bulletin of Missionary Research* 39 (2015) 28–30.

Klein, Ezra. "Why the Media is So Polarized—and How it Polarizes Us." Vox.com. January 28, 2020. https://www.vox.com/2020/1/28/21077888/why-were-polarized-media-book-ezra-news.

Mangalwadi, Vishal. *The Book that Made Your World: How the Bible Created the Soul of Western Civilization*. Nashville: Thomas Nelson, 2012.

Martin, Glenn. "How Africa Might Save Global Christianity." In *Mission and Evangelism in a Secularizing World: Academy, Agency, and Assembly Perspectives from Canada*, edited by Narry F. Santos and Mark Naylor, 105–18. Eugene, OR: Pickwick, 2019.

———. "Technology as Loose Cannon on the Deck of Secularization's Ship." In *Mission and Evangelism in a Secularizing World: Academy, Agency, and Assembly Perspectives from Canada*, edited by Narry F. Santos and Mark Naylor, 149–62. Eugene, OR: Pickwick, 2019.

Moon, W. Jay. "Evangelism in a Secular Age: Complexities and Opportunities." In *Against the Tide: Mission Amidst the Global Currents of Secularization*, edited by W. Jay Moon and Craig Ott, 53–73. Pasadena: William Carey, 2019.

Netland, Harold A. "Secularization, Multiple Modernities, and Religion." In *Against the Tide: Mission Amidst the Global Currents of Secularization*, edited by W. Jay Moon and Craig Ott, 1–13. Pasadena: William Carey, 2019.

Newbigin, Lesslie. *The Gospel in a Pluralist Society*. Grand Rapids: Eerdmans, 1989.

Ott, Craig. "Introduction." In *Against the Tide: Mission Amidst the Global Currents of Secularization*, edited by W. Jay Moon and Craig Ott, ix–xxvi. Pasadena: William Carey, 2019.

Pew Research. "America's Changing Religious Landscape." May 12, 2015. http://www.pewforum.org/2015/05/12/americas-changing-religious-landscape/.

———. "In U.S., Decline of Christianity Continues at Rapid Pace." October 17, 2019. https://www.pewforum.org/2019/10/17/in-u-s-decline-of-christianity-continues-at-rapid-pace/.

Reimer, Sam. "Conservative Protestants and Religious Polarization in Canada." *Studies in Religion/Sciences Religieuses* 46 (2017) 187–208.

Stark, Rodney. *The Rise of Christianity: How the Obscure, Marginal Jesus Movement Became the Dominant Religious Force in the Western World in a Few Centuries*. New York: Harper Collins, 1997.

Stetzer, Ed. "Ministering to International Students." *Christianity Today*. August 16, 2019. https://www.christianitytoday.com/edstetzer/2019/august/ministering-to-international-students.html.

Taylor, Charles. *A Secular Age*. Cambridge, MA: Harvard University Press, 2007.

Winter, Ralph D. "The Kingdom Strikes Back: Ten Epochs of Redemptive History." In *Perspectives on the World Christian Movement: Reader*, edited by Ralph D. Winter et al., 195–213. Pasadena: William Carey, 1999.

Winter, Ralph D., and Bruce A. Koch. "Finishing the Task: The Unreached People's Challenge." In *Perspectives on the World Christian Movement: Reader*, edited by Ralph D. Winter et al., 509–24. Pasadena: William Carey, 1999.

Zurlo, Gina A., and Todd M. Johnson. "Unaffiliated, Yet Religious: A Methodological and Demographic Analysis." *Annual Review of the Sociology of Religion* 7 (2016) 50–74.

5

The Proper Place for a Woman

Submitting to the Original Ideals of the Chinese and Korean Church

Lisa Hamni Pak and Xenia Ling-Yee Chan

Introduction

WOMEN IN MINISTRY, PARTICULARLY in leadership positions, continues to be a contentious issue in many churches and denominations. While doors have been opening for women in ministry and leadership, many non-Western women remain restricted because of cultural values and norms. This is the lived experience of many current women ministers in Chinese and Korean church cultures. This chapter will present a historical-theological overview of the place of Asian women, specifically Chinese and Korean, in God's Kingdom and further apply a suitable appropriation to the current Chinese and Korean Canadian context.

Nineteenth-Twentieth Century Korea

In the late 1800s, American missionaries, many of whom were women, came to the peninsula to bring "light to the presumed darkness of Korea" and were seen to be ushering in the world in which a new woman could emerge from under the "hierarchical Confucian gender relations in which women had been regarded as inferior to men."[1] The arrival of these missionaries and the contemporary socio-political backdrop is significant in Korea's attempt

---

1. Choi, *Gender and Mission*, 2; though not the very first missionaries to Korea, American missionaries brought with them the social changes that affected the lives of Korean women.

to reject the Chinese influence of Confucianism and to accept the liberty of Western values. In particular, Confucian gender ideology secluded women in the home, prohibited education, forced them into early marriage, and exposed them to the abuses of the concubine system.[2] Western culture brought new ideas and new possibilities.

Western missionaries and their criticism of Confucian gender ideology, however, neither resulted in domestic emancipation nor established gender equality since gender discrimination existed, though more veiled, in the American presentation of Christianity.[3] They rightly observed that Christian women "assumed unequal, subordinate positions within the larger church organizations."[4] However, these missionaries had not divorced themselves from Victorian norms and so Korean women essentially traded one form of gender ideology for another, under the guise of liberation, education, and enlightenment. This "women's-rights-but-not-fully" approach presented by Western missionaries influenced Korean intellectuals who expressed their "enlightened" thoughts in contemporary newspaper editorials, where the argument that "women are equal but as the weaker sex needed to be protected," and the merging Confucianism with Christianity was propagated.[5]

In response to this rhetoric, a circulation of the *Yohhakkyo Solsi Tongmun* in September 1898 stands as the first public demand for equal rights for Korean women, by Korean women.[6] This was a cry from Korean women for equality and, particularly, the right to be educated and many point to the establishment of girls' mission schools as evidence of how Christianity positively impacted women's liberation and women's rights.[7] Mary Fitch Scranton, an American Methodist missionary, founded Korea's first school

---

2. Choi, *Gender and Mission*, 33–34.

3. Choi, *Gender and Mission*, 3.

4. Choi, *Gender and Mission*, 3.

5. Choi, *Gender and Mission*, 34–37; Young J. Allen was known for his very progressive views on gender equality, including women's education and suffrage. Warren Candler, on the other hand, supported women's education but stood against women's suffrage and women's right to vote. Also, "Korean intellectuals" refer only to men. The *Tongnip Sinmun* (*The Independent*), was founded in 1896 and was the first Korean newspaper with an English edition. So, Chae-Pil intended the paper to be the voice of the most disenfranchised of Korean society, including women.

6. Choi, *Gender and Mission*, 38–39.

7. Choi, *Gender and Mission*, 3.

for women, *Ewha Hakdang*, in 1886.[8] This was a monumental achievement in a culture where even women of nobility were limited in education. Still, these social advances proved to be a double-edged sword. While the promise of girls and women's education was so appealing that the king himself named the school, there was concern that Western education might cause Korean women to reject Korean traditions and desire the liberal Western lifestyle.[9] The missionaries recognized that if they were even perceived to be overthrowing Korean tradition, all their Gospel work on the peninsula could come to an end. Hence, in an effort to alleviate public concern and prevent misconception, the "missionaries strategically emphasized that they trained girls not to become Westernized ladies but rather to become better Koreans and model housewives," which meant recognizing, at the core of their curriculum, that a woman's place was in the domestic sphere.[10] This, of course, was well-supported by Victorian ideals of womanhood.[11]

Thus, despite the establishment of mission schools for women, "in retrospect, early Christianity and modern education in Korea failed to challenge, but rather confirmed the traditional self-images of Korean women, even as they introduced modern knowledge to those women."[12] In the end, the purpose for missionary school education for girls and women was to make them "good wives and wise mothers."[13] This educational philosophy was eagerly adopted and further perpetuated by native Koreans. Male scholars from the intellectual class "urged" educators to teach girls how to prepare a creative dinner table, using a variety of ingredients.[14] Thus, while Korean leaders encouraged and even welcomed change across the country—new ideas, cultural exchange, and avant-garde technologies that promised exciting possibilities for future generations— these opportunities, were limited only to men. Women were, yet again, relegated to the domestic sphere.

---

8. Kim, *Women Struggling for a New Life*, 13–14.

9. Choi, *Gender and Mission*, 97–100.

10. Choi, *Gender and Mission*, 99; One *Ewha* teacher explained, "Whatever may be the private opinion of any one concerning woman's sphere and proper occupation we must, for the present, at least act under the supposition that in Korea domestic life is her sphere and destiny . . . "

11. Kim, *Women Struggling for a New Life*, 16.

12. Kim, *Women Struggling for a New Life*, 13–15.

13. Choi, *Gender and Mission*, 101–3.

14. Choi, *Gender and Mission*, 102.

Nineteenth-Twentieth Century China[15]

Western incursions into China were met with hostility. The end of the Opium Wars left China humiliated and the Taiping Revolution only accelerated tensions.[16] From the Opium Wars until 1949, the gospel in China was "proclaimed in the context of power."[17] Westerners did not separate Christianity from Western culture, viewing Chinese culture as heathen.[18] Hudson Taylor made significant effort to adapt, as he thought this was the most effective way to reach Chinese people.[19] This effort to learn Chinese culture revealed the influence of Confucianism shutting women off from the gospel. As such, female missionaries—especially championed by Taylor—became key to the movement, and their work included reforms in education and healthcare. Westerners also gave the Chinese a new perspective on family structures and the role of women.[20] Where previously women were restricted to the home, their worth deriving from their kinship to the male figure (son, husband, or father), they were now free to enter society as individuals and could pursue careers previously inaccessible to them. Chinese women responded to these missionary efforts; by 1921, women represented about 37 percent of the Christian population.[21]

By the 1860s, female missionaries were recruiting Chinese women ("Bible women") to evangelize to their own people.[22] By the 1880s, Bible women were teaching, publicly evangelizing, and preaching to

---

15. There is evidence of Christianity arriving in China as early as the seventh century. However, the scope of the chapter is limited to only the Protestant missionary efforts of the nineteenth century onward.

16. Leung, "China," 141.

17. Noll and Nystrom, *Clouds of Witnesses*, 195. One tangible consequence of the Opium Wars was that Chinese Christian converts were seen as no longer Chinese, because the terms dictated at the end of the Opium Wars made provisions for them (Leung, "China," 141).

18. Leung, "China," 142; Foreigners were not the only ones who thought that these practices were abhorrent. Early Chinese feminists like Qiu Jin (1875–1907) wrote "China's women still remain in the dark and gloom, mired in the lowest of all the levels of hell's prisons." (Wo de er wan wan nu tongbao, hai yiran hei'an chenlun zai shiba ceng diyu).

19. Leung, "China," 142. This was a means to an end rather than respect for the culture itself.

20. Spence, *Modern China*, 208–9.

21. Kwok, *Chinese Women*, 1.

22. Chow, "Remarkable Story." These were often employees or the wives and mothers of Chinese male evangelists.

mixed-gender groups, without the direct supervision of foreign female missionaries. Other women trained as doctors—both in China and overseas—to push the mission forward.[23] The stories of Chinese women in ministry in this time largely shows that women went to places men were often unwilling to go, sometimes to their detriment and even death.[24] This prompted questions about formal female leadership. After the May Fourth Movement, there was an increasing push for women to be raised up in the church as much as they had been liberated in broader society.[25] Others appealed to the work of the Spirit, enabling women to prophesy and appealing to female leadership within the Scriptures. Opposing this were missionaries influenced by Victorian ideals and locals influenced by Confucian ideals, arguing that women should not be in formal leadership and should assume their traditional roles of being in the home—though they were happy to accept the informal leadership of women because such ministries pertained to the kitchens, children, and women.[26] By the 1930s, the impact of women in the story of Christianity became largely superseded by male evangelists' narratives.[27]

Current Experiences of Korean and Chinese Women in Ministry

While the Korean and Chinese contexts are different, there are common themes between these two demographics when it comes to the experience of women in ministry.[28] First, women's roles within the home are directly transferred into the local expression of the church, producing a sense of second-class citizenship. Second, the women in ministry question is largely viewed as a Western construct. Third, women who question the system are viewed as arrogant, power-hungry, overly ambitious, and disruptive. Fourth, women continue to face gender-based violence and harassment even in

---

23. Examples include Dora Yu Cidu, Mary Stone (Shi Meiyu), and Victoria Cheng (who was born in Canada).

24. E. L., "Women in China's Protestant Church."

25. Chow, "Remarkable Story"; Kwok, *Chinese Women*, 83–84.

26. Kwok, *Chinese Women*, 83.

27. Wu, "Dora Yu," 86.

28. Korean, Korean American, and Korean Canadian experiences of women in ministry will be discussed. As for the Chinese experience, Hong Kong and Hong Kong Canadian diaspora will be examined.

their ministries. Fifth, the rise of popularity of New Calvinist norms have revived an anti-women-in-ministry sentiment. Lastly, the women-in-ministry question is seen to compromise witness and evangelism.

The assumptions of modern Christian womanhood stemming from old-world Confucian gender ideology reinforced by Victorian Christian values is deep-seated in the Chinese and Korean churches.[29] One such assumption is that the women should remain in the home. While this is not often taken literally, it often translates into women being relegated to women, caring, and children's ministries. Some have been ordained in these positions, while others are only given the title pastor, minister, or intern. Many are disallowed from positions of formal leadership and decision-making positions. Wai-Lin Lau recounts being placed consistently at the bottom of the hierarchy, even below a new seminary graduate.[30] Rank and position in Asian culture is significant and indicates one's place or lack thereof. Congregants often mistake female pastors for office staff because the respect given to male pastors is not extended to female pastors.[31] One experienced woman pastor was, according to denominational requirements, eligible for ordination. However, she was told that her junior male colleague would be pursuing ordination first. When she persisted, the senior pastor finally told her that she was not eligible for ordination in his church because she is a woman. Unfairly, while the church may appreciate the work of women pastors, they withhold full recognition and acknowledgement of their calling, theological and pastoral training, and years of service.[32] In the 1970s, CCOWE noted that the majority of seminarians in Hong Kong were women, but made a point of inquiring about ministry options; for instance, pastors' wives, volunteers, lay leaders, and missionaries, and tentatively proposed that the option for female ministerial workers was an "issue to be pondered."[33] Many more women have heard the call of ministry on their lives since then.

---

29. There are cases of Chinese and Korean churches where women are empowered. However, these are rare, and there are a number of assumptions which cause difficulties for women in vocational church ministry.

30. Lau, "Am I a Pastor," 2.

31. Lau, "Am I a Pastor," 2.

32. Law, *Chinese Churches Handbook*, 64. Churches associated with CCOWE in North America have since ordained women.

33. Law, *Chinese Churches Handbook*, 64.

Christine Hong shares an experience that further illustrates the cultural challenges for women pastors in the Asian church.[34] Hong had looked to church leaders and mentors to help discern and affirm her call to ministry, however, the responses she received, ranged from, "You aren't practical enough for ministry" to "Isn't what you really feel a call to be a pastor's wife?"[35] Still, she was certain of her calling and had the courage to continue. After graduating from seminary and returning to her Korean American roots, what she experienced was, in her own words, "bizarre."[36] They would ask about her age, whether or not her parents were "okay with this?", playing the piano, liking children and planning for marriage. This line of questioning was par for the course and assumed to be feminine skills. She also recalls:

> When I asked why they posed these questions, their response was, "Well, women follow their husbands when they get married, so you wouldn't stay here long." One interview ended with an elderly Korean American pastor giving me a paternalistic pat on my rear end as I left his office. He handed me a hundred-dollar bill, saying, "Go have something good to eat."[37]

These interview questions betray the undergirding Confucian gender ideology that had oppressed Asian women for centuries. The expectation of women to be "good wives and wise mothers," reinforced by the Victorian Christian values of the American missionaries, transferred all too easily into the sphere of ministry and lingers there even today. In short, women called to ministry were assumed to be called to the church equivalent of the domestic sphere.

The assumption is that because the father is the head of the household, in both the Christian complementarian and Confucian ideal, *he* is therefore suitable to be a pastor.[38] Even in the churches where women are allowed to be pastors or even ordained, only men can be senior pastors. In other words, a "glass bamboo ceiling" still exists, and is reinforced by both men and women. Lau confesses that she thought that the administrative assistant, as a fellow woman, would support her effort to be recognized as

---

34. Hong, "Go Somewhere Else," 58–62.

35. Hong, "Go Somewhere Else," 58; Hong later understood that being "practical" meant being male.

36. Hong, "Go Somewhere Else," 58.

37. Hong, "Go Somewhere Else," 58–59.

38. Lau, "Am I a Pastor," 158.

a pastor in the church. Unexpectedly, she reported Lau to the senior pastor as a troublemaker.[39] Similarly, Hong shares an experience that forced her to reckon with her own glass bamboo ceiling. She writes:

> The worst was when one interviewer asked if I had any ambitions to become a senior minister someday. Initially, I thought that this was a prodding encouragement, as if to say that I *should* be thinking about such things. However, I realized that he was checking to see if I would fall in line. He was checking to see if I would try to reach beyond the boundaries set for me.[40]

In the same way that women were relegated to the private, domestic sphere in neo-Confucianism, women in the church have boundaries and are passive-aggressively "encouraged" to fall in line. Men belong in the public sphere and, therefore, positions of senior leadership are expected to be filled by men. Women should not presume to reach too far or too high. Just like the walled homes of Confucian Korea, a woman should know her proper place in the church.[41]

Even when Hong found her place of ministry, there were other challenges that she had to overcome. For instance, Hong was not allowed to drive a van and had to find a man to drive in her place.[42] The assumption was that a van was too "manly" a vehicle for her to drive. She was also told to "cut her hair shorter, wear less makeup, and dress more modestly," and, just like the lack of female support Lau faced, Hong confesses that these comments stung the most because they were given by "well-meaning women who claimed they saw me as a daughter and they would not want their daughter running around that way."[43]

Another obstacle in the Asian church is that female leadership is seen as a Western construct. However, as we have seen, the traditional role for women is both a Confucian and Western construct and there are varying responses. Among the first generation, many churches support women pastors; however, there is a significant power imbalance and, in some cases, abuse. Among the second generation, there is a growing discontentment

---

39. Lau, "Am I a Pastor," 222–23. Other women pastors have also reported that they thought they were unable to be senior pastors because women are too emotional and not rational enough.

40. Hong, "Go Somewhere Else," 59.

41. Hong, "Go Somewhere Else," 59.

42. Hong, "Go Somewhere Else," 60.

43. Hong, "Go Somewhere Else," 60.

with the first generation, and their rejection of the first generation has also included some rejecting women in formal leadership. While it may be tempting to dismiss the second generation's response as reactionary, it is more helpful to see their response as simply another outcome of the same discipleship continuum that has been passed on from the time of the initial Protestant mission to Asia.

Hong's ordeal with her ordination as a woman pastor in the Korean American church reveals the deeply enculturated mindset of Korean church leadership. When she and another female minister approached the senior pastor about ordination, not only did he seem aggravated, but he suggested that they have a 20-minute ordination service on a day when many people would be away.[44] When Hong gently countered by expressing her desire to celebrate her well-earned ordination and her spiritual journey with her mother, grandmother, youth, teachers, and mentors, the senior pastor dismissed her saying, "Go somewhere else! If you want to make this a show, go somewhere else. Rent out a gym or a room somewhere, but don't invite anyone from the church. No one will come."[45] The effects of his words on Hong were deeply personal: "Was a pastor's first call always like this—humiliating, belittling, frightening? Did this response come because I was a woman and did not fit into the preconceived mold of Korean American femininity? Did my male counterparts go through this? Maybe it was normal."[46] Confucian gender ideology reinforced by culture and Christian doctrine has deeply damaging and humiliating consequences.[47]

When women do seek to be formally recognized in leadership, they are seen as being power-hungry, disruptive, attention-seeking, prideful, and overreaching.[48] The onus of asking for ordination, even in denominations that ordain women, is often placed on the woman. In one case at a Chinese diaspora church, a female pastor was asked to take over as acting senior pastor during the senior pastor's leave. Given the inconveniences of trying to accomplish her responsibilities without being given the proper credentials, she applied for ordination but was accused of overstepping and of coveting the senior pastor's position.[49]

44. Hong, "Go Somewhere Else," 60.
45. Hong, "Go Somewhere Else," 62.
46. Hong, "Go Somewhere Else," 61–62.
47. Hong, "Go Somewhere Else," 60.
48. Lau, "Am I a Pastor," 168.
49. Lau, "Am I a Pastor," 143. In another case in Toronto, the senior pastor supported

Moreover, gender-based violence and harassment pervade the church as well. According to a brief survey, of the forty-nine women in ministry surveyed in Hong Kong and Vancouver (or those who had significant cross-over between the two cities), forty-eight women answered that they had experienced sexual harassment in ministry from both colleagues and congregation members.[50] Lau's response that, "a mature woman in seminary should be taught by mature clergywomen how to cope firmly, but graciously, with minor verbal abuse and unwelcome joking relationships", exemplifies the normalization of this behavior within the church.[51]

There has also been a shift in theological orientation towards New Calvinism, which is notable for its complementarian orientation. Fenggang Yang notes that where there were missions for Chinese people in America, those churches tended to stay in those denominations.[52] The churches established by Chinese pastors, however, tended to either be independent or belonged to denominations that allowed for autonomy, and were known for their theological conservatism.[53] Yang makes several observations: within independent or autonomous *Chinese* churches, Chinese people could establish their North American identity on their own terms.[54] Secondly, the association with the Southern Baptist Convention was in part because of the influence of Southern Baptist missionaries in China as well as their emphasis on the homogeneous unit principle.[55] Thus, Chinese churches were able to establish respectability in the North American church as well as keep their theological conservatism, congregational autonomy, and preserve their language and culture.[56] In the 1980s, as Hong Kong students emigrated en masse to study in North America, they converged upon a

---

a woman pastor's ordination. He even advocated for her only to have his efforts stymied by the deacons. It took almost a decade for her to be ordained.

50. Lau, "Am I a Pastor," 214. An example of this in the Korean church: Hong's experience with the senior pastor who gave her a hundred dollars and patted her on the rear.

51. Lau, "Am I a Pastor," 215.

52. Yang, *Chinese Christians in America*, 6–7; these are mostly mainline denominations.

53. Yang, 7; these were the Southern Baptist and the Christian and Missionary Alliance. Also, given that Canada and the US were treated as one district by CCOWE, it is not a far stretch to imagine that what was influencing the States also made its way into the Chinese Canadian church.

54. Yang, *Chinese Christians in America*, 127.

55. Yang, *Chinese Christians in America*, 130.

56. Yang, *Chinese Christians in America*, 130.

Southern Baptist movement that was beginning to craft a complementarian response in opposition to "liberal" evangelicalism and "feminism."[57] While there had previously been a deep history of Chinese women empowered and released for ministry, Chinese women began to be suppressed by this desire to defend Christianity at this time. As the structures began to form, the openness exemplified in missions was verbally proclaimed but the structures meant to facilitate that openness began to harden. Complementarianism was thus adopted by the Chinese (-diaspora) church because it presented a logical, consistent, seemingly biblical justification for the particular Confucian values that pertained to gender and the home. The practicality of Chinese (in particular, Hong Kong-diaspora) churches leads to a teaching of the conservative position on women in leadership. However, in application, they are more open.[58] Therefore, the second-generation adoption of New Calvinist values and norms should also not be a surprise. In fact, they are only bearing the fruit of what they have been raised in. In insisting that the structure be entirely coherent to unreservedly prevent women from formal leadership in the church, they are merely asking for consistency and authenticity.

With Reformed traditions and doctrine dominant in Korean churches, the leap to New Calvinism has been a more obvious pathway than in Chinese churches. It remains rare today—even among the second generation—to see a female elder in a decision-making position or as a senior pastor. It remains true that a noble, biblically Christ-like, and culturally becoming woman serves her male counterparts. A woman who overreaches and disrupts the accepted norm is thoroughly shamed by her peers and elders.

Still, the Chinese and Korean church remains a place of hope and belonging for many women. Korean American Aram Bae shares how meaningful the Korean church community was to her in her formative years.[59]

---

57. Piper and Grudem, *Recovering Biblical Manhood and Womanhood*, xiii. By 1989, the Danvers Statement had been published and the Council for Biblical Manhood and Womanhood was established.

58. Lau, "Am I a Pastor," 260; there is diversity in response too, dependent on the senior pastor's theological education. The first Chinese female pastor to be ordained in the Canadian Baptists of Ontario and Quebec was Rev. Dorothy Wong in the late 1990s. Shortly thereafter, the Association of Christian Evangelical Ministries ordained a number of women in the early 2000s. Anita Leung was the first Chinese woman to be ordained in the C&MA in Vancouver.

59. Lee, "Foolishness of Wisdom," 80–89.

However, later when she returned to the Korean American church as a pastor, the "once-upon-a-happy-place" had become toxic:

> I want to run away from the overt sexism and stifling nature of patriarchy found in the church. I want to run away from the ageism that works against me. I want to run away from the sometimes subtle but always telling way certain older adults have when they speak to me, or rather, *at* me.[60]

Bae also adds, "And I really want to stay away from adults who, having been spoiled by both their parents and culture, still expect women to remain ignorantly agreeable, alluringly quiet, and alarmingly thin."[61] It would seem that the more things change, the more things stay the same.[62] Like Hong, and despite her inclination to run away from her diaspora home church, Bae returns with hope, seeing herself as an agent of change "of the place that has loved and nurtured" her.[63] Both Hong and Bae are courageous women, confronting and challenging Confucian gender norms that have defined traditional Korean culture for centuries. There is still a long way to go. However, changes are being made and more young women, and older women, are recognizing the significant role that women have played and must play in the Korean church, both on the peninsula and throughout the diaspora communities.

Despite the frustrations, it is encouraging to know that Asian women are finding their voice to share their experiences. Overcoming obstacles, women have and are still stepping into positions of leadership: formally recognized or not, some within the church, as lay ministers, and in the parachurch world. In 1929, the ratio of female and male missionaries was two to one in and from China.[64] In the last century, two-thirds of all missionaries have been women.[65] Women are not leading to merely fill a gap that men have been unable to fill. The reality is that the church needs both

---

60. Lee, "Foolishness of Wisdom", 82.

61. Lee, "Foolishness of Wisdom," 83.

62. Bae, "Home Sweet Diaspora Home," 84–87. Jung Ha Kim, notes some significant observations in the history of the Korean American church, namely, "patterns of feminization, the permanence of patriarchy, and an ethos of religion (one's actions) over faith (one's beliefs)." The Korean diaspora churches in North America have imported and preserved the Confucian gender ideology of traditional Korea, perhaps as an unconscious way of preserving Korean culture as an immigrant population in North America.

63. Bae, "Home Sweet Diaspora Home," 88–89.

64. Lau, "Am I a Pastor," 176.

65. Lau, "Am I a Pastor," 176.

men and women, empowered by the Spirit and released in their giftings so that the world might come to know Jesus. No longer should the Asian woman be relegated to the private domestic sphere, but rather, she ought to be confident in her calling to minister and serve in the communities that she calls home. Her place is not hidden and silent. Her place is where God has called and placed her—for his Kingdom and his glory.

The Proper Place for a Woman in Ministry Leadership

The proper place for a woman in ministry leadership is not limited to the kitchen or to children's ministry. There is "no immovable sex line drawn on God's employment sheet."[66] Women are not only to be in the "inner place" and domestic sphere, but also in the public sphere: to lead, to teach, to preach, and to serve. With every passing generation of Korean and Chinese women and their daughters, the confidence and willingness to challenge the established gender norms builds. As women distinctly feel God's calling and the Spirit's leading in their life, they are discovering that their place in ministry leadership is not dictated by culture and tradition but rather by God and where he places them.

But just "getting" a ministry leadership position is not the goal. Rather, the calling of Korean and Chinese women for the good of the Body is at stake. Hence, with the wisdom of experience, Unzu Lee cautions women leaders about getting used to the established leadership even if they eventually become insiders.[67]

An intentional effort by women leaders to continue to push for change is needed, especially to open doors of opportunity that they never had for emerging women leaders. Women should be given the opportunity to lead, not only because they bring "a woman's perspective," but because they bring many different perspectives, experiences, talents, gifts, and skills. Therefore, global leaders should aim to be mindful in making space for women to raise their voices and have opportunities to lead in order to optimize all the gifts that God has given to the church for the *missio Dei*.

The relationship between Christian liberty and gender roles remains a tense tightrope for many women, not just for Chinese and Korean women. The call to leadership and ministry is also very personal and God's prerogative; this "divine ministry placement" neither belongs to man, nor

---

66. Lau, "Am I a Pastor," 141.
67. Lee, "Foolishness of Wisdom," 122.

woman, nor cultural tradition. What the Chinese and Korean churches have failed to do, in varying degrees, is to recognize, encourage, and empower women in their calling to lead and to minister. Perhaps now, in the twenty-first century, it is time to restore women to their proper place as full participants, ministers, and leaders, in God's mission.

Reflection Questions

1. How can constructive discussions take place about cultural gender norms and women as leaders in ministry?

2. What are some ways your community can engage in this potentially challenging conversation?

3. How can the church community do to encourage young women to pursue God's calling on their lives?

Bibliography

Bae, Aram. "Home Sweet Diaspora Home." In *Here I Am: Faith Stories of Korean American Clergywomen*, edited by Grace Ji-Sun, 80–89. Valley Forge, PA: Judson, 2015.

Chan, Joyce Chung-yan. *Rediscover the Fading Memories: Early Chinese Canadian Christian History*. Burnaby, BC: Chinese Christian Missions, 2013.

Choi, Hyaeweol. *Gender and Mission Encounters in Korea: New Women, Old Ways*. Los Angeles: University of California Press, 2009.

Chow, Alexander. "The Remarkable Story of China's 'Bible' Women." *Christianity Today*, 2018. https://www.christianitytoday.com/history/2018/march/christian-china-bible-women.html.

E. L. "Women in China's Protestant Church and Missions." *China Source*, 2017. https://www.chinasource.org/resource-library/articles/women-in-chinas-protestant-church-and-missions/.

Hattaway, Paul. "Li Chouzi." *Biographical Dictionary of Chinese Christianity*, 2005–2020. http://bdcconline.net/en/stories/li-chouzi.

Hong, Christine J. "Go Somewhere Else." In *Here I Am: Faith Stories of Korean American Clergywomen*, edited by Grace Ji-Sun, 58–62. Valley Forge, PA: Judson, 2015.

Kim, Ai Ra. *Women Struggling for a New Life: The Role of Religion in the Cultural Passage from Korea to America*. Albany, NY: State University of New York Press, 1996.

Kwok, Pui-lan. *Chinese Women and Christianity, 1860–1927*. Atlanta: Scholars, 1992.

Lau, Wai Lin. "Am I a Pastor? Woman in Ministry in a Chinese Church in Canada." DMin diss., Western Seminary, 1999.

Law, Gail. *Chinese Churches Handbook*. Hong Kong: CCOWE, 1982.

PART 2: PAST CHRISTIAN MISSION AND ITS RELEVANCE TO PRESENT MISSION

Lee, Unzu. "Foolishness of Wisdom." In *Leading Wisdom: Asian and Asian North American Women Leaders*, edited by Su Yon Park and Jung Ha Kim, 115–37. Louisville: Westminster John Knox, 2017.
Leung, Ka-lun. "China." In *A Dictionary of Asian Christianity*, edited by Scott Sunquist. Grand Rapids: Eerdmans, 2001.
Li, Yading. "Dora Yu." In *Biographical Dictionary of Chinese Christianity*, 2005–2020. http://bdcconline.net/en/stories/yu-dora.
Noll, Mark, and Carolyn Nystrom. *Clouds of Witnesses: Christian Voices from Africa and Asia*. Downers Grove, IL: InterVarsity, 2011.
Piper, John, and Wayne Grudem, eds. *Recovering Biblical Manhood and Womanhood*. Wheaton: Crossway, 1991.
Spence, Jonathan D. *The Search for Modern China*. New York: Norton, 1990.
Wu, Silas. "Dora Yu (1873–1931): Foremost Female Evangelist in Twentieth-Century Chinese Revivalism." In *Gospel Bearers, Gender Barriers: Missionary Women in the Twentieth Century*, edited by Dana L. Roberts, 85–98. Maryknoll, NY: Orbis, 2002.
Yang, Fenggang. *Chinese Christians in America: Conversion, Assimilation, and Adhesive Identities*. University Park, PA: Pennsylvania State University Press, 1999.

Part 3
Present Evangelical Mission and its Relevance to Future Mission

6

"Diversity is a Fact; Inclusion Is a Choice"

Is Multiculturalism "Bad" for the Church in Canada?

SHERMAN LAU

"Diversity is a Fact. Inclusion is a Choice."

ON SEPTEMBER 21, 2016, Stéphane Dion, then Canadian Ambassador to Germany and special envoy to the European Union, addressed the United Nations at the General Assembly on the high-panel topic of inclusion and diversity. He begins his speech by quoting Prime Minister Justin Trudeau, who had addressed the assembly the day before, "In Canada, we see diversity as a source of strength, not weakness. Our country is strong not in spite of our differences, but because of them. Because what is the alternative? To exploit anxiety? To turn it into fear and blame? To reject others because they look or speak or pray differently than we do?"[1] Furthermore Dion states, "Diversity in Canada is a fact. Canada is home to people of every race, religion, sexual orientation, shape and size. Inclusion is a choice. This choice is guided by the many benefits that diversity can bring. I believe that diversity in our communities and countries can lead to higher rates of economic growth, better social cohesion and tremendous cultural and civic benefits."[2]

Dion adds, "Multiculturalism is sometimes criticized on the basis that it means closed ghettoes of people who import their home cultures without any adaptation. This is not multiculturalism. In a multicultural

1. Global Affairs Canada, "Address by Minister Dion."
2. Global Affairs Canada, "Address by Minister Dion."

society, the people you pass on the street are virtually all fellow citizens, with full and equal rights, whether their families have been in a country for a hundred years or they recently arrived in their new home."[3] In summation, multiculturalism is believed to be the ideal that brings out the best of every culture represented in Canada toward making Canadians more complete humans in a global world.

As Canadian Christians, how do we interpret and apply Mr. Dion's viewpoint and the Liberal Party's social progressive advocacy of multiculturalism in relation to the church? Can appealing for inclusion in church (to bolster a fledging attendance) be able to supplement church budget through rental income or to check off the diversity box? For Dion, his admonition for inclusion of the "other" is to challenge the rising tides of xenophobia, discrimination, and racism in Western society. We must then ask the questions, "Are faith communities immune from these attitudes towards the 'other'? Is the call for inclusion, an anchor of multiculturalism, *really* a choice for the Christian, individually and corporately?"

In order to understand what multiculturalism is, we begin by clarifying its definitions as the term may be interpreted "descriptively (as a sociological fact), prescriptively (as an ideology) or politically (as a policy)."[4] Richard J. Konieczny and Enoch Wan define multiculturalism as follows:

> **1. A Descriptive Definition:** Multiculturalism connotes referencing the undeniable varieties of cultures both international and intranational. In its most basic sense then, multiculturalism is the recognition that a variety of cultures co-exist in a given context.
>
> **2. An Ideological Definition:** Multiculturalism can be defined ideologically "as the stipulation of the procedural and substantive principles ordering a multi-cultural society" (Goldberg 1994:7; cf. Lee and Rice 1991:73ff.). It is more than that envisioned in the first definition outlined above. It foresees social engineering.
>
> **3. An Ideological Definition based on Power:** Multiculturalism is "primarily a movement for change" that involves theoretical analysis and the development of a conceptual framework to challenge the "cultural hegemony of the dominant ethnic group" (Turner 1994:407). In this sense it is related to power (Baum 1977:101).[5]

---

3. Global Affairs Canada, "Address by Minister Dion."
4. Brousseau and Dewing, *Canadian Multiculturalism*, 1.
5. Konieczny and Wan, "Theology of Multiculturalism", 1.

The *Canadian Multiculturalism Act* was passed into law on July 21, 1988. This policy not only recognized the diversity of Canada both in ethnicity and culture (descriptive) but also placed multiculturalism as a high value (ideology): Clauses 3(1)(a) and (b) of Bill C-93 which recognizes the cultural diversity of Canada, states that Canadians are free to *preserve and share their cultural heritage* [emphasis mine] and affirm that multiculturalism is a fundamental characteristic of Canadian identity.[6] In short, to be Canadian is to be multicultural. Within this fundamental characteristic lie the roots of multiculturalism as stated in the Act:

> Whereas the Constitution of Canada provides that every individual is equal before and under the law and has the right to the equal protection and benefit of the law without discrimination and that everyone has the freedom of conscience, religion, thought, belief, opinion, expression, peaceful assembly and association and guarantees those rights and freedoms equally to male and female persons.[7]

Thus, multiculturalism is the offspring of *liberalism*, which is "the culmination of developments in Western society that produced a sense of the importance of human individuality, *a liberation of the individual from complete subservience to the group* [emphasis mine], and a relaxation of the tight hold of custom, law and authority."[8]

In contrast, David E. Stevens states in *God's New Humanity*, Paul's exhortation to live not as strangers and aliens in Ephesians 2:19 "is because God has graciously through the sacrificial death of his Son, made Jew and Gentile one new man (v.15)."[9] In essence, Jesus' disciples form a new humanity who are fellow citizens of the saints and members of the household of God. The walls of xenophobia, discrimination, and segregation are deconstructed not by human will to overcome these evil attitudes but in Jesus Christ alone, and never allowed to be reconstructed (Eph 4–6). While I appreciate the desire to include aliens and strangers in multicultural congregations that serve as a pragmatic witness of God's heart for the nations, we must instead seek to develop an intercultural ecclesiology. Inclusion is not a choice. It is *the* reality.

---

6. Canadian Multiculturalism Act, 13.
7. Canadian Multiculturalism Act, 3.
8. Encyclopedia Brittanica, "Liberalism."
9. Stevens, *God's New Humanity*, 98.

A Brief History of Canadian Multiculturalism

As Canadians, we cherish our multicultural value, proudly celebrated every Canada Day.

We encourage ethnic diversity in the workplace, schools, and communities—believing that this will strengthen us as a society. The diversity that Canada enjoys is primarily due to immigration. However, a survey conducted by the Canadian Broadcasting Corporation,

> suggest a majority of Canadians believe the federal government should limit the number of immigrants it accepts . . . [furthermore], the government should prioritize limiting immigration levels because the country might be reaching a limit in its ability to integrate them.[10]

The issue of immigration is not a new one and has been contentious since the confederation of Canada. "Canadians can never agree on how many immigrants the country needs, how many refugees it should welcome, where immigrants should come from, and what role they should play in Canadian society."[11] At this juncture, it would be important to understand the history of immigration in Canada and the events that influenced the development of multiculturalism as a national policy.

Pre-Confederation Canada was less about immigration than it was about trade and settlement. Europeans would arrive during the Age of Exploration (1500–1700) with the Portuguese and Spaniards leading the way, motivated by the search for greener shores, trade routes to the East, and conversion of the "heathen." Portugal would be the first Europeans to navigate the Northern Atlantic and settled on Cape Breton Island, but they were swiftly dispatched by the local natives.[12]

Jacques Cartier, a French explorer who entered the Gulf of St. Lawrence in 1534 and settled in present-day Prince Edward Island, would be the first to make headway into North America. He established French presence by erecting a fort—an act that infringed on the Indian's land rights, which he chose not to recognize. His voyages laid the foundation for France's claim on the territory, recognized with the first permanent French settlement under the leadership of Samuel de Champlain. However, the perception of France was that "colonies existed to enrich the mother country by

---

10. Wright, "Limiting Immigration Levels."
11. Francis et al., *Destinies*, 464.
12. Francis et al., *Destinies*, 29.

exporting raw materials and by importing finished manufactured products from the mother country."[13]

Early English exploration into the North Atlantic began with Henry Hudson in 1610, who was also tasked with seeking the Northwest Passage to the East. However, he too met an untimely demise but at the hands of his crew. It would not be until 1668 that a group of English merchants under the patronage of Prince Rupert and guided by two renegade French *coureurs de bois*, Pierre-Esprit Radisson and Medard Chouart Des Groseilliers, that the English presence was formalized with the establishment of the Hudson's Bay Company. In 1690, Charles II gave the Hudson's Bay Company exclusive trading rights and property ownership to all the lands with the areas of Hudson and James Bays, although no one consulted the Indians about this charter to "Rupert's Land."[14]

The English settlements would continue to grow and threaten the fur trade for New France, even though fur was no longer an economic benefit to France, who wanted to maintain their territory to contain the British from expanding westward. However, New France was outnumbered militarily, economically precarious, and still dependent on supplies from France. The Treaty of Utrecht in 1713 would establish French and English territories, theoretically planting the seeds for a bicultural "nation" while marginalizing the indigenous nations or using them as pawns in their expansion efforts.

The period of 1713–1744 would provide relative peace for New France until the outbreak of war in Europe between France and England, yet again. The attack on the long-standing French fortress of Louisbourg and its fall signaled the beginning of the end of French occupation in the New World. In the summer of 1759, the French and the British met at the Plains of Abraham, where the British army defeated the French militia and entered the gates of Quebec on September 18. A year later, on September 8, Montreal also fell to the British, and Canada passed into their hands.

This brief early history of Canada's formation serves not only as an example of the drive for European expansion but also the cultural attitudes of the time that would lead to ethnic hostility and racism that plagues our society today, especially towards the First Nations peoples of Canada. Paul Hiebert in *The Gospel in Human Contexts* states that during the Age of Exploration (1500–1700),

13. Francis et al., *Origins*, 50.
14. Francis et al., *Origins*, 109.

> The Western commercial world saw the newly discovered Others a source of goods and labor—of gold and slaves.... What right did Europeans have to enslave other peoples? Many argued that these Others were like children. Therefore, the Europeans were justified in colonial expansion in which they acted as parents, educating and managing the native's wealth for their natives' own good.[15]

We have noted two instances in the formation of Canada that both French and British occupiers settled on land without consultation of the First Nations Amerindians.

The defeat of New France presented a new problem for the English, as they inherited a former French colony and assimilation would prove to be difficult. This set in motion the Quebec Act, a policy of concession adopted by the British Parliament in 1774,[16] which restored civil laws and trading practices established under the French but more importantly allowed for the former French colonies to form their own Legislative Council with councilors appointed by the Governor. This would infuriate the English settlers who had been denied the same request. This early legislative Act would be the first of many concessions to the future province of Quebec and highlights the difficulty in governing a bicultural nation divided by language, culture, and religion.

After the War of 1812, which established Canadian (Upper Canada) and American borders, the British government made a concerted effort to encourage British immigration and discourage American immigration. The period from 1815 to 1840 was one of growth and consolidation for Upper Canada,[17] with immigration primarily from the British Isles: Protestants from the north of Ireland, Roman Catholics from the south, Lowland and Highland Scots, Welsh, and English. These immigrants brought British customs and attitudes to create a unique British North American character. By 1867, three of the four major groups that make up Canada's multicultural society were well established—the Native peoples, French and British (though there were already German, Dutch, and American black settlements in the new Dominion).[18] People of British descent accounted for 60 percent of Canada's population while 31 percent were French Canadian, who still mostly resided in Quebec.

---

15. Hiebert, *Gospel in Human Contexts*, 64.
16. Francis et al., *Origins*, 179.
17. Francis et al., *Origins*, 221.
18. Francis et al., *Destinies*, 1.

On the eve of World War I, Canada was still divided linguistically and culturally between English-Canada and French-Canada, though they had similar views regarding the systemic eradication of indigenous identity. This would result in the establishment of the Residential School System with the cooperation of the Anglican, Presbyterian, United and Roman Catholic churches, which operated from the 1880s into the closing decades of the twentieth century, with the expressed objectives of indoctrinating Indian children with Euro-Canadian and Christian ways of living and assimilating them into mainstream Canadian society.[19] This event continues to affect Indigenous and Canadian relations negatively.

Early European immigrants were also suspect in their ability to assimilate, who were enticed by the Canadian government to settle the West with the promise of land ownership. On April 12, 1901, the House of Commons debated this issue with the Honorable Member Mr. Frank Oliver stating,

> I have heard hon. members say that these strange people, these Slavs, will assimilate with the other people. Do you know what the word "assimilate" means? It is a nice sounding word. Do you know that it means the intermarriage of your sons to daughters with those who are of an alien race and of alien ideas?[20]

To contextualize the debate, Oliver was not in favor of accepting Galicians or Doukhobors as the "best" immigrants for Canada. This prejudice would extend to Chinese and Indian immigrants as well.

Canada's involvement in both World Wars, opened the door to more immigration from Europe, particularly displaced refugees. From 1946–1962, Canada admitted nearly a quarter of a million refugees as sponsored relatives, contract labor, or sponsorship by government and churches.[21] However, many Canadians

> were reluctant to receive a sizeable influx of immigrants. By 1954, only 45 percent of Canadians looked positively upon immigration, down from 51 percent in 1947. Many Canadians of British origin feared that immigration would weaken the British element in Canada. Workers often viewed immigrants as competitors willing to work for lower wages."[22]

---

19. University of British Columbia, "Residential School System."
20. Library of Parliament, "House of Common Debates."
21. Canadian Council for Refugees, "Brief History."
22. Francis et al., *Destinies*, 447.

These views continue today and the main contention to immigrants by "established" Canadians are speaking their own ethnic languages or wearing traditional dress in public. They tended to see immigrants as ignorant of Canadian cultural practices and unwilling to "act like Canadians," and they have expressed discomfort with the changes in Canadian society that have been brought about by immigration.[23] This last reaction has seen legislation introduced in Quebec, known as Bill 21, which bans public servants from wearing "religious symbols" but has been interpreted as discrimination of Muslims and Sikhs, for whom the *hijab* and *kirpan* are not only part of their religious identity; it also defines their ethnic identity.[24]

This right to maintain one's cultural heritage, ethnic identity, language, beliefs (and in 2019, gender) was so entrenched that, in October 1971, Prime Minister Pierre Trudeau admonished his government to accept, "other cultural communities [as they too] are essential elements in Canada and deserve government assistance in order to contribute to regional and national life in ways that derive from their heritages."[25] The Canadian Multiculturalism Act, formalized the government's commitment to "promote the full and equitable participation of individuals and communities of all origins in the continuing evolution and shaping of all aspects of Canadian society."[26] Incidentally, the Act coincided with a shift in immigration trends for 1971, as for the first time, the majority of new immigrants were of non-European ancestry—a precedent that has persisted ever since.[27]

Immigration and Religious Canada

In the 1980s, 90 percent of Canadians self-identified as Christians (Roman Catholics, United Church, Anglican, "Christian", Baptists, Orthodox), which decreased to 67 percent by 2011. It is projected that affiliation with Christianity will continue to decline by 2036 to between 52–56 percent, while the number of unaffiliated people with any religion will continue to increase from 28.2 percent to 34.6 percent. However, non-Christian religions (Muslim, Hindu, and Sikh faiths) are predicted to see the most rapid increase, their population doubling in almost all the scenarios selected

23. Francis et al., *Destinies*, 454.
24. Wells, "Quebec's Bill 21."
25. Francis et al., Destinies, 457.
26. Burnet and Driedger, "Multiculturalism."
27. Burnet and Driedger, "Multiculturalism."

from 2011 to 2036.[28] Reginald Bibby, renowned Canadian sociologist from the University of Lethbridge, states, "In the last ten years of Statistics Canada data, 25 percent or so of immigrants are Roman Catholic, another 20 percent are Protestant."[29] In effect, immigrants are reinvigorating Canadian Christianity, especially the Roman Catholic Church.

As Canadian Christians, we should rejoice that there are more global Christians immigrating to Canada, and secondly, the rise in immigration from Asia Pacific has provided access to formerly closed groups. However, this begs the question, "Why are there not more multicultural churches per capita in Toronto, Vancouver, and Montreal, where most immigrants settle?" To answer this question, we must now devote our attention to the history of Christianity in Canada.

The pre-Christian history of Canada would be Aboriginal spirituality, followed by the introduction of Roman Catholicism by the French settlers and missionaries. With the succession of Canada to England, the Anglican Church would be the main Christian denomination until 1812. "The first challenge to the Anglican's ecclesiastical monopoly came from the Presbyterians. As the established Church of Scotland and a major Protestant denomination, they demanded a share of the revenues from the Clergy reserves, which were approved in 1829."[30] The other challenger was Methodism, which was perceived to be a threat to the elitist Anglican church. In 1825, Archdeacon John Strachan described Methodists as, "ignorant, incapable, idle and, above all, disloyal because of their emotionally charged and 'republican' views."[31]

Other Protestant denominations would arrive in Upper Canada bringing along their brand of Christianity, such as, Baptists, Quakers, Dunkards, Millerites, Campbellites, Christian Universalists, Mormons, and German-speaking Mennonites, creating greater Christian pluralism.[32] With the immigration of Irish Catholics, the Roman Catholic church strengthened its position as well. An analysis of these different denominations would reveal their ethnic attachments (i.e., French and Irish Catholics, English Anglicans, Scottish Presbyterians, Swiss Baptists, German Lutherans and Mennonites, and Dutch Huguenots). In essence, the push to settle Canada

---

28. Statistics Canada, "Immigration and Diversity."
29. Faith Today, "FT Interview."
30. Francis et al., *Origins*, 227.
31. Francis et al., *Origins*, 227.
32. Francis et al., *Origins*, 227.

through immigration allowed for the establishment of ethnic communities, practicing their particular brand of Christianity.

Ironically, Canada's multicultural policy which promotes tolerance and accommodation created a false solidarity, where little was done to overcome barriers to integration in homily or ecclesial leadership. Roland Kawano states this dichotomy well in *The Global City*. He writes,

> Curiously, the churches in the host society have always been the initiators of spiritual movements in societies in other parts of the world. But when people from those other countries come to the host country, the church in the host society frequently become afraid. It is unable or unwilling to cross the barriers in its own multicultural society.[33]

Toward an Intercultural Ecclesiology

For Canadian-Christians, the need to embrace the "other" should not be driven by economic, political, or population sustainability reasons. However, it is my observation that an "unconscious bias" exists within our mainstream evangelical congregations that can be traced to the mindsets of their Western European forefathers who were the initial "immigrants" to North America. Furthermore, unspoken racial prejudice toward non-Europeans that developed during periods of colonialism hinder the development of an egalitarian faith community.

It is my personal conviction that this "unconscious bias" and unspoken ethnocentrism contradicts Scripture, which promotes an ethic and praxis of integrating the nations into the Body of Christ (see Matt 28:19–21; Isa 55:5; Gal 3:26–29; Col 3:11; Rev 7:9). These verses suggest that God's ideal for his church is to be intercultural, regardless of ethnicity, gender, and socio-economic status. Safwar Marzouk in *Intercultural Church: A Biblical Vision for an Age of Migration*, states, "Migration holds the possibility and the promise that the church can rediscover its identity as envisioned in the Bible."[34] Furthermore:

> From its inception, the church was meant to be a diverse community. On the day of the Pentecost, the Holy Spirit inaugurated the church by proclaiming the Gospel in a multiplicity of languages.

---

33. Kowano, *Global City*, 95.
34. Marzouk, *Intercultural Church*, loc. 69.

> In the eschatological vision of the church in Revelation 4–7, the worshipping community, which offers God and the Lamb praises of glory and honor, comes from many nations, tribes, languages, and peoples. While the church in North America might see migration as an opportunity to serve God's kingdom by showing hospitality to the migrant and the alien, migration offers the church an opportunity to renew itself by rediscovering the biblical vision of the church as a diverse community. This biblical vision views cultural, linguistic, racial, and ethnic differences as gifts from God that can enrich the church's worship, deepen the sense of fellowship in the church, and broaden the church's witness to God's reconciling mission in the world.[35]

In addition, Marzouk asserts that "an intercultural church is a church that fosters a just diversity, integrates different cultural articulations of faith and worship, and embodies in the world an alternative to the politics of assimilation and segregation."[36] In regards to the question posed by this paper, "Is multiculturalism 'bad' for the church in Canada?," Marzouk states, "Although multiculturalism is a great step towards accepting cultural and linguistic difference, the concern is that people will end up forming islands within the same community while avoiding deep engagement with one another."[37] Pentecost then become the prescription for this malady of dis-ease with the "other," as the gift of languages enabled the Jerusalem church to become intercultural through the power of the Holy Spirit. A Kingdom community is made possible "not because one language [or one culture] dominates but rather because of the ability to speak each other's languages [and integrate each other's cultures]."[38]

In conclusion, the apostle Paul admonished the Corinthian church for their attitude and treatment of the "other" in 2 Cor 5:17–21. He states in verse 16, "From this time on, we don't think of anyone as the world thinks" (2 Cor 5:16, ERV). In Christ, Canadian Christians do not have to continue to adopt and have the mindset of their forefathers toward immigrants and global Christians, nor apply our secular multicultural conditioning to our ecclesiology. We can learn to speak each other's language by intentionally seeking to increase our intercultural awareness, repent of our prejudice, and start integrating voices that are missing from our churches.

35. Marzouk, *Intercultural Church*, loc. 76.
36. Marzouk, *Intercultural Church*, loc. 82.
37. Marzouk, *Intercultural Church*, loc. 1552.
38. Marzouk, *Intercultural Church*, loc. 1565.

PART 3: PRESENT MISSION AND ITS RELEVANCE TO FUTURE MISSION

Reflection Questions

1. "Inclusion" has become the catchphrase in workplaces, schools, and public institutions. In particular, the inclusion of the LBGTQ+ community has become the issue of the age. For the church, this issue has created division among the various denominations but more poignantly, has caused confusion among our youth who struggle with the tension of same-sex attraction and faithfully following God. How does the church navigate the practice of inclusion along with its traditional orthodox position?

2. At its core, multiculturalism as a liberal policy exists to protect the natural rights and freedoms of the individual or individual community. Thus, it is perfectly acceptable to maintain one's ethno-cultural heritage at the exclusion of others, although it is encouraged that said heritage be shared. However, the problem of multiculturalism is when opposing rights and freedoms come into tension with one another. Whose rights and freedoms do we then protect?

3. With the diversity of ethnic communities, there are few intercultural churches, though these are commonly described as multicultural churches. Most mainstream, evangelical, Protestant churches are predominantly homogeneous. Does multiculturalism hinder or promote Christian ethnocentrism?

Bibliography

Brousseau, Laurence, and Michael Dewing. *Canadian Multiculturalism*. Ottawa: Library of Parliament, 2018.

Burnet, Jean, and Leo Driedger. "Multiculturalism." *The Canadian Encyclopedia*. https://www.thecanadianencyclopedia.ca/en/article/multiculturalism.

Canadian Council for Refugees. "Brief History of Canada's responses to refugees." https://ccrweb.ca/sites/ccrweb.ca/files/static-files/canadarefugeeshistory3.htm.

The Canadian Multiculturalism Act: A Guide for Canadians. Ottawa: Multicultural and Citizenship Canada, 1990.

Encyclopedia Brittanica. "Liberalism." https://www.britannica.com/topic/liberalism.

Faith Today. "The FT Interview." July/August 2015. http://digital.faithtoday.ca/faithtoday/20150708?pg=26#pg26.

Francis, R. Douglas, et al., *Origins: Canadian History to Confederation*. 2nd ed. Toronto: Harcourt Brace, 1992.

Francis, R. Douglas, et al., *Destinies: Canadian History since Confederation*. 3rd ed. Toronto: Harcourt Brace, 1996.

Global Affairs Canada. "Address by Minister Dion at the High-Level Panel on Inclusion and Diversity, Sep. 21, 2016." https://www.canada.ca/en/global-affairs/news/2016/09/address-minister-dion-high-level-panel-inclusion-diversity.html.

Hiebert, Paul G. *The Gospel in Human Contexts*. Grand Rapids: Baker Academic, 2009.

Kawano, Roland. *The Global City*. Winfield, BC: Wood Lake, 1992.

Konieczny, Richard J., and Enoch Wan. "An Old Testament Theology of Multiculturalism." *Global Missiology* (last modified July 2004). http://www.enochwan.com/english/articles/pdf/An%20Old%20Testament%20Theology%20of%20Multiculturalism.pdf.

Library of Parliament. "House of Common Debates, 9th Parliament, 1st Session: Volume 1." parl.canadiana.ca/view/oop.debates_HOC0901_01/1482?r=0&s=4.

Statistics Canada. "Immigration and Diversity: Population Projections for Canada and its Regions, 2011–2036." Catalogue no. 91-551-X, 2017.

Stevens, David E. *God's New Humanity*. Eugene, OR: Wipf & Stock, 2012. Kindle.

University of British Columbia. "The Residential School System." Accessed on Nov. 22, 2019. https://indigenousfoundations.arts.ubc.ca/the_residential_school_system/.

Wells, Paul. "The Battle against Quebec's Bill 21." *Macleans* (November 8, 2019). https://www.macleans.ca/news/canada/the-teachers-taking-on-quebecs-bill-21/.

Wright, Teresa. "Polls Suggest Majority of Canadians Favour Limiting Immigration Levels." *The Canadian Press* (June 16, 2019). https://www.cbc.ca/news/politics/canadians-favour-limiting-immigration-1.5177814.

7

Churches Together

Mission-Engaged Differentiated Unity
as a Hermeneutic of the Gospel

Dave Witt

Introduction

For the past sixteen years, the TrueCity network of churches in Hamilton, Ontario, has pursued the collective mission to be *churches together for the good of the city*. In this chapter, I describe how the advent of the Missional Conversation led this group of churches to partner around a vision of collaborative mission. Desiring unity for the sake of collective mission, we set out to find church-based models for engaging missionally in our city. I explore the nature of the differentiated unity that resulted, and how it energized this network beyond the instrumental results that we were initially looking to achieve. I bring our experience into dialogue with the ecclesiological literature that links this dynamic of differentiated unity to the characteristic of catholicity attested to by the historic creeds. I consider how these churches, in overcoming the separatist tendencies of their ecclesiological roots, have given the Spirit freedom to deepen this differentiated unity, unleashing the life-giving dynamic of catholicity and making it a visible, participatory reality.

The second part of the chapter explores the partnership and network methodologies we have used to develop this differentiated unity. The formal and structural practices of building partnerships and the informal and relational practices of network development have both proven essential. Learning to integrate and sustain them over time is challenging, but

I believe it is the key to developing missional church networks that create vibrant differentiated unity.

Missional Church Roots of TrueCity

It was the advent of the Missional Conversation that led to the creation of TrueCity. I arrived in Hamilton in 1998 after spending ten years doing mission work focused on church planting and community organizing among the urban poor in Manila, Philippines. I came to Hamilton looking for churches interested in reaching out to their neighborhoods in ways that matched the ethos of what had been formed while I was in Manila.

The book *Missional Church* tapped into a shift from an ecclesial-centric to a theocentric understanding of mission.[1] This *missio Dei* insight—that God is on mission to bring his shalom-intention to fulfillment in all of creation and how churches are called to partner with God in this mission shifted how churches understood their part in the mission venture.[2] Mission was no longer conceived as a specialized calling of a few within the church in order to expand the church but was understood to be the calling of the whole church wherever she exists.[3]

TrueCity started in 2004 when three of the churches that I had been coaching around their missional engagement asked the organization that I work for, International Teams Canada (iTeams), to facilitate collaboration between them in order to strengthen church-based neighborhood engagement. By the end of the first year, three more churches had joined, and a year later, a seventh church committed to being part of the network. We developed regular rhythms to bring pastors and other church leaders together. We held a conference on the first year and found it to be a powerful vehicle for bringing more people in our congregations together. We have held a conference each year since. Those gatherings create space to connect, share stories, and learn from each other.

The cooperative engagement that has resulted has included such initiatives as volunteering in neighborhood schools, welcoming refugees, walking with those facing mental health challenges, engaging the arts community, caring for creation, youth ministry, Indigenous reconciliation, and other such ventures. We refer to these as "arenas of mission." The innovation

1. Guder, *Missional Church*, 81–83.
2. Guder, *Missional Church*, 82.
3. Guder, *Missional Church*, 83.

was to recognize all this work as collective mission, even though the various churches involved were not all focused on the same arenas. We have found that together we can engage a growing number of these arenas if each of our congregations identifies and focuses on a few of them.

This has not been a panacea. Discerning which arenas to focus on and how to sustain engagement remains a work in progress for all congregations involved. Finding effective ways to do evangelism in the midst of missional engagement remains challenging, as does sustaining intentionality in how we pursue discipleship in the midst of mission, but we continue to face and engage these challenges together. In all of this, the churches involved in TrueCity challenge each other to work from the understanding that they are joining God in his mission. I believe this has been key to the larger sense of church that has taken root.

Exploring the Ecclesiological Implications of TrueCity

All of the churches involved in the startup of TrueCity had ecclesiological distinctives that the other churches did not share. Some of these differences (such as beliefs around baptism, the gifts of the Spirit, and views on female leadership) were considered significant, but it was agreed that there was enough alignment to be in relationship. The openness to relationship was a clear sign that God was at work among us. As one of the pastors of a founding church noted: "You know God is at work when a group of churches from different traditions, which have defined themselves by who they don't associate with, choose to partner with each other." Though I did not recognize it then, this statement named how this network of churches was moving against the tide of their Free Church ecclesiology in opening themselves up to an enriched expression of catholicity.

Two of the key founding voices of the missional movement, Lesslie Newbigin and David Bosch passionately contend for the deep connection of unity and mission. George R. Hunsberger summarizes this theme in Newbigin's writing:

> The calling of the churches made it a missionary necessity to resolve disunity. And to say that it is a missionary necessity is to say that unity most importantly comes to form locally as "all who confess Christ as Lord [are] recognizably one family in each place."[4]

4. Hunsberger, *Bearing the Witness of the Spirit*, 28.

Bosch concurs when he contends: "We have to confess that the loss of ecclesial unity is not just a vexation but a sin. Unity is not an optional extra. It is in Christ, already a fact, a given."[5] These are not perspectives that the churches involved in TrueCity had traditionally lived out. While this missional input motivated us, it is only over time that we have come to recognize that the unity of the church is an established reality that we are called to live into rather than a secondary goal that we can work at if things are going well.

The ecclesiological distinctives of nearly all of the churches involved in TrueCity come from the Free Church tradition of congregationalism with its emphasis on local church self-determination. Churches formed in this Free Church tradition have a strong tendency toward suspicion of churches from other denominations.[6] While this dogmatic separatism is not inherently necessary to the Free Church ecclesial self-understanding, it has been so characteristic that moving beyond it feels like compromise to those formed within this tradition. And yet we cannot escape the reality that the historical pattern of separation goes directly against Scripture's call to glorify Christ by maintaining the unity of the Spirit.[7] With this, our practice has been deeply at odds with our commitment to the authority of Scripture. As Tim Keller writes: "To be estranged in ministry from other true believers who are members of the 'wrong' denomination is to fail to welcome those whom Christ himself has welcomed."[8] A besetting sin of the Free Church framework and the theology it generates is how our idolatrous belief in the certainty of our grasp of knowledge has led us to the conclusion that we have (or can discover) the one right perspective on how to be a "Bible-believing" church.[9]

In his book *After Our Likeness*, Miroslav Volf develops a Free Church ecclesiology that can lead us beyond this separatist pattern while remaining true to the theological roots of the Free Church tradition. In laying out what constitutes a church, Volf introduces the condition of the "interecclesial minimum," which contends that for any church to be a true church it must recognize all other churches. In so doing, each church sets out on the eschatological path to its future, which will include communion

---

5. Bosch, *Transforming Mission*, 465.
6. Keller, *Center Church*, 368.
7. Kärkkäinen, *Introduction to Ecclesiology*, 61–62.
8. Keller, *Center Church*, 368.
9. Keller, *Center Church*, 368.

with all of these churches.[10] Volf links this communion to the importance of developing a differentiated unity among churches.[11] The development of this "interecclesial minimum" as a mark of a true church coming from within a Free Church ecclesiology provides a very helpful launching point for working out a deeper sense of why unity is essential from within a Free Church ethos and how developing a network of congregations aligns with God's heart for his church in any given context.

As I reflect on the history of the TrueCity network, I see how the separatist impulse of the churches involved was suspended in pursuit of a viable response to the changing culture, where competing denominational distinctives had become increasingly irrelevant and the congregational practices of evangelism were no longer contextually effective. This created an openness to cooperative mission when it was accompanied by a clear vision for missional engagement that left initiative and control with the leadership structures of each of the churches.

As our network has grown and diversified, the challenges to our unity have grown. In order to continue to live well into our calling to be "churches together for the good of the city," we have needed to recognize and develop a more conscious and robust ecclesiology, one which recognizes how our collective reality is enriched and made more compelling when it is characterized by the differentiated unity that Volf highlights.[12] One of my co-workers has described this reality as the "thickening of the social and spiritual fabric" in our city.

A Theology of Reconciling Catholicity

While the local congregation remains the primary experience of church for those involved in TrueCity, participation in the network is growing our awareness of this broader collective reality that Volf identifies as *catholicity*.[13] This word points to the totality of the interconnected reality of the global expression of the Church and to the fullness that God intends for this totality to become part of the new creation.[14] By forming a network and learning to collaborate we have given the Spirit space to enrich our

10. Volf, *After Our Likeness*, 156.
11. Volf, *After Our Likeness*, 157.
12. Volf, *After Our Likeness*, 157.
13. Volf, *After Our Likeness*, 262.
14. Volf, "Catholicity," 527–28.

understanding of what God intends his church to be. In describing catholicity, Keller notes that unity is not simply the work of the Spirit but the very instrument through which the Spirit works.[15] This describes the reconciling reality that is deepening our unity in the midst of diversity and has a transforming impact on our churches and in our city.

Volf unpacks how different streams of the church define catholicity in ways that fit with their own agenda but argues that in order to recognize it for the core characteristic of the church that it is, we have to affirm that there is a fundamental relationship between unity and plurality. The church is a heterogeneous whole, which means that we are called to pursue a differentiated unity.[16] Catholicity is the way in which every particular community points toward the full expression of the global church throughout time.[17] In reflecting on the implications of catholicity for how the church lives in any given context, Craig Van Gelder writes:

> The starting point for thinking about the church is to recognize that it is already a community that possesses an essential oneness. In working from this starting point, it is as if God says to the diversity of churches in any context, "You are one. Now learn how to affirm each other's distinctiveness while you work out your differences."[18]

This is what we have been learning to pursue through TrueCity. It has been messy and often uncomfortable, but it has enriched our network as we have benefitted from the cross-pollination that has resulted.

Catholicity most often is used in reference to the unity amid diversity of the global church.[19] Coming to recognize that this dynamic is important at a local level—as diverse congregations risk associating across their differences—has proven a vital new perspective. In an important way, TrueCity has made catholicity visible for a group of churches, which given their Free Church ecclesiology, do not have categories for this reality as a lived, local experience. The experience we have gained over the past sixteen years would suggest that all congregations are called to and would benefit from being in relationship with other congregations across their default affinity lines of denomination and doctrinal alignment by

15. Keller, *Center Church*, 368.
16. Volf, "Catholicity," 527.
17. Guder, *Missional Church*, 257.
18. Van Gelder, *Essence of Church*, 122.
19. Volf, *After Our Likeness*.

finding overlap that allows them to join more closely together in mission as God leads. In order to do this, however, structures and practices are needed that make it possible to live out the differentiated unity that we have come to find deeply life-giving.

Ecclesiology and Unity Methodologies

Volf's articulation of how differentiation is essential to the biblical call to unity and Van Gelder's exhortation to learn to affirm distinctives while working out differences, have provided greater depth of insight into our sense of God's presence and favor in the work to see churches collaborate. It more clearly names for us why this work is important. Yet, how to best to operationalize this work is an equally important and often more challenging question. I started into this work naively expecting it to be straight forward, only to find it fraught with challenge. In this section I will explore two methodologies that we have used. We have found that both the formal, structural work of building partnerships, and the informal, connective process of developing a network have much to offer. But while they both have important contributions to make, it is only as we have begun to learn to hold them in creative tension that they have proven most fruitful.

Literature on Partnership

While partnership is a pervasive and positive concept in our culture, there has been and still remains a lack of clarity around how best to define it.[20] In her article, "The Theology of Partnership," Cathy Ross suggests that partnership is constituted of three factors: genuine involvement, acceptance of responsibility, and a willingness to accept liability.[21] She highlights how the triune nature of God is the basis of and pattern for partnership, and how in Christ, God lives out involvement, responsibility, and liability in order to establish authentic partnership with humanity. She sees this as providing us with the pattern for how partnership is to be

---

20. See Mendel, "Achieving Meaningful Partnerships," 66; Pietroburgo, "Doing Good," 139; Lister, "Power in Partnership," 228; Stott, "Partnership and Social Progress," iii.

21. Ross, "Theology of Partnership," 145.

lived out in our relationships as well, highlighting the call to listen, give, and forgive as core to partnership.[22]

In his article, "The Mission of God and Global Partnerships," César García uses the concept of partnership to name the way in which the church lives out the mission of God. He writes:

> "Partnership" is the term I use to refer to the kind of *relationship* that can be found among the people of God when we serve together interdependently in the mission of God. *Partnerships* require a solid *relationship* and a *shared purpose* that fosters *joint plans* and the *sharing of resources*.[23]

As García suggests, partnership in mission proved quite powerful over the first three years of our work developing TrueCity. The collaborative work of naming and defining the network and running a yearly conference was challenging, but it was the kind of challenge that built strong relational bonds across boundaries that used to feel insurmountable. Ross and García theologically ground partnership in such a way that makes it almost interchangeable with the attribute of differentiation. This provides an important bridge to our theological foundations.

Like García, we understand partnership to be a straightforward task of establishing strong relationships, shared purposes, joint plans, and shared resources, and for the first few years that proved to be the case. In 2006 (TrueCity's second year), the pastoral leadership of the six churches involved framed a set of core values in an attempt to name what it was that had brought us together. These core values have been invaluable and remain at the heart of the network. The following year, we framed a Covenant Agreement template and process that sought to operationalize the core values calling for church structures to commit to the network. This was our version of a partnership agreement. That we created this process was important and formative. I am convinced that the network would not have continued without this. But there were significant weaknesses in the process that the literature on partnership has helped me to recognize. There was very little in the template that defined common practice.[24] We did not recognize how significant variations in understanding the partnership make the tasks of defining and working together as partners challenging.[25]

22. Ross, "Theology of Partnership," 148.
23. García, "Global Partnerships," 18 (emphasis in original).
24. Mendel, "Achieving Meaningful Partnerships," 74.
25. Stott, "Partnership and Social Progress," 37.

Our grasp of the organizational implications of partnership were lacking.[26] In retrospect, it is clear that our practice of partnership was not robust enough to avoid organizational pitfalls.

Partnership in Social Development and Non-Profit Leadership Disciplines

The academic literature in the social development and non-profit leadership disciplines provides insightful input that provides the basis for critiquing our initial work. Mendel introduces the term *meaningful partnership* and defines it as a form of partnership that leads to benefits that strengthen the participating organizations in specific ways.[27] He provides three insightful recommendations for recognizing and organizing around the attributes that make a partnership meaningful. These are:

1. Timing: the process of developing trust is time consuming and is not well served by short-term oriented funding models.
2. Shared Values: meaningful partnerships are those that endure because of shared values and functions between the participants, and so there is a need for trust building by leaders.
3. Adaptive Nature: successful partnerships will nurture an open-ended, flexible, and adaptable process leading to more intense connections between the collaboration members.[28]

Building trust, establishing shared values, and nurturing open-ended, adaptable processes is in fact what took place over the earlier years of developing the TrueCity network, and I would affirm that this was essential for its development.

Mendel highlights the reality that there are costs for participants in forming a partnership that need to be recognized and accounted for. There are also organizational competencies that need to be developed.[29] Tennyson insightfully writes:

> Partnering is practised by many as if it is simply "business as usual" with a new name, instead of a significantly different way of

---

26. Tennyson, "Partnership Brokers," 22–25.
27. Mendel, "Achieving Meaningful Partnerships," 73–74.
28. Mendel, "Achieving Meaningful Partnerships," 74–75.
29. Mendel, "Achieving Meaningful Partnerships," 68–69.

planning and operating that requires changes in mindset, courage to challenge assumptions and willingness to break the habitual behaviour patterns.[30]

We did not recognize this during the early years of TrueCity. Given the lack of definition to how partnership would function (given clear agreed-upon objectives), it is not surprising that we found the way forward more challenging.

Partnerships require structure and administrative capacity, but this is often not adequately recognized or planned for.[31] The financial, HR, and legal structures needed to run the TrueCity network were provided by iTeams, which was willing to stay behind the scenes—allowing for the network to start and develop. Stott recognizes the importance of this *Servant Organization* role and shares best practice input.[32] One key practice is having someone to provide facilitative leadership, which is described as someone "who provide the 'connective tissue' that enables the partners involved in collaborative alliances to work together optimally and augment their ability to achieve positive societal transformation."[33] For TrueCity, we have given this role the title of *Network Developer*.

Network Weaving

The partnership methodology had created formal relationships between multiple congregations, but we needed a different methodology, one that demanded less centralized, goal-oriented activity in order to see the network grow and flourish. We came to recognize that our network structures were weighing down our congregational leadership and structures. We needed ways to facilitate more informal, relational connections based on affinities. In his book, *Thy Kingdom Connected*, Dwight Friesen provided a vision for how the paradigm of networks can give robust direction to the kind of work we were doing.[34] Coming to understand TrueCity as a social–spiritual network and learning of methods for strengthening networks provided a way forward.

30. Tennyson, "Partnership Brokers," 20.
31. Hundal, "Partnership Brokers as Planners," 88.
32. See Stott, *Shaping Sustainable Change*.
33. Stott, *Shaping Sustainable Change*, 12.
34. Friesen, *Thy Kingdom Connected*, 85.

Up to this time, we had been focused on the way churches were connected through their leaders. A network paradigm pushed us to recognize that there were numerous other connections and that these were in many ways more important. A core tenet of social network theory is the counterintuitive reality of the importance to a network of weak links. Friesen writes that "a strong network is made up of many weak links. In fact, a network comprised of many weak links is stronger and more enduring than a network made up of fewer but stronger links."[35]

June Holley's *Network Weaver Handbook* helped provide the practical direction for a network methodology.[36] Holley identifies three aspects of networks, relational, action, and support that need to be woven together to create robust networks and identifies the roles that are central to each aspect. The relational aspect is the web of relationships that defines the shape of the network. Connectors are especially important to this aspect. They are the ones who help people get more involved in the network, by connecting them to others who have similar passions and experience. The action aspect is focused on the way that networks get things done. Implementers are people who gather clusters to take collaborative initiative on projects. The support aspect is the system and culture created to strengthen and enrich the network. The role associated with this aspect is that of a *Guardian*. They support project work and leadership action by strengthening communication systems and ensuring accountability.[37]

In 2015, in response to this input, we set out to identify those in our congregations who enjoy and are particularly gifted connectors. By bringing these people together four times a year, we have been able to multiply the relational bridges between churches and strengthen communication links. This Church Connectors group has been particularly good at naming the ways that God is at work at the grassroots level. Working with the Connectors, we began to recognize the traction that a significant number of missional initiatives had through the community that TrueCity had catalyzed and strengthened. These were not projects that TrueCity leadership groups organized, but the network created by TrueCity was energizing them.

---

35. Friesen, *Thy Kingdom Connected*, 138
36. Holley, *Network Weaver*, 71.
37. Holley, *Network Weaver*, 18–23, 30–39.

Integrating Paradigms

The literatures on partnerships and networks do not seem to engage with each other. This is unfortunate because not only is there significant overlap in the postures they advocate for, but they also seem to have distinct but complementary strengths that reflect the Spirit's initiative to develop differentiated unity among us. The partnership methodology recognizes the importance of organizations establishing mutually beneficial relationships, ones which recognize and organize around the differing strengths of those involved as well as laying out procedures and goals that serve all involved. It pays closer attention to formal structures and the ways that collaboration can best be established. The network methodology, on the other hand, is particularly powerful in involving a broader group of people, recognizing and tapping the creativity latent in the periphery of a network and building more robust alignment. It functions more powerfully in informal settings and stimulates cooperation. The partnership methodology's emphasis on structures is important for congregational leadership to buy-in but runs the danger of stifling grassroots initiative (or failing to recognize it). The network methodology's emphasis on building cooperation through relational connections is powerful but too easily bypasses church leadership in a way that diminishes congregational ownership and participation. I have come to the conclusion that in order for a network of congregations like TrueCity to flourish, an integration of partnership and network approaches are needed.

What TrueCity has to Offer

In this chapter, I have shared the story of the surprising way that the Spirit moved in Hamilton in bringing together a group of churches, characterized by Free Church ecclesiology with its normal separatist impulse, and weaving them into the TrueCity network that embraced cooperative mission. Engaging as a network of partnered congregations has encouragingly led to the original goal of increased congregational involvement in mission, but it is the vibrant witness of the differentiated unity that has developed and which this network of churches is increasingly learning to put into practice through building partnerships and engaging in network development that has been most compelling. In his seminal book *The Gospel in a Pluralist Society*, Newbigin asserts, "I have come to feel that the primary reality of which we have to take into account in seeking for a Christian impact on public life is the Christian congregation."[38] He summarized this with the phrase "the congregation as hermeneutic of the gospel." We have found that this hermeneutical reality is powerfully amplified when congregations connect and collaborate in pursuit of expressions of the Kingdom that Jesus inaugurated. Jesus's prayer was that we would be one, and that by that unity the world would know that the Father sent him (John 17:23). We are finding that when in answer to this prayer, a cross-denominational group of congregations commit to pursue collective mission, learning from and collaborating with each other, their differentiated unity becomes a visible and participatory reality, amplifying their witness so that their city becomes more acutely aware of how God is at work in their midst.

Reflection Questions

1. Are there expressions of differentiated unity between churches in your area? What shape does it take?

2. Are there further opportunities for churches to work together in your community? What are the barriers to this happening?

3. What practices have you seen that were used to operationalize a commitment to unity? Which ones have been most effective?

Bibliography

Bosch, David J. *Transforming Mission: Paradigm Shifts in Theology of Mission.* Maryknoll, NY: Orbis, 1997.

Friesen, Dwight J. *Thy Kingdom Connected: What the Church Can Learn from Facebook, the Internet, and Other Networks.* Grand Rapids: Baker, 2009.

Garcia, Cesar. "The Mission of God and Global Partnerships." *Anabaptist Witness* 5 (2018) 15–25.

Guder, Darrell L., ed. *Missional Church: A Vision for the Sending of the Church in North America.* Grand Rapids: Eerdmans, 1998.

Holley, June. *Network Weaver Handbook: A Guide to Transformational Networks.* Athens, Ohio: Network Weaver, 2012.

Hundal, Surinder. "Partnership Brokers as Planners, Managers, and Administrators." In *Shaping Sustainable Change*, 88–94. New York: Routledge, 2019.

Hunsberger, George R. *Bearing the Witness of the Spirit: Lesslie Newbigin's Theology of Cultural Plurality.* Grand Rapids: Eerdmans, 1998.

---

38. Newbigin, *Gospel*, 227.

Kärkkäinen, Veli-Matti. *An Introduction to Ecclesiology: Ecumenical, Historical and Global Perspectives*. Downers Grove, IL: IVP Academic, 2002.

Keller, Timothy. *Center Church: Doing Balanced, Gospel-Centered Ministry in Your City*. Grand Rapids: Zondervan, 2012.

Lister, Sarah. "Power in Partnership? An Analysis of an NGO's Relationship with Its Partners." *Journal of International Development* 12 (2000) 227–39.

Mendel, Stuart C. "Achieving Meaningful Partnerships with Non-Profit Organizations: A View from the Field." *Journal of Non-Profit Education and Leadership* 3 (2013) 66–81.

Newbigin, Lesslie. *The Gospel in a Pluralist Society*. Grand Rapids: Eerdmans, 1989.

Pietroburgo, Julie. "Doing Good Across Faith and Global Borders." *Journal of Non-Profit Education and Leadership* 6 (2016) 127–43.

Ross, Cathy. "The Theology of Partnership." *International Bulletin of Missionary Research* 34 (2010) 145–48.

Stott, Leda. "The Case for Partnership Brokering." In *Shaping Sustainable Change*, 11–19. New York: Routledge, 2019.

———. "Partnership and Social Progress: Multi-stakeholder Collaboration in Context." PhD diss., The University of Edinburgh, 2017.

———, ed. *Shaping Sustainable Change*. New York: Routledge, 2019.

Tennyson, Ros. "What do Partnership Brokers Do?" In *Shaping Sustainable Change*, 20–34. New York: Routledge, 2019.

Van Gelder, Craig. *The Essence of the Church: A Community Created by the Spirit*. Grand Rapids: Baker, 2000.

Volf, Miroslav. *After Our Likeness: The Church as the Image of the Trinity*. Grand Rapids: Eerdmans, 1998.

———. "Catholicity of 'Two or Three': Free Church Reflections on the Catholicity of the Local Church." *The Jurist* 52 (1992) 525–46.

8

Healing of Memories
Reconciling the Church for the Reconciliation of Community

Manuel Böhm

Church in a World of Non-Christian and Hurt People

The Church is in decline, not just in Europe but also in Canada.[1] In "Not Christian Anymore," Rick Hiemstra reveals recent poll results that 43 percent of Canadians today have some kind of Christian religious affiliation, though when they were 12 years of age, this same group reported it had 71 percent affiliation.[2] Many people across generations and denominations are not part of the church anymore. Though churches may tend to look to some "superstar" pastors, others try to adapt their approach to find fresh ways to stay alive.[3]

A phenomenon build on migration is the constant arrival of newcomers in Canada. Some of them hope for a better future, but they observed that their "new neighbor" might belong to their "old enemy" from the land where they just fled. Others may not carry struggles of past trauma but with their new challenges in a different cultural context, some devoted Christians may find it hard to recognize that their methods of mission, which were successful in their home country, do not work in Canada. Robert Cousins notes that "we are living in a changing cultural context where the proven solutions of the past no longer relate to the

---

1. For the European context, see Reimer, "Healing Memories in the City."
2. Hiemstra, "Not Christian Anymore."
3. As example, see Stiller and Metzger, *Going Missional*.

questions being raised in the present."⁴ What are the approaches for doing church in this constant evolving multiplicity?

In the past century, two almost opposite approaches were pursued: social transformation and evangelism—either through social activity churches tried to be part of society's transformation so that churches were known as intermediary agents in communities among "other societal powers of change,"⁵ or churches put all efforts into evangelistic crusades.

In the 1990s, with David Bosch's call for paradigm shifts in mission came newer missiological approaches that turned toward a more holistic view of helping the church see outside the box and back to what church was meant to be as "a fellowship of those called out of the world to accept responsibility for the world."⁶

The Peace and Reconciliation Network (PRN)⁷ has observed three reasons why the church has not become effective in society: she is preoccupied with her own matters; she has lost her theological calling; and she is involved in foreign business.⁸ Thus, the church needs to relearn her God-given mission. PRN has proposed three aspects in this regard.

First, the church is a response to God and the world—God's creation and agent in this world sent to take over the responsibility for the world (Matt 16:18; 28:18–19). God's people are called a holy nation and priesthood that presents the worldly matters in front of God and his presence among his people (1 Pet 2:9–10). Having lost that calling, the church has defined her identity apart from God's intention and has started building her own kingdom.

Second, God called his people to be ambassadors of reconciliation. Paul described how God through his minister of reconciliation, Jesus Christ, reconciled the whole world with himself (2 Cor 5:18–20). This ministry is given to his church to invite people to a restored life in fullness. When the church excludes this aspect from her mission, she ends being God's ambassador and is dependent on her own authority and abilities.

Third, the church has a clear calling. Jesus said, "As the father has sent me, I am sending you" (John 20:21). Being effective depends highly on

---

4. Cousins, "Foreword", vii.

5. Reimer, "Healing Memories in the City."

6. Reimer, "Healing Memories in the City." See more in Reimer, "Die Welt umarmen," 42–47.

7. For more about PRN, see https://wea.peaceandreconciliation.net.

8. Reimer, "Healing Memories in the City."

following Christ and his mission, plus relying on the Holy Spirit to show the way. When the church gets involved in matters outside of being salt and light in the world (Matt 5:13), she loses her effectiveness and impact. To be an effective witness for Christ in the world and to follow the calling that God gave the church, she ought to be reconciled with her given mission of being an ambassador for reconciliation, and therefore, bringing holistic healing and peace to communities.

Reconciliation as Central to the Church's Mission

What is the basis for the assumption that the ministry of reconciliation is central to the church? A theology of reconciliation can be derived from Paul's letter to the church in Corinth, particularly in 2 Cor 5:14–21,

> For Christ's love compels us, because we are convinced that one died for all, and therefore all died. And he died for all, that those who live should no longer live for themselves but for him who died for them and was raised again. So from now on we regard no one from a worldly point of view. Though we once regarded Christ in this way, we do so no longer. Therefore, if anyone is in Christ, the new creation has come: The old has gone, the new is here! All this is from God, who reconciled us to himself through Christ and gave us the ministry of reconciliation: that God was reconciling the world to himself in Christ, not counting people's sins against them. And he has committed to us the message of reconciliation. We are therefore Christ's ambassadors, as though God were making his appeal through us. We implore you on Christ's behalf: Be reconciled to God. God made him who had no sin to be sin for us, so that in him we might become the righteousness of God. (NIV)

The concept of reconciliation used by Paul is rooted in a bigger picture. Paul starts the paragraph with the love of Christ and his death that brings together the separated (Eph 2:11–22). Reconciliation (Greek: *katallassō*)[9] describes an exchange "of hostility, anger, or war for friendship, love, or peace"[10] and "involves a process of overcoming alienation through identification and solidarity with the other, thus making peace and restoring

---

9. Balz and Schneider observes, "The verb καταλλάσσω is used six times in the Pauline Epistles; it is used once of human relationships (1 Cor 7:11) and five times of the God-human relationship (Rom 5:10; 2 Cor 5:18–20). The noun καταλλαγή is found four times (Rom 5:11; 11:15; 2 Cor 5:18, 19)" ("καταλλάσσω," 261).

10. Balz and Schneider, "καταλλάσσω," 261.

relationships."¹¹ This includes the notion of "exchanging places with the other, having solidarity instead of being against the other."¹²

Along with other voices,¹³ Craig Ott defines mission as "the sending activity of God with the purpose of reconciling to himself and bringing into his kingdom fallen men and women from every people and nation to his glory."¹⁴ This way, 2 Cor 5:18 points out three basic propositions. First, God is working reconciliation through Christ. God knows that humans have forgotten their original design as the image of God and to be in relationship with him. They have lost this vision and have fallen into self-destruction and follow their corrupted mind (Rom 1). God with his loving heart does not want sinners to perish (Ezek 33:11) and therefore brings restoration of the broken relationship through Jesus Christ (2 Cor 5:18).

Second, the aim of reconciliation is to restore the relationship between God and the world. Reconciliation means bringing back the original imagery in the human heart, to restore that memory of being a child of God (2 Cor 6:18), and giving people their new identity (2 Cor 5:17). "The fullness of reconciliation is friendship with God in Jesus Christ,"¹⁵ which brings the renewal of the mind and the potential to live a life in harmony with God (Rom 12:1–3). Third, the ministry of reconciliation is given to the church. "God desires peace with his creation and, therefore peace is at the heart of his mission."¹⁶ Robert Schreiter suggests that reconciliation is a central way to explain God's work in the world and to make reconciliation a paradigm of mission through combining it with the concept of the *missio Dei*.¹⁷

According to Schreiter, this reconciliation does not eliminate other elements of God's mission but could become a frame of reference for evangelism, *diakonia*, dialogue, and further aspects.¹⁸ At PRN, we propose

---

11. De Gruchy, *Reconciliation*, 51.
12. Reimer, "Healing Memories in the City".
13. See Breytenbach, *Versöhnung*.
14. Ott, *Theology of Mission*, 155.
15. Rice, *Reconciliation as Mission of God*, 11.
16. Reimer, "Healing Memories in the City."
17. Schreiter, *Mission as Ministry of Reconciliation*, 14.
18. Scheiter states further: "Reconciliation as a paradigm of mission does not replace the other paradigms, but can bring them into closer connection with one another within the larger frame of God's intentions for the world. So this twofold contribution—to the larger questions of reconciliation in the world today and to the dialogue between paradigms of mission within the churches—assures a continuing role for this paradigm of reconciliation on missionary thinking for the coming decades" (Schreiter, *Mission as*

PART 3: PRESENT MISSION AND ITS RELEVANCE TO FUTURE MISSION

that peace and reconciliation work as a matrix for the mission of the local church; this matrix relates the reconciliation rooted in God's outreach to restore brokenness to the implications for human relationships and creation.[19] The Christian work of reconciliation needs a holistic approach. Reconciliation therefore means one "has to deal with root causes of conflicts if it is to be considered genuine."[20]

Joining the Wounded to Bring the Alienated to the Table

Wounded people often claim justice as either finding revenge or integrating it as a part of their healing journey. Even in societies that claim to have laws and fair processes, people feel left behind and alienated. Why should one stand up for those outsiders?[21]

Looking into the past, one could argue with the words of the German protestant pastor Martin Niemöller, who stood up—somewhat belatedly—to resist the Nazi regime and then spent eight years in a concentration camp:

> First, they came for the socialists, and I did not speak out because I was not a socialist. Then they came for the trade unionists, and I did not speak out because I was not a trade unionist. Then they

---

Ministry of Reconciliation, 29).

19. Other papers read at the EMS conference 2020 in Toronto, ON, and Langley, BC, relate to this issue: Reimer, "Reconciliation—Matrix for Christian Mission"; and Wagler, "Agents of Peace and Reconciliation."

20. See Schreiter, "Reconciliation", 25–26.

21. But what if there is no one that speaks up for the hurting and they must fight for their own healing? Is it then just the hurt one who needs to learn to overcome a victim perspective and come to a point of forgiveness? An important topic, which would go beyond the scope of this chapter, that should be elaborated more is the question of power dynamics. In conflict transformation, both parties have to lay down their past perspectives, and especially the party with power needs to come to the place of laying down their opportune position. Power and conflict seem closely related; see more about this in Blalock, "Power and Conflict." Conflict relates to both misuse and absence of power. More on this in Wallace, "Control in Conflict." Is a power position always evil or how can power be seen in a Christian perspective? More on the correlation of power and conflict in Himes, "Conflict Management"; more on perspectives on power in LaGuardia, "Transforming Christology," and Wood, "Theology of Power." How can a view on Jesus and his use of power help for reconciliation efforts? More on the power in the ministry of Jesus in Moore, "Kenotic Politics," and Wright, "Day the Revolution Began."

came for the Jews, and I did not speak out because I was not a Jew. Then they came for me, and there was no one left to speak for me.[22]

But instead of a negative-driven perspective, one could rather focus on Jesus and how his mission gives a framework for reconciliation, to leaving the past behind, and creating a new future. Jesus says: "You will see the truth and the truth will set you free" (John 8:32). This includes the past and the future—with Paul's image, the old man (made according to the flesh) is stripped down and a new man (made in the Spirit) is put on (Col 3:5–15). "Thus, restoration is a two-step process: we realize what is old in us and leave it, and we understand what God's new creation for us is and put it on."[23]

Recovering our Sinful Memory

"Every conflict has its story."[24] To find healing and restoration of the vision that God intended for us, we must recover our own past. "To see our own life story, our own biography from God's perspective, to read the pages of our past together with God's Spirit, will uncover our sinful ways and set us on His paths."[25] To overcome the past requires the recognition of sin and confession—both prerequisites for forgiveness—"and forgiveness breaks the chain of bad memory and inferiority complexes."[26]

Recovering God's Vision

Paul encourages those who believe in Christ that God reveals to them what this new identity means and what gifts they received with this new status (Eph 1:3–23). In this way, we leave the "demonic cycle" and through reconciliation step into "God's cycle"[27] and receive a new vision.

> Reconciled people will find here their orientation for their all-day life. They will accentuate the mind of Christ and steadily build up a recovered memory of God's plan for their life. Thus,

---

22. http://www.forerunner.com/champion/X0006_5._Martin_Niemller.html.
23. Reimer, "Healing Memories in the City."
24. Baumberger, "Lasst es uns noch mal versuchen," 114.
25. Reimer, "Healing Memories in the City."
26. Reimer, "Healing Memories in the City."
27. Baumberger, "Lasst es uns noch mal versuchen," 116.

memories are healed, and the past no longer influences the present and future.[28]

Healing of Memories: A Methodology for Reconciliation

It lies within the human nature to perceive situations through a subjective lens, having the potential to strive for a life in fulness or into culturally driven psychological and physiological pathologies. This often happens to conflicting parties that read historical events through their understanding, shaping certain narratives of the conflict, or so called "collective memory,"[29] which may not be accurate. As a result, polemics dominate a relationship and hinder the parties from seeing their own portion of guilt in the basket. Reading history together helps to discover the alternative views relativizing predefined positions and opening a road for mutual understanding.[30] It is crucial to name wrongdoing as sin, regardless of what the motivation may have been. Sin can never be excused. The only way to overcome sin is forgiveness.[31] The calling of the church is to bring the healing to the nations, discipling people, and introducing them to the fulness of life found in Jesus Christ. How can we achieve that and change those narratives? The concept of Healing of Memories (HoM) can help to step into that gap.

In the beginning, HoM was developed in South Africa to bring healing and reconciliation into the broken post-apartheid relationships between victims and offenders.[32] Since then, it has been used globally to bring conflict resolution and reconciliation.[33] The main focus, though, was to reconcile individuals with each other.

With entering the European context in the late 1990s,[34] HoM was first used in Northern Ireland[35] and then found its way to be used in Serbia, Ukraine, Slovakia, and Finland.[36] In 2004, the Conference of European

28. Reimer, "Healing Memories in the City."
29. Assmann and Czaplicka, "Collective Memory and Cultural Identity," 125–33.
30. One example for such historical understanding is the blanket exercise: https://www.kairoscanada.org/what-we-do/indigenous-rights-2/blanket-exercise.
31. Reimer, "Healing Memories in the City."
32. Botman, *To Remember and to Heal*.
33. For an overview, see Garzon and Burke, "Healing of Memories."
34. Gutierrez, "Friedens-und Versöhnungsarbeit," 152–56.
35. McEvoy, "Making Peace with the Past," 144–55.
36. Brandes, *Healing of Memories in Europe*.

Churches and the Community of Protestant Churches in Europe started an HoM-project in Romania.[37] The important step happened through the Irish School of Ecumenics to use HoM for reconciling groups and cultures, based on the *charta ecumenica*. In September 2007, with the third Conference of European Churches in Sibiu, Romania, a call for all European Christian Churches to cooperate in peace and reconciliation efforts was made. In 2008, the foundation Reconciliation in South East Europe and the Ecumenical Institute of Healing of Memories were established in Sibiu. These concepts have successfully been used in various conflicts, including Central African ones such as in Burundi, Rwanda and Congo.[38]

Through contextual adaption, the HoM approach uses three steps.[39] The first step is walking together through history. In this phase, the parties work together in an interdisciplinary way through the socio-cultural and religious backgrounds of evolution of conflicts. The aim is to understand how conflicts arise and develop and what does influence them. It is crucial that all conflict parties work in this together. The second is taking the time to share in the pain of others. In this phase of the process, the parties hear the stories of pain and suffering of each other and develop a sense of understanding why the common history causes so much pain on the one hand but also a sense of understanding why the offense happened. The aim is to open ways for apology and forgiveness, understanding, and acceptance. The third step is preparing the future together. Solving the problems of the past opens ways to work on a common peaceful future. In order to work together, the parties will have to discover the richness of the other, along with the gifts and competences of each other. Active and peaceful participation in the life of each other is the aim of this step. The result is an expected reconciled community.

Through the model of HoM reconciliation can extend into healing of memories in which the conflicted past is not excused, but through confession of sin a clear step towards forgiveness is possible. At the same time an alternative future is brought to the table—God's vision. This is the common base for peaceful connivance; healing of our memories leads to a common future.

37. The focus was on reconciling Western and Eastern European cultures.

38. HoM was also used successfully in recent years to bring reconciliation among Christians and different church denominations or confessions. In particular, the Mennonites and the Roman-Catholics discussed their understanding of each other, the past, the conflicts, and how to overcome it through common reading of history.

39. Brandes, "Heilende Erinerungen," 179–86.

PART 3: PRESENT MISSION AND ITS RELEVANCE TO FUTURE MISSION

The Church in a Multi-Optional Community

Today's life in a globalized world happens in a multi-optional, multi-religious, multicultural orientation, resulting not only in potential for tension but also conflicts. Therefore, community development needs to include reconciliation work,[40] and Christian mission of the future will work for the ministry of reconciliation as its core competence.[41] Today's approaches of mission also need to use a more integrated approach. To work in non-Christian contexts, one may consider using different terms and concepts. De Gruchy suggests "primary" expressions of reconciliation for those based on Scripture and "secondary" expressions that "are visible in social and political reality."[42] For this, HoM provides a method of naming and understanding the hurtful history together, finding forgiveness, and developing a future together "without referring to our religious convictions verbally [as] an active way to live the gospel out. This is evangelism through being and doing."[43]

An example from global partners of PRN is Building Leaders for Peace (BL4P). This was developed to create a third space for conflicting parties of Muslims, Christians, and other faith communities in the Middle East. BL4P creates a safe space, organized by Christians, where participants live and learn together in a week-long peace camp. People share honestly their own personal or collective story of hurt, ask for forgiveness, and together, not only learn about but also start to collaborate for peace. A different narrative is created together for a better future. In this trusting atmosphere, Muslims use the opportunity to pose their questions about the spiritual underpinning and the motivation of the Christian faith. They are pointed to Isa, the Messiah, Jesus Christ, the Prince of Peace.

Practicing HoM as Christian Community Development and Church Approach

A church that acts as an ambassador of reconciliation and accepts it as her source of being will then, as pointed out by Walter Freitag,[44] focus less on

40. Haspel, "Rechtfertigung, Versöhnung und Gerechtigkeit," 472–90.
41. Reimer, "Healing Memories in the City."
42. DeGruchy, *Reconciliation, Restoring Justice*, 18.
43. Reimer, "Healing Memories in the City."
44. Freitag, "Mission of the Church."

her own internal matters but accept this calling and seek the wellbeing of the people around (which of course include those who belong to the church as well). Consequently, the church will speak prophetically into the lives of people, societies, and even nations,[45] uncover personal, collective and structural sin, leading the people to confession. The church will also invite people to a new way of life and process of life transformation based on an alternative for life.

According to Robert Schreiter, the church can use four practices. The first practice is healing. Healing refers to three dimensions: healing of memories, healing of victims, and healing of wrongdoers.[46] Healing leads to rebuilding trust and restoring right relationships."[47] The second practice is truth-telling, which involves sharing testimonies to what really happened in the past and a common effort to reconstruct a public truth.[48] The third practice is the pursuit of justice, which distinguishes itself from punitive justice (pursuing the wrongdoer) but rather brings a restorative justice in play that "may involve restitution and reparation, as well as opportunities to explore how to rebuild a just and meaningful society."[49] After that, a structural justice proceeds into other areas, such as the social sphere. The last practice is forgiveness, which is directed toward the wrongdoers and not their actions. This process addresses the individual and societies, providing forgiveness that is not cheap nor forced upon the victim.[50]

In conclusion, the Christian understanding of reconciliation can help the church to develop her own approach to local conflict transformation that is tailored for the people. When people start seeing Christians pursue a relational way of healing, they may hopefully open their doors and ask questions on hope, forgiveness, and reconciliation that are ultimately found in Jesus Christ.

Reflection Questions

1. How do you think HoM relates to the mission of God and the mission of the church?

---

45. Reimer, *Missio Politica*, 53–62.
46. Schreiter and Jørgensen, *Mission as Reconciliation*, 19.
47. Schreiter and Jørgensen, *Mission as Reconciliation*, 19.
48. Schreiter and Jørgensen, *Mission as Reconciliation*, 19.
49. Schreiter and Jørgensen, *Mission as Reconciliation*, 20.
50. Schreiter and Jørgensen, *Mission as Reconciliation*, 20.

PART 3: PRESENT MISSION AND ITS RELEVANCE TO FUTURE MISSION

2. In the light of the multicultural context and religious diversity in Canada, how can HoM be an opportunity for the Canadian church to bring good news to hurting people in conflict?

3. How can a church become a facilitator or participant in uncovering history together with people, and what would a roadmap to reconciliation look like for the church?

Bibliography

Ahrens, Theodor. "Versöhnung in der ökumenischen Diskussio." *Zeitschrift für Mission* 3 (2005) 162–73.

Assman, Jan, and Czaplicka, John. "Collective Memory and Cultural Identity, New German Critique." *Cultural History/Cultural Studies* 65 (1995) 125–33.

Balz, H. R., and Schneider, G, eds. *Exegetical Dictionary of the New Testament*. Grand Rapids: Eerdmans, 1990.

Baumberger, Mariane. "Lasst es uns noch mal versuchen: Mediation als Weg, Beziehungen wieder zu ordnen." In *Das Buch vom Frieden*, edited by Tom Sommer. Witten: Brockhaus, 2012.

Bieringer, R. "2Kor 5,19a und die Versöhnung der Welt." *EthL* 63 (1987) 295–326.

Blalock, Hubert M. *Power and Conflict: Toward a General Theory*. Newbury Park, CA: Sage, 1989.

Bohler, Frieder. "Begegnung wagen. Eine Kultur des Friedens entwickeln." In *Das Buch vom Frieden*, edited by Tom Sommer, 123–27. Witten: R. Brockhaus, 2012.

Bosch, David J. *Transforming Mission: Paradigm Shifts in Theology of Mission*. American Society of Missiology Series 16. Maryknoll, NY: Orbis, 1991.

Botman, Russel H., and Robin M. Petersen, eds. *To Remember and to Heal: Theological and Psychological Reflections on Truth and Reconciliation*. Johannesburg: Human & Rousseau, 1996.

Brandes, Dieter, ed. *Healing of Memories in Europe: A Study of Reconciliation between Churches, Cultures and Religion*. Leipzig: Evangelische Verlagsanstalt, 2008.

———. "Heilende Erinnerung." In *Gerechtigkeit: Jahrbuch Mission*, edited by Bettina von Clausewitz, 179–86. Hamburg: Missionshilfe Verlag, 2011.

Brandes, Dieter, and Olga Lukács, eds. *Die Geschichte der christlichen Kirchen aufarbeiten. Healing of Memories zwischen Kirchen, Kulturen und Religionen. Ein Versöhnungsprojekt der Kirchen in Rumänien*. Leipzig: Evangelische Verlagsanstalt, 2009.

Breytenbach, Cilliers. *Versöhnung. Eine Studie zur paulinischen Soteriologie. Wissenschaftliche Monographien zum Alten und Neuen Testament*. Neukirchen-Vluyn: Neukirchener Verlag, 1989.

Brunner, Emil. *Vom Missverständnis der Kirche*. Stuttgart: Evangelisches Verlagshaus, 1951.

Cousins, Robert. "Foreword." In *From the Margins to the Centre: The Diaspora Effect*, edited by Michael Krause et al., vii. Toronto: Tyndale Academic Press, 2018.

De Gruchy, John W. *Reconciliation, Restoring Justice*. Minneapolis: Fortress, 2002.

Escobar, Samuel. *La Palabra—Vida de la Iglesia*. Atlanta: Editorial Mundo Hispano, 2006.
Engelsviken, Tormod. "Reconciliation with God: Its Meaning and its Significance for Mission." In *Mission as Ministry of Reconciliation*, edited by Robert Schreiter and Knud Jørgensen, 79–89. Oxford: Regnum, 2013.
Enns, Fernando, ed. *Heilung der Erinnerungen—befreit zur gemeinsamen Zukunft. Mennoniten im Dialog. Berichte und Texte ökumenischer Gespräche auf nationaler und internationaler Ebene*. Frankfurt: Lembeck & Paderborn, Bonifatius Verlag 2008.
Enns, Fernando, and Hans Joachim, eds. *Gemeinsam berufen Friedensstifter zu sein: Zum Dialog zwischen Katholiken und Mennoniten*. Schwarzenfeld: Neufeld Verlag and Paderborn, Bonifatius Verlag, 2008.
Enns, Fernando, and Jonathan Seiling. *Mennonites in Dialog: Official Reports from International and National Ecumenical Encounters*. Eugene, OR: Pickwick, 2012.
Freitag, Walter. "Mission of the Church." *Consensus* 15 (1989) 5–6.
Garzon, Fernando L., and Lori Burke. "Healing of Memories: Models, Research, Future Directions." Faculty Publications and Presentations. Paper 37. http://digitalcommons.liberty.edu/ccfs_fac_pubs/37.
Gutiérrez, Juan. "Friedens-und Versöhnungsarbeit. Konzepte und Praxis, Unterwegs zu einer dauerhaften, friedensschaffenden Versöhnung." In *Agenda for Peace: Reconciliation*, edited by Jörg Calließ, 152–96. Loccum: Evang. Akademie, 1999.
Haspel, Michael. "Rechtfertigung, Versöhnung und Gerechtigkeit. Die Globalisierung als Herausforderung christlicher Sozialethik." *ÖR* 52 (2003) 472–90.
Hiemstra, Rick. "Not Christian Anymore." http://www.faithtoday.ca/Magazines/2020-Jan-Feb/Not-Christian-anymore.
Himes, Joseph S. *Conflict and Conflict Management*. Athens, GA: University of Georgia Press, 1980.
LaGuardia Aoanan, Melanio. "Transforming Christology in a Changing Church and Society." *CTC Bulletin* 53–54 (October 1995–April 1996) 32–42.
Lausanne Occasional Paper 51. *Reconciliation as the Mission of God: Faithful Christian Witness in a World of Destructive Conflicts and Divisions*. https://www.lausanne.org/wp-content/uploads/2007/06/LOP51_IG22.pdf.
McEvoy, Kieran. "Making Peace with the Past. Healing through remembering. Options for truth recovery regarding the conflict in and about Northern Ireland." In *Healing of Memories in Europe: A Study of Reconciliation between Churches, Cultures and Religion*, edited by Dieter Brandes, 144–55. Leipzig: Evangelische Verlagsanstalt, 2008.
Matthey, Jacques. "Versöhnung im ökumenischen missionstheologischen Dialog." *Zeitschrift für Mission* 3 (2005) 174–91.
Moore, Mark E. *Kenotic Politics: The Reconfiguration of Power in the Jesus´ Political Praxis*. Library of New Testament Studies. London: Bloomsbury T. & T. Clark, 2013.
Ott, Craig. *Encountering Theology of Mission: Biblical Foundations, Historical Developments, and Contemporary Issues*. Grand Rapids: Backer, 2010.
Pope Benedict XVI. "Post-Synodal Apostolic Exhortation Africae Munus." 2011. http://w2.vatican.va/content/benedict-xvi/en/apost_exhortations/documents/hf_ben-xvi_exh_20111119_africae-munus.html.
Reimer, Johannes. "Die Welt umarmen: Theologie des gesellschaftsrelevanten Gemeindebaus." In *Transformations studien* 1. 2., 42–47. Aufl. Marburg: Francke Verlag, 2013.

PART 3: PRESENT MISSION AND ITS RELEVANCE TO FUTURE MISSION

———. "Der Dienst der Versöhnung—bei der Kernkompetenz ansetzen. Zur Korrelation von Gemeinwesenmediation und multikulturellem Gemeindebau." *Thelogisches Gespräch* 35 (2011) 19–35.

———. "Healing Memories in the City—Correlation between Reconciliation and Transformation in the Mission of the Local Church." Paper at a symposium on Peace and Reconciliation in Wiedenest, Germany, 2018. Now edited and published in: *Reconciliation as Healing of Memory—A Missionary Task of the Church*, edited by Tobias Faix et al., 100–14. RECONCILIATION: Christian Perspectives—Interdisciplinary Approaches. Interdisziplinäre und theologische Studien—Interdisciplinary and Theological Studies 3. Zürich: LIT Verlag, 2020.

———. *Missio Politica: The Mission of the Church and Politics*. Carlisle: Langham Global Library, 2017.

Rice, Chris, ed. "Cape Town 2010: Reconciliation, Discipleship, Mission, and the Renewal of the Church in 21 Century." In *Mission as Ministry of Reconciliation*, edited by Robert Schreiter and Knud Jørgensen, 9–29. Oxford: Regnum, 2013.

———. *Reconciliation as the Mission of God: Christian Witness in the World of Destructive Conflicts*. Durham, NC: Duke Divitity School, 2017.

Schreiter, Robert. "Reconciliation and Healing as a Paradigm for Mission." In *International Review of Mission* 94 (2005) 74–83.

Schreiter, Robert, and Knud Jørgensen, eds. *Mission as Ministry of Reconciliation*. Oxford: Regnum, 2013.

Stiller, Karen, and Wilgard Metzger. *Going Missional: Conversations with 13 Canadian Churches Who Have Embraced Missional Life*. Winnipeg, MB: Word Alive, 2010.

Sundermeier, Theo. "Konvivenz als Grundstruktur ökumenischer Existenz heute." In *Ökumenische Existenz Heute*, edited by Wolfgang Huber et al., 1:49–100. München: Kaiser Verlag, 1986.

Vicedom, Georg. "Missio Die: Actio Dei." In *Additional essays of Brandl, Bernd und Wagner, Herwig*, edited by Klaus W. Müller, 115–230. Mission Classics 4. Nürnberg: VTR, 2002.

Wallace, John. *Control in Conflict*. Nashville: Broadman, 1982.

World Council of Churches. *Participating in God's Mission of Reconciliation—A Resource for Churches in Situations of Conflict*. Faith and Order document 201. Geneva: WCC, 2005. https://www.oikoumene.org/en/resources/documents/commissions/faith-and-order/vi-church-and-world/Faith-and-Order-201?set_language=en.

Wood, James E., Jr. "A Theology of Power." *Journal of Church and State* 14 (1972) 107–8.

Wright, Tom. *The Day the Revolution Began: Reconsidering the Meaning of Jesus's Crucifixion*. San Francisco: HarperOne, 2016.

9

Power and Participation in Evangelical Mission

Marilyn Draper

Introduction

THOSE INVOLVED IN EVANGELICAL activities often state that they are "doing things for God." While this indicates an underlying and positive emphasis on wholehearted dedication to God and the Gospel, the result has often been a misunderstanding of the human role in mission. When the church does mission "for God," mission risks becoming a human-powered enterprise characterized by human misuses of power and methodologies.

Jacques Ellul's prophetic discussion of "technique" provides a helpful lens for contemporary missiologists to critique current church planting efforts and missional models in order to help us reframe this human-powered understanding of mission. This chapter will define "technique," show how evangelical mission unintentionally adopted "technique," and suggest how this adoption reflects an unexamined accommodation to Western cultural values. In terms of its implications, this unexamined adoption of "technique" has proven detrimental for mission. Fortunately, Ellul also suggests there is potential for change. It is possible for the evangelical church to shift from doing mission "for God," based on human initiative, to participating more fully in God's initiative through connecting with God's greater purposes in the *missio Dei* and the coming of God's Kingdom.

The chapter suggests that a theological and spiritual reorientation that examines mission through the lens of *participating* in Christ's mission offers a helpful step forward for a new understanding and approach to evangelical mission. When mission is perceived through the lens of participation, the work of mission is best described as an act of worshipful engagement, offered in weakness, which seeks to discern where God's Spirit is already at work within a population or neighborhood in order to live into the Gospel as good news for all.

"Doing Things for God"

During a day devoted to visioning or mission involvement, the conversations in a congregation often contain the phrase "doing things for God." Carolyn Arends provides an example in *Faith Today*. Arend's friend, Sally, looks at Arends with envy and says: "You're out there *doing things for God* and I'm just here teaching . . ."[1] Arends then helpfully explains that all vocations provide possibilities to be involved in God's ongoing story. However, Arends does not investigate the specific phrase "doing things for God." Reflecting upon the phrase is essential if we are to understand how evangelicals tend to perceive mission through the lens of human-powered activity.

Since "activism" is one of the four qualities of evangelicalism as described by David Bebbington (the other three being crucicentrism, biblicism, and conversionism),[2] we should perhaps not be surprised that the phrase "doing things for God" encapsulates the evangelical perception of outreach. In fact, reflecting on the phrase encourages us to consider that many evangelical Christians have a positive desire to be involved in mission-related activity but may hold an inaccurate understanding of mission itself.

Positively, the words, "doing things for God," point to a desire to be involved in sharing the Gospel and being active in the ministry of the local church. Christians who are "doing things for God" are eager to share their faith and serve others. These followers of Jesus perceive their ministry as acts done for God's purposes. Thus, the phrase is meant to be a response of obedience to the call of the Great Commission (Matt 28:18–20), because evangelicals have historically assumed that this call to go into all the world "clearly expresses our obligation to make Christ known to all."[3]

While we applaud the enthusiasm and the concern that all the nations be introduced to Jesus Christ, we recognize that over time negative aspects have also emerged out of the evangelical impulse to take the Gospel to all nations. Thus, we must consider a detrimental aspect to the

---

1. Arend, "Butchers, Bakers," 19 (emphasis added).
2. Bebbington, *Evangelicalism*, 2–3.
3. Mott, *Evangelization of the World*, 22.

phrase when the emphasis on obedience results in evangelicals, often unintentionally, taking the burden of mission upon themselves. The emphasis "for God" becomes focused on the preposition's meaning of doing an action in the place of another. In other words, Christians are acting on God's behalf. Christians are doing mission so that God does not have to do so. The end result is a subtle shift in thinking about the empowerment of mission. When Christians assume that they are "doing things for God," they potentially over-emphasize their human role.

An over-emphasis on human responsibility skews both the goals and the manner of mission. The goal of mission empowered by human effort emphasizes numbers and success. Evangelicals assume that we are achieving mission "for God" when the numbers rise, and we see people responding. Higher numbers are interpreted as evidence of God's blessing. In *Purpose-Driven Church*, Rick Warren emphasizes the importance of quantifying the congregation's results through asking a series questions all focused around: How many? Warren states: "These questions measure our success and force us to evaluate if we are really fulfilling the Great Commandment and the Great Commission."[4] Congregations seeking to be involved in local mission look for numbers to substantiate their efforts, and the success can be misconstrued as a validation of their own faithfulness. In other words, the congregation is perceived as "doing things for God" if there are growing numbers of participants, a greater public presence, and a sense of influence in the larger Christian community. When the emphasis is on numbers, competition subtly emerges. In fact, congregations who see the outreach programs at another ministry being recognized and rewarded might become a little envious, like Arend's friend. In turn, those who are not gathering the numbers perceive their own efforts as unsuccessful. In an effort to avoid failure, these evangelical leaders are tempted to adopt unexamined methodologies. A program that "worked" in one area is adopted unreflectively in another location. A desire for more numbers is the main reason for the program choice.

Further, when the goal is numbers, then the temptation is to use any available influence and power to accomplish the objective more quickly. Not surprising, potential misuse of power may emerge in the manner by which the congregation implements a particular program. An evangelical leader can justify the use of any available method as long as he or she perceives it is the most effective in encouraging the largest number to accept Christianity.

---

4. Warren, *Purpose-Driven Church*, 107–8.

"For church leaders, numerical growth is powerfully intoxicating justification. It impairs sound judgment and makes you vulnerable to just about anything that will help you achieve your success."[5] In short, when mission becomes a human-powered enterprise, methodologies are measured by success of numbers and are potentially characterized by misuse of power.

In fact, over the last 150 years, we have seen the tendency for an emphasis on power to enter into evangelical mission in a variety of ways, including the language of political, military, and economic power. John Mott's influential booklet, *The Evangelization of the World in this Generation*, from the early 1900s, states: "The Church of God is in the ascendant. She has well within her control the power, the wealth and the learning of the world. She is like a strong and well-appointed army in the presence of the foe. The only thing she needs is the Spirit of her Leader and a willingness to obey His summons to go forward. The victory may not be easy but it is sure."[6] Victory in evangelical circles became equated with the gathering of numbers and the increase of influential power.

The assumption was that throughout the twentieth century, the numbers and influence of the Protestant evangelical church would continue to grow. The Church Growth Movement developed strategies to increase the numbers entering congregations and encouraged a church planting emphasis in North America.[7] However, in recent years, increased numbers of church attenders have not materialized in spite of this church planting emphasis. Throughout the last 50 years, percentages of those attending North American church services have continued to fall. In Canada, people attending weekly service declined from 50 percent to less than 10 percent.[8] Given these figures, it is not surprising that Christian leaders fell prey to the temptations of misusing power and seeking prestige in their desire to attract more of the declining numbers.[9] As long as obeying a command and increasing the numbers was seen as the goal, human strategy and methods became central.

---

5. Chadwick, *Stealing Sheep*, 18.

6. Mott, *Evangelization of the World*, 131, quoting a letter from Calvin Mateer.

7. "The single most effective evangelistic method under heaven is planting new churches." Wagner, *Church Planting*, 11.

8. https://www.intrust.org/Magazine/Issues/New-Year-2016/Religious-affiliation-and-attendance-in-Canada.

9. James McDonald of Harvest Bible Chapel provides one example.

Fortunately, this situation of declining numbers provides an opportunity for those involved in evangelical mission and church planting to stop and rethink how to move forward. In fact, Jacques Ellul's prophetic discussion of "technique" provides a helpful lens for contemporary missiologists to critique current church planting efforts and missional models in order to help reframe this human-powered understanding of mission and correct the tendency to "do things for God."

Helpful Lens of "Technique"

Jacques Ellul, a Christian social theorist and French scholar, provides insight into evangelical mission's unintentional adoption of "technique." He suggests this appropriation reflects an unexamined accommodation to Western cultural values. Fortunately, Ellul also offers hope.

Rationality, progress and product, efficiency and effectiveness, predictability, measurement and success, method and control can all be encompassed in a single word. The word "technique," adopted by Ellul, explains the organizing force behind Western culture that emerged forcefully during the twentieth century. According to Ellul, "technique" refers to the fact that Western culture promotes ever expanding rational systems in order to help things run more efficiently, but the teleology, or purpose, behind those systems is now lost.[10] Because the purpose disappears, the methodology is no longer questioned. Thus, whatever methodology works most efficiently and effectively is the method that is sought and adopted.

Further, "technique" is not simply a method, "is not just a practice, it also presupposes values—an intellectual or a spiritual attitude consistent with the demands of technology."[11] This combination of a loss of *telos*, with the adoption of a rational system of means, accompanied by an emphasis on methodology, helps to explain the current way that missional models and church planting strategies are often understood and practiced in evangelical circles.

The proponents of many missional and church planting models have accepted particular means for the purpose of growth and success, but in the process of that adoption, have lost the doxological *telos* of church and mission. For example, Donald McGavran's homogeneous unit principle emphasizes that when people are similar to one another, they are more likely to

10. Ellul, *Presence*, 54–55.
11. Ellul, *Perspectives*, 42.

attend a congregation. "They prefer to join churches whose members look, talk, and act like themselves."[12] However, while meeting the practitioner's desire for growth, reflective scholars criticize the homogenous unit principle because it ignores the Kingdom *telos* that highlights the diversity of nations gathered together in worship before God's throne. Roger Bowen writes: "A church that insists on being homogeneous denies its own nature and the gospel . . . Heterogeneity [in crossing both social and racial barriers] was an essential mark of the church from the outset."[13] When mission innovators and church planters unintentionally give their allegiance to "technique," when they emphasize numbers over the greater vision of the gospel, this promotes human agency in mission. They rely on human effort and the implementation of methodology, rather than deferring to the unpredictable and often unobservable work of the Holy Spirit.

The Subversion of Christianity addresses Ellul's concerns about the church and its relationship with "technique." He suggests that the church has helped to birth a society, Western culture, which in turn has influenced the church, so that now we find the behavior of the church opposite to what we find described in the Gospel of Jesus Christ.[14] "We have to admit there is an immeasurable distance between all that we read in the Bible and the practice of the church and of Christians."[15] He argues that this immeasurable distance is because the church has promoted human agency and sought her own glory.[16] Rather than being subversive of political, economic, and cultural power, Christianity has been subverted by them, wandering away from the Gospel of Jesus.[17] The current behavior of the church reflects a lack of understanding of the Gospel.[18] In essence, Ellul's argument is that the church has wandered from God's Spirit, absorbed the values of Western culture, surrendered itself to the "technique" it helped to create, and now lives "a Christianity that is remodeled by the world."[19] As a result, mission, even evangelical mission, runs the risk of being a human-powered exercise.

---

12. McGavran, *Understanding*, 198.
13. Bowen, "Church Growth," 56–57.
14. Ellul, *Subversion*, 3.
15. Ellul, *Subversion*, 7.
16. Ellul labels this process as "human aggrandizement," Ellul, *Subversion*, 13.
17. Ellul, *Subversion*, 13.
18. Ellul, *Subversion*, 17.
19. Ellul, *Subversion*, 12.

"When we act, we want our action to serve some end, to succeed, to bring progress. We want to do it all ourselves."[20]

Ellul is not alone in his critique. Lesslie Newbigin expressed concern for this tendency of the church to rely on human agency and seek success through methodology. Newbigin challenged congregations to think theologically in order to deliver us "from being impressed by the various proposals which are frequently made to the effect that if we will adopt the proper techniques for evangelism, we can be assured of success."[21] He suggested that the church cannot simply exercise power in the way the world does, and it cannot simply respond to "the aspirations of the people."[22] For Newbigin, this meant the exclusion of "ideas which have been too prevalent in 'evangelical circles,' ideas which portray the Church in the style of a commercial firm using modern techniques of promotion to attract members."[23] Even though he refers to "techniques," rather than "technique," Newbigin is expressing the need for evangelical mission to recognize that it has been, and is being, shaped by the assumptions underlying contemporary society; he encourages us to acknowledge that the conversion of the world will *not* "be our achievement."[24] He calls the church to a reorientation of mission, "to be fully open to the needs of the world and yet have its eyes fixed always on God."[25] Newbigin reminds evangelicals of the importance of seeing ourselves as part of God's greater story where the congregation exists as a foretaste of God's glorious Kingdom.

Fortunately, both Newbigin and Ellul retain hope for the future of evangelical mission. They both look to the work of God's Spirit to bring forth a theological and spiritual reorientation to correct our tendency of "doing things for God."

Reorientation

Ellul suggests that our reorientation requires a new set of glasses. "We put on the world's glasses in order to see only what the world sees," but the

---

20. Ellul, *Subversion*, 171.
21. Newbigin, *Gospel in a Pluralist*, 224.
22. Newbigin, *Gospel in a Pluralist*, 226.
23. Newbigin, *Gospel in a Pluralist*, 226.
24. Newbigin, *Gospel in a Pluralist*, 224.
25. Newbigin, *Gospel in a Pluralist*, 226.

Spirit offers us a greater clarity of vision.[26] When we invite the Holy Spirit to reorient our evangelical perception, we come to understand that as individuals, and as the church, we participate in mission through our union with Christ utilizing cruciform power exhibited in weakness.

In order to approach mission more appropriately, we need to see the world differently, but we also need to see the church anew. A theological reorientation encourages the church to situate itself within God's story, and indeed within the intimacy of Trinitarian life, so that the church participates in mission not as the goal, but as the outcome of a discipleship that is situated "in Christ." Participating in God, and in God's mission in Jesus Christ through the Spirit, is based on Paul's conception that new life and involvement in ministry emerge out of our union with Christ, which "functions as the connecting fabric of Paul's theology."[27]

The theme of union with Christ is pervasive and foundational to the Pauline corpus, as expressed by the idiom "in Christ," which Paul uses throughout the epistles.[28] "Scholars unanimously regard this phrase to be central to the theme of union with Christ."[29] According to Richard Longenecker: "Being 'in Christ' is the essence of Christian proclamation and experience."[30]

The phrase "in Christ" describes the starting place of our involvement in mission, as well as the manner in which that mission unfolds. Michael Gorman suggests that while the precise meaning changes slightly depending on the context, *"to be 'in Christ' principally means to be under the influence of Christ's power, especially the power to be conformed to him and his cross, by participation in the life of a community that acknowledges*

---

26. Ellul, *False Presence*, 48.

27. Campbell, *Paul and Union*, 443.

28. Campbell, *Paul and Union*, 21, writes: "The theme of union with Christ in the writings of the apostle Paul is once dazzling and perplexing. Its prevalence on every page of his writings demonstrates his proclivity for the concept, and yet nowhere does he directly explain what he means by it." Campbell, *Paul and Union*, 67, states that there are 73 occurrences of "in Christ." However, when scholars add the related phrases "in him," "into Christ," "with Christ," and "through Christ," the number of usages by Paul increases greatly. Plus, Campbell, *Paul and Union*, 267–324, points to a series of related metaphors that do not have the phrase but are linked by theme. Deissmann, *St. Paul*, 128, a pioneer in Pauline studies, suggests that Paul uses the phrase 164 times. In his commentary, George, *Galatians*, 275, suggests that there are 172 instances of "in Christ."

29. Campbell, *Paul and Union*, 25.

30. Longenecker, *Galatians*, 159.

his lordship."[31] Thus, the term being "in Christ," includes personal salvation, our incorporation into the church through God's Spirit, and living in the reality of God's Kingdom now. The key item is that we are involved in God's mission as a by-product of being firmly identified with and adopted into the life of this Trinitarian God who initiates and enacts mission. The mission belongs to God and not to us.

Further, Gorman identifies the manner and method in which this Christian discipleship unfolds as involving a new understanding of power. We are given through the Spirit *"the power to be conformed to [Christ] and his cross."*[32] Our new set of glasses provides an understanding of power with implications for mission. Power here is not a triumphal vision of grasping and taking over the world. Instead of seeing power as a limited entity to be grasped in a zero-sum game, we discover power is a gift that when expended in love expands to invite others to experience the power of creative flourishing and worship of the living God.[33] God's Kingdom is evident in power that appears as weakness and vulnerability, undergirded by love and creativity. Thus, our mission also moves forward in a manner characterized by frailty but results in transformation empowered by the God we worship.

Marva Dawn explains the relationship between mission and weakness, a willingness to place our power under the tutelage of the Spirit:

> Even as Christ accomplished atonement for us by suffering and death, so the Lord accomplishes witness to the world through our weakness. In fact, God has more need of our weakness than of our strength. Just as powers overstep their bounds and become gods, so our power becomes a rival to God . . . . By our union with Christ in the power of the Spirit in our weaknesses, we display God's glory.[34]

When we operate not out of self-sufficiency, but out of our dependence upon God, acknowledging our needs, brokenness, infirmities, and humility, then it is God's grace and power that bring forth new life. In other words, when our power comes to an end, Christ's power is given freedom to work.[35]

---

31. Gorman, *Cruciformity*, 36 (emphasis original).
32. Gorman, *Cruciformity*, 36 (emphasis original).
33. Crouch, *Playing God*, 51.
34. Dawn, *Powers*, 47.
35. Dawn, *Powers*, 41. Dawn translates 2 Cor 12:9: "My grace is sufficient for you, for [your human] power is brought to its end in weakness."

Seeing mission through the lens of being "in Christ" and living in our weakness provides an important reorientation for evangelical mission. This reorientation has three major implications: purpose, alignment, and direction. First, congregations are reminded of their purpose for being. The church does not exist for the purpose of obedience to a command to enact mission. Rather, the church exists so that we might love and worship God and bear witness to God's character. Second, congregations might experience a new alignment with God's purposes. As the church lives "in Christ," the church lives as a foretaste of God's Kingdom. The Kingdom is good news for all, including the oppressed and the oppressors, a place of shalom, reconciliation, and hope. Finally, reorientation allows for a new direction. Rather than implementing programs, evangelical congregations can take time to build relationships with those inside and outside, and to discern how the Spirit of God might already be working in the neighborhood. In sum, a new perspective of mission through our life "in Christ" enables us to resist the cultural tendency to adopt "technique" and become realigned with God's vision for the church.

Conclusion

We are tempted to think that mission is about advancing the Kingdom through gathering numbers. However, when mission becomes a human oriented and empowered task, we risk missing God's purposes for the church and for the world. Fortunately, when evangelicals understand mission as participation rather than misuse of power, we have a renewed vision of the church. We see a church that moves forward on its knees. The church kneels in worship for it recognizes that it exists for God alone. The church kneels in prayer asking that the Kingdom might come in greater fulness. Finally, the church kneels in dependence knowing that God will reveal where God's Spirit is already at work so that the congregation might bear witness to God's person and God's mission in the world.

Reflection Questions

1. Think of three ways that "technique" has influenced the development of mission in your congregation.

2. How might spiritual disciplines both fall prey to "technique" and help us recognize and resist "technique"?

3. How might the concept of "cruciform power" be helpful in guiding the way we interact with our neighbors and community?

Bibliography

Arends, Carolyn. "Butchers, Bakers and Candlestick Makers." *Faith Today* (2016) 19.
Bebbington, David W. *Evangelicalism in Modern Britain: A History from the 1730s to the 1980s.* London: Routledge, 1989.
Bowen, J. Roger. "Church Growth." In *Dictionary of Mission Theology: Evangelical Foundations*, edited by John Currie, 55–58. Downers Grove, IL: IVP Academic, 2007.
Campbell, Constantine. *Paul and Union with Christ: An Exegetical and Theological Study.* Grand Rapids: Zondervan, 2012.
Crouch, Andy. *Playing God: Redeeming the Gift of Power.* Downers Grove, IL: InterVarsity, 2013.
Dawn, Marva. *Powers, Weakness, and the Tabernacling of God.* Grand Rapids: Eerdmans, 2001.
Deissmann, Adolf. *St. Paul: A Study in Social and Religious History.* Translated by Lionel Strachan. London: Hodder & Stoughton, 1912.
Ellul, Jacques. *False Presence of the Kingdom.* Translated by C. Edward Hopkin. New York: Seabury, 1972.
———. *Perspectives on our Age: Jacques Ellul Speaks on His Life and Work.* Translated by Joachim Neugroschel. Toronto: Canadian Broadcasting Corporation, 1981.
———. *The Presence of the Kingdom.* Translated by Olive Wyon. 2nd ed. Colorado Springs: Helmers & Howard, 1989.
———. *The Subversion of Christianity.* Translated by Geoffrey Bromiley. Grand Rapids: Eerdmans, 1986.
George, Timothy. *Galatians.* New American Commentary 30. Nashville: B & H, 1994.
Gorman, Michael. *Cruciformity: Paul's Narrative Spirituality of the Cross.* Grand Rapids: Eerdmans, 2001.
Longenecker, Richard. *Galatians.* Word Biblical Commentary 41. Dallas: Word, 2002.
McGavran, Donald. *Understanding Church Growth.* Grand Rapids: Eerdmans, 1970.
Mott, John. *The Evangelization of the World in This Generation.* New York: Student Volunteer Movement, 1905. https://www.questia.com/read/3165271/the-evangelization-of-the-world-in-this-generation.
Newbigin, Lesslie. *The Gospel in a Pluralist Society.* Grand Rapids: Eerdmans, 1989.
Wagner, Peter. *Church Planting for a Greater Harvest: A Comprehensive Guide.* Ventura, CA: Regal, 1990.

Part 4
Present and Future of Workplace Mission

10

An *Imago Dei* Model for Workplace as Mission

Laurie George Busuttil and Susan J. Van Weelden

Introduction

Jesus's command to go into all the world, preach the Gospel, and make disciples (Matt 28:19) has occupied the church since his resurrection. The first disciples quickly dispersed, sharing the good news of salvation in person and through the Scriptures. Romans 1:20 tells us that we also understand and see God through his creation, thus recognizing that individuals will come to know Christ through his word and through his world. As the crowning glory of God's creation (Ps 8:1), the very image of God (Gen 1:27), our role is to live in such a way that we preach the Gospel by who we are and how we act, including at work.

Workplace as mission is founded on being and acting as image bearers of God and recognizing that others are also made in his image. In unfolding the model, we begin by describing three theological perspectives on *imago Dei*. We then discuss how truly and fully living as image bearers of God in the workplace will enable Christians to reveal Christ, using three areas of business as examples. Lastly, we identify what this means for preparing the next generation for the workplace.

Current Approaches to Mission

Believers have been called to share the good news of salvation with others since Christ's ascension. In numerous forms and under many models, missionaries have traditionally been sent to those who have not yet heard the Gospel.

European missional models have assumed "the primary location of God's activities is inside the church."[1] Consequently, few traditional models recognize a field ripe for harvest: the workplace. When they do, it is from the vantage of actively evangelizing co-workers. However, even though there is a move for individuals to bring "their whole selves" to work, it is becoming increasingly less acceptable for Christians to openly evangelize. Canada is becoming secularized, with more millennials abandoning religion and identifying as agnostic or atheist.[2] More people are embracing spirituality, but fewer are claiming Christ as their personal Savior. Church attendance and membership are declining.[3] There has been a "sea change . . . march toward secularization" over the past forty years; in 1971, only one percent of Canadians indicated no religious affiliation on national surveys, rising to 23 percent of Canadians by 2009.[4]

The face of mission is also changing because of the unprecedented rate of movement among the world's populations. The World Migration Report 2020 indicates that 3.5 percent of the world's population—272 million people—were mobile in 2019.[5] We no longer have to go into the world to preach the Gospel; people from around the world now live and work in Canada.

The Workplace as Mission

The fields everywhere are ready to harvest. Christians in the workplace have an exciting opportunity to winsomely live Christ before their colleagues, opening another way to partner with traditional approaches to mission.

Therefore, we should intentionally help Christians to recognize that the role of missionary should not be left to paid clergy or institutionally ordained missionaries. Steven Fettke wonders whether the church in the West is facing a crossroads: has the professional pastorate tightly held the work of ministry for themselves, or have Christians sitting in Sunday

---

1. Roxborough, *Leaders*, 191.
2. Samek, *Millennials*.
3. Lipka, *Facts*.
4. Valpy and Friesen, *Secularization*, lines 1–6.
5. IMO, *Migration*, 3.

services chosen to participate by paying the pastor's salary so the pastor can do the work of ministry?[6] It is likely both.

Already in 1958, Hendrik Kraemer recognizes that the laity is the church in the world.[7] He reviews the history of the professional pastorate, perspectives on the laity, and the movement of the Gospel. He discusses Joseph Oldham's theology of work, indicating it "was quite new, because for the first time it was not the mobilization of active laymen for various purposes considered *quite apart* from the Church . . . but as an *expression* of the Church and its calling and function in the world."[8] Henrik Kraemer also cites the World Council of Churches' question whether " . . . most of the Church-members live a schizophrenic life having two different sets of ethics, one for the private Sunday life and the other for their behaviour in the workaday world?"[9]

Despite these workplace challenges to become a channel of mission, the response of the church has remained largely organizational. Jo Plummer writes that Business as Mission, one such approach, comprises businesses that are profitable and sustainable, are intentional about Kingdom purposes and their impact on peoples and nations, see holistic transformation through economic, social, environmental, and spiritual outcomes, and seek the welfare of the world's poorest, least evangelized peoples.[10]

The Business 4 Transformation (B4T) network, established by Operation Mobilization, helps businesses use biblical values to transform their communities. Working in a variety of countries, B4T provides investors, subject-matter experts, developers, and business coaches who work with local entrepreneurs to have an expanded impact in their communities. The organization seeks to "see Kingdom business playing its vital role in fulfilling the Great Commission."[11]

As we consider the role of the laity in sharing the Gospel, an *imago Dei* workplace-as-mission approach equips individual Christians to unite their private Sunday life with their Monday-to-Friday life. By understanding what it means to be image bearers of God, Christians will be prepared to bear witness to Christ in the workplace—where we spend one third of our

6. Fettke, *Empowered*.
7. Kraemer, *Laity*, 149.
8. Kraemer, *Laity*, 33 (emphasis in original).
9. Kraemer, *Laity*, 37.
10. Plummer, *BAM*, lines 19–23.
11. B4T, *About Us*, lines 2–4.

waking hours. In turn, this will invite questions about why we are different as we live our lives in a winsome, transparent manner.

The Meaning of *Imago Dei*

According to Paul Sands, Christians are in agreement that we are created in God's image; however, that is where the agreement ends.[12] The foundational passage in the Old Testament, Gen 1:27, simply states that humans are created in the image of God. This is further developed in Gen 2:7, which states, "the Lord formed man from the dust of the ground, and breathed into his nostrils the breath of life" (NRSV). Additional passages give us glimpses of *imago Dei*, moving from a pneumatological perspective in the Old Testament (Gen 5:1–3 and 9:6; Ps 9:5–6) to a Christocentric confession in the New Testament (1 Cor 15:47–49; Col 3:10–11; Rom 8:29; 1 John 3:2).

As discussed in previous articles,[13] three main approaches to *imago Dei* have developed among theologians: structural, relational, and functional (or ambassadorial). The structural perspective describes who we are created to be as we reflect the characteristics and attributes of God. The relational approach identifies how we are to live communally, in relationship with one another as we model the triune God. The functional perspective defines what we are created to do as we steward the earth's resources and co-create alongside God, using the diverse gifts that he has crafted within us.

To elaborate, the structural perspective describes an image bearer as one who possesses attributes and characteristics of God. Sands identifies several such characteristics: reason, self-consciousness, freedom, moral sense, and spirituality.[14] Richard Chewning lists several more: holiness, righteousness, and true knowledge.[15] In Ephesians 4:23–24, we are encouraged to "be renewed in the spirit of your minds and to clothe yourselves with the new self, created according to the likeness of God in true righteousness and holiness." Col 3:10 exhorts us to clothe "yourselves with the new self, which is being renewed in knowledge according to the image of its creator."

Relationally, we reflect God, his image, and our experience of him while in relationship with others. Sands indicates, "Human beings reflect

---

12. Sands, *Vocation*.
13. Busuttil and Van Weelden, *HRM* and Van Weelden and Busuttil, *Accountants*.
14. Sands, *Vocation*, 32.
15. Chewning, *Practice*, 134.

the divine image not as solitary individuals but in social relatedness."[16] He then describes Karl Barth's affirmation that humans repeat God's relational behaviors.

A functional or ambassadorial perspective suggests that we are co-creators with God because we are commanded as his image bearers to have dominion over the rest of creation. As his children, we care for his possessions, steward his work, and safeguard his reputation as ambassadors sent to represent him in a foreign country. According to J. Richard Middleton (as summarized by Sands), we function as ambassadors as we share in the administration of resources and creatures.[17] Michael Pregitzer uses 2 Corinthians 5:20 to encourage believers to "approach the world from the perspective of an ambassador: someone who goes out into the world representing not himself but the King, Jesus Christ."[18]

The richest understanding of *imago Dei* integrates all three perspectives because they are closely connected. As we apply the three perspectives of *imago Dei* to the workplace and mission, we recognize that to be created in God's image means we possess specific character traits of God (who we are created to be), which shape the ways in which we relate to God and to one another (how we are created to live), as we fulfill the roles of co-creators and stewards of God's world (what we are created to do).

The Heart of Work: *Imago Dei*

As image-bearers of God and as stewards of his creation, we are created to work (Gen 2:15; Exod 23:12; Col 3:23–24; 2 Thess 3:10b). While work became toilsome as a result of human's fall into sin, the command to tend God's garden was given to Adam and Eve before the fall.

Lee Hardy summarizes the views of three key Reformers on work. Luther stresses that, "having fashioned a world filled with resources and potentials, God chose to continue his creative activity in this world through the work of human hands."[19] Calvin's view is

> that we express the image of God within us, that we become most Godlike not when we turn away from action, but when we engage

---

16. Sands, *Vocation*, 35.
17. Sands, *Vocation*, 37.
18. Pregitzer, *Scorecard*, 49.
19. Hardy, *Fabric*, 48.

in it . . . When we shape and administer his creation in service to others and pursue his righteousness in the context of human society, we express something of his nature in our lives.[20]

Zwingli claims that "it is those who exercise themselves in righteousness that they may 'serve the Christian community, the common good, the state, and individuals' that are 'the most like to God.'"[21]

Hardy's own conclusion is that work is a "social place where we can employ our gifts in service to others . . . Our jobs ought to engage us as whole persons, as creatures with high-level capacities for thought, imagination, and responsible choice as well as motor abilities."[22]

In a similar vein, John Bernbaum and Simon Steer conclude, "[We] work to serve God and to bring glory to his name to fulfill our distinctiveness as humans by being stewards and co-creators with God in the world, to provide for our needs and those of our families because that is what God intended, and to help others who are in need."[23] Hardy also indicates that work is "one of the chief integrators of persons in our society. It orients our lives; it organizes our time; it puts us in touch with people."[24]

Imago Dei in the Workplace-as-Mission Model

The implications of *imago Dei* for how we do our work are profound. If we truly believe that we are created in God's image, by the very breath of God, then the character we seek to develop within ourselves at work, how we design work and manage people in organizations, the products that we develop and the way in which we advertise them, and even how we record transactions and measure success are all opportunities to display Christ in us.

The Business Roundtable, a group of Chief Executive Officers (CEOs) of some of the United States' leading companies, recently published an unmistakable call to do business differently. Rather than focus strictly on profits, 180 CEOs signed a "Statement on the Purpose of a Corporation," in which they committed to deliver value to their customers, invest in their

---

20. Hardy, *Fabric*, 57.
21. Hardy, *Fabric*, 57.
22. Hardy, *Fabric*, 174.
23. Bernbaum and Steer, *Careers*, 87.
24. Hardy, *Fabric*, 6.

employees, deal fairly and ethically with their suppliers, support the communities in which they work, and generate long-term value for shareholders.[25] This approach to doing business is not new; biblical principles have called us to structure work in this way for millennia. What is sometimes overlooked is that individuals who adopt these practices in the workplace—whether at the employee or management level—can intentionally emulate Christ in such a way that Christ will be revealed to others.

When we recalibrate our understanding of what God is calling us to do in the workplace, we bring honor and glory to God and generate questions about why we are different and why our work is different. Whether or not others in the workplace recognize that they, too, are created in the image of God, we behave toward them in ways that are worthy of their status as image bearers. Below we provide examples of what that looks like in just three functional areas of business. However, this can also apply in all areas—from leadership practices to purchasing practices, from production to financial management, from research and development to organizational design.

Imago Dei and People Management

People-managers have perhaps the most direct opportunity to display God's character to those whom we lead in organizations. If we are thinking, creative, productive people who desire to develop healthy relationships and to make wise decisions about the resources that God has entrusted to us, we see the people in our organizations as also being created in God's image. Therefore, we treat people with the respect and dignity due them because they are made in his image. We develop relationships with employees that enable us to understand who God created them, as individuals, to be. We look for his character traits in our employees and seek to develop them further.

When we design jobs, we consider the individual capabilities of employees as well as their psychological and physiological needs. This reflects a structural approach to image-bearing—one where the focus is on the attributes and characteristics that God created within us. Relationally, we build meaning into jobs when we enable people to serve others. When we align stewardship of resources with empowerment to make decisions, we recognize that image-bearing implies acting as an ambassador of the Creator.

25. Business Roundtable, *Statement*.

Structurally, when we fill specific job openings, we match job requirements with the God-given characteristics and attributes of applicants, their unique manifestation of *imago Dei*. Relationally, we seek candidates who will fit with the culture of the organization. From a functional perspective, godly managerial practice means that we wisely steward the talents of people seeking to work with the organization. Likewise, training and development allows managers the privilege of getting to know each of their team members (relational), of discerning how God created each of them (structural), and of equipping them to become effective ambassadors as they share in developing and sustaining God's creation (functional).

Perhaps the greatest opportunity for people-managers to reflect God is when managing performance. Structurally, we identify and help expand the abilities of each employee, justly promoting—or holding back—employees. Relationally, these discussions lead to information sharing and problem solving through relationships of trust and networks that we have intentionally created. Functionally, we hold each other mutually accountable, develop the complementary gifts of employees to replicate the body of Christ, and together operate as wise stewards.[26]

First and foremost, recognizing the imprint of God's character on our own character shapes who we become as people-managers. Moreover, it influences how we interact with others as we care for them and their jobs and careers. By doing so, we reveal glimpses of Christ to others.

Imago Dei and Accounting

From a structural perspective, accountants bring glory to God when we are just, righteous, and honest. These characteristics mirror God's character traits and reflect the type of information that accountants provide. Trust is critical in business relationships; and for accountants, our word—the financial statements and other information we produce—is our bond. It enables business relationships to succeed. It protects all parties to a contract from borrowing or lending too much, or from asking for or offering pay increases that a firm cannot afford.

Relationally, we show a concern for justice for all stakeholders, not just owners. In this way, we also recognize that financial statements users are also made in God's image. We show love as we translate organizational events (such as making sales and incurring costs) into financial language,

---

26. Busuttil and Van Weelden, *HRM*.

so progress can be measured. We provide financial statements that reflect a concern for the welfare of our neighbor, information that we ourselves would want to receive.

Functionally, we steward the resources of the organization, putting spending safeguards in place and holding managers accountable for that spending. We work to ensure a long-term focus on the stewardship of resources—including human and environmental resources—instead of a short-term focus on profits.[27]

Employees who do not know Christ should not observe Christian business owners and managers making unethical accounting choices, nor should they be asked by Christians to do something unethical, like manipulating the financial statements towards a specific end. Users of financial statements, including bankers, lenders, investors, and suppliers, should recognize a higher standard in accountants, organizations, and the financial statements that we produce.

Imago Dei and Marketing

As marketers with an *imago Dei* mindset, we build effective relationships, which satisfy individual, organizational, and societal objectives. We seek the shalom of the community through the products that we develop, the prices that we set, and the advertising that we undertake. We develop normative marketing practices that shape industry standards and provoke questions about why our approach to marketing differs from that of others.

By remembering that our customers are made in God's image, we develop products that meet moral criteria. Our advertising provides complete and fair information so customers can make appropriate buying decisions. We ensure that cultural distinctions are justly balanced in branding and advertising decisions. We consider the buyer as an equal partner in the marketing process and an image bearer of God.

Structurally, our character reflects that of God, practicing marketing with integrity and doing so in a righteous and truthful manner. We do not tolerate unethical pricing, slandering competitors, or stretching the truth about our products. Relationally, we develop long-term relationships with customers, honor warranties, and do not profit from those who cannot afford to make purchases. Finally, from a functional perspective, we develop

---

27. Van Weelden and Busuttil, *Accountants*.

products that meet the needs of buyers, are efficient in the use of resources, and enhance the shalom of God's Kingdom in our communities.

Training the Next Generation: *Imago Dei*

In a workplace-as-mission model, training the next generation of employees, managers, and entrepreneurs is crucial. First, we must intentionally develop a normative approach of *imago Dei* in business. If we are to consider the workplace as the largest mission field that individual Christians will encounter, then we must help students to understand the characteristics and actions that will repel non-believers from Christ and those that will attract people to him. We must learn to work and do business in such a way as to engender a curiosity about our motives and, in the context of a relationship, open opportunities for witness.

Fully living as image bearers of God requires deliberate efforts to reflect the characteristics and attributes that mirror those of our Creator (structural perspective). We must intentionally develop workplace relationships that are characterized by an agape love (relational perspective). It means actively serving as co-creators with God and stewards of his world (functional perspective).

While we are created to live in this way, the impact of sin in our world means that our ability to reflect God's image becomes distorted. We must intentionally safeguard relationships from being characterized by mistrust and abuse instead of love. We must stop ravaging and pillaging the resources we are given and instead wisely steward them. When non-Christians see sinful characteristics and behaviors in us, they will have no reason to inquire of the hope that lies within us (1 Pet 3:15). This draws us back to the need to focus on our relationship with God so that we can be effective witnesses for him in the workplace.

As professors at a Christian university, our mission is to prepare students to enter the workplace with a clear understanding of God's character and how to mirror those character traits in their daily interactions—as accountants, marketers, entrepreneurs, production managers, human resource managers, financial analysts, and more. We are called to help students discern the differences between healthy, respectful, and loving relationships and those that take advantage of others. We want them to develop curiosity and creativity that will allow them to innovate in products and processes to achieve better stewardship of resources. Our goal is to develop well-rounded, thoroughly equipped business people, who are fit for every good work to which God calls them, able to live in such a way as to spark curiosity from those with whom they work.

So, then, how does all of this happen? It happens by the grace of God, by his presence in our own lives and those of our students, by our effectiveness in bearing witness to God, and by a well-developed curriculum that not only includes the what and the how of business, but the why. It requires training and equipping young people not only with sound business skills but with a good understanding of *imago* Dei. It requires recognizing that despite the ongoing impact of sin on God's good creation—including his image bearers—we are part of God's redemptive work that is transforming all of creation.

Recently, Andrea, a student, shared that she had been approached by her manager at work, who asked if she was a Christian. She responded that yes, she was, and wondered why he was inquiring since she knew he was not a believer. The manager responded that a new employee had asked. At the first opportunity, Andrea spoke with the new employee. She was not a Christian, but she saw something different in Andrea and she knew that Christians were "different." Over time, Andrea built a relationship with her and invited her to church. She ultimately gave her life to Christ and is actively serving in the church. This is the type of impact that hundreds of Redeemer University business students are having because of who they are and what they do in the workplace. We praise God for how he is using them in fields that are ripe for harvest.

Conclusion

"Ever since the creation of the world his eternal power and divine nature, invisible though they are, have been understood and seen through the things he has made" (Rom 1:20). As the crowning glory of all of God's created things and beings, our very character and behavior in the workplace can show Christ to those around us. When we reflect the structural, relational, and functional dimensions of *imago Dei*, we present a revelation of Christ that is not read from the words of a book nor preached from a pulpit but that is seen in the attributes and the actions of his followers.

For some, the workplace will be the only opportunity to see him and we may be the first revelation of Christ that some people may encounter.

Then, more traditional forms of evangelism and discipleship can "water the seeds that have been sown."

May God give us the strength to be faithful in our respective witnesses.

Reflection Questions

1. In the workplace, what characteristics of *imago Dei* do you manifest that are likely to cause others to ask what is different about you? Are you prepared to give a reason that witnesses effectively?
2. How do you see God's image in your team members and colleagues, and what difference does that make to how you relate with them?
3. What behaviors would lead others to view you as an ambassador? Would they know for whom?

Bibliography

Bernbaum, John A., and Simon M Steer. *Why Work? Careers and Employment in Biblical Perspective.* Grand Rapids: Baker, 1986.

Bowen, John, ed. *Green Shoots Out of Dry Ground: Growing a New Future for the Church in Canada.* Eugene, OR: Wipf & Stock, 2013.

Business 4 Transformation, n.d. "About." http://www.b4t.org/about-2/.html.

Business Roundtable. "Statement on the Purpose of a Corporation." https://opportunity.businessroundtable.org/wp-content/uploads/2020/06/BRT-Statement-on-the-Purpose-of-a-Corporation-with-Signatures.pdf.

Busuttil, Laurie George, and Susan J. Van Weelden. "*Imago Dei* and Human Resource Management: How Our Understanding of the Breath of God's Spirit Shapes the Way We Manage People." *Journal of Biblical Integration in Business* 21 (2018) 9–20.

Chewning, Richard C. ed. *Biblical Principles and Business. The Practice. Volume 3.* Colorado Springs: NavPress, 1990.

Fettke, Steven M. *God's Empowered People: A Pentecostal Theology of the Laity.* Eugene, OR: Wipf & Stock, 2010.

Hardy, Lee. *The Fabric of This World: Inquiries into Calling, Career Choice, and the Design of Human Work.* Grand Rapids: Eerdmans, 1990.

International Organization for Migration. "World Migration Report 2020." https://publications.iom.int/books/world-migration-report-2020.

Kraemer, Hendrik. *A Theology of the Laity.* Vancouver: Regent College, 1958.

Lipka, Michael. "5 Facts about Religion in Canada." Pew Research Center 2019. https://www.pewresearch.org/fact-tank/2019/07/01/5-facts-about-religion-in-canada/.

Plummer, Jo. "What is Business as Mission?" https://businessasmission.com/get-started/.

Pregitzer, Michael. "Introducing the Ambassador Scorecard: A Christian Approach to HR Professional Excellence." *Christian Business Academy Review* 3 (2008) 48–60.

Roxburgh, Cam. "What Kind of Leaders Do We Need?" In *Green Shoots Out of Dry Ground: Growing a New Future for the Church in Canada*, edited by John Bowen, 183–95. Eugene, OR: Wipf & Stock, 2013.

Samek, E. "The Canadian Millennials Choosing God in a Secular World." *The National Post* (Toronto), March 4, 2019. https://nationalpost.com/life/the-canadian-millennials-choosing-god-in-a-secular-world.

Sands, Paul. "The *Imago Dei* as Vocation." *Evangelical Quarterly* 82 (2010) 28–41.

Van Weelden, Susan J., and Laurie R. Busuttil. "Imago Dei: How Accountants Glorify God." *Christian Business Review* (2019) 45–54.

Valpy, M., and J. Friesen. "Canada Marching from Religion to Secularization." *Globe and Mail* (Toronto), December 10, 2010. https://www.theglobeandmail.com/news/national/canada-marching-from-religion-to-secularization/article1320108/.

11

Renewing the Role of the Canadian Church in Cross-Cultural Marketplace Ministry

Jonathan Fuller

Introduction

The sushi was delicious, one of the perks of dinner meetings in Tokyo, but it was the conversation that I was looking forward to the most. Dave and Phil have worked in Japan for many years, forging a friendship around their common passion to introduce their Japanese colleagues to Jesus. Dave works for a large international accounting firm, and Phil is a software developer. Although they were somewhat jealous of more traditional foreign missionaries who had more time and flexibility for witness, they also recognized that their full-time jobs gave them opportunities to share Jesus with Japanese working men whom the traditional missionary would rarely meet. I was enjoying their stories of discipleship in the workplace, when Phil asked Dave how his Japanese language was coming along. Dave bemoaned his lack of deep Japanese and explained that he had arranged to take six months off for Japanese language study in order to strengthen his ability to witness. His work had given him an unpaid leave of absence and was holding his job for him because they were supportive of him improving his Japanese. I asked Dave how much it was going to cost for the Japanese training and living costs for the six months and he said that he had been saving for two years to set aside the US$40,000 he would need. While I was reeling a bit from that expense, Phil suggested that Dave's church might be willing to help with the cost of the language learning as it would clearly increase his ministry effectiveness. "I've lost touch with my church back in Australia," Dave replied, "and they wouldn't care anyway." Noticing that both Phil and I were a bit dismayed, Dave explained that his church had never seen him as involved in real mission work. Although they supported traditional missionaries working in Japan, they saw Dave as someone who had moved to Japan for his career. Dave had given up trying and had lost touch with the church over the years.

That conversation has stuck with me, especially as the following discussion included stories from Phil about all the ways in which his church has encouraged and supported him, even though he is self-supported financially. I left the restaurant asking how we can encourage more churches to have a vision for working with a purpose, for promoting and supporting their people to practice their vocation in least reached corners of the world.

Reflecting on Mission and Vocation in Today's Global Context

The Bible has lots to say about work. A cursory search of the New International Version results in over 500 references to the English word "work," and that is without exploring various related words. It is significant, though, that the first reference to work in the Scriptures is not to man's work but to God's work. "By the seventh day God had finished the work he had been doing; so on the seventh day he rested from all of his work" (Gen 2:2).

The Scriptures invite us to a spiritual life that is inextricably linked to God's glory and to a participation in the delight of his work. Paul Stevens emphasizes this in his book, *The Other Six Days: Vocation, Work and Ministry in Biblical Perspective*:

> The Old Testament is rich in metaphors to describe God as worker . . . These metaphors, while limited, offer a correspondence of meanings between the work of God and the work of humankind. They suggest that our work is a point of real connection with God and therefore a source of meaning and spirituality.[1]

Andrew Scott strongly affirms this biblical vision of work in his book *Scatter: Go Therefore and Take Your Job with You*. However, he articulates a stinging critique of the Western mission movement and its marginalization of vocation. Starting with the Genesis account, he argues persuasively

---

1. Stevens, *Other Six Days*, loc. 978.

from Scripture that work with rest is how God intends us to reflect his image to show his glory.

> God set an example of six days of work and one of rest. He set it up that 85 percent of the days of the week were to be used for work. If you work a typical number of hours each week you spend close to half of your waking hours working. That was God's plan. And His plan for your work is wrapped up in His plan for you to reflect His glory and goodness. The two cannot be separated. Your workplace is your place to reflect His image.[2]

Scott's concern with the western missionary movement is that we have allowed a false dichotomy between work and mission to marginalize the majority of God's people whose created gifts and talents should be his means of mission.

> A new paradigm is needed— one in which we recognize that all of life is where every believer gets to be a "full-time" follower of Jesus. Paul tells us that "everything comes from him and exists by his power and is intended for his glory" (Romans 11: 36 NLT). So everything that was created has a purpose, and that purpose is God. That includes us. We were created by God, for God. Everything we have was created and given to us by God, for God. Music was created by God, for God. Art was created by God, for God. The earth, the Milky Way, the universe was created by God, for God. When Paul says "everything," he means everything. Including our talents, our gifts, and our passions. All of life was created by Him, for Him, and is held together by Him, and all of life has the potential and was intended to bring glory to God. There is no dichotomy.[3]

Scott's argument points to what can go wrong when we forget that God delights in work done for his glory, whatever that work and wherever that work is done. This does not minimize the importance of missionaries serving cross-culturally among the unreached, but it does underline the great truth that their work is no less a delight and delightful to God than any other disciple's obedient work done for his glory. Jesus said that the world will know his disciples by their love, by the fruit they bear (John 15:8–14). There is nothing more compelling than God's people living out acts of unexpected redemptive service with deep joy driven by their love for him and for each other.

2. Scott, *Scatter*, loc. 115.
3. Scott, *Scatter*, loc. 187.

Since the days of William Carey and Hudson Taylor, mission work has been closely linked with mission agencies—specialized, parachurch, and volunteer communities. Churches partnered with mission agencies to identify, send and support "missionaries," who were generally involved in full-time "ministry," and usually fully dependent on funding from their sending context. God has wonderfully used this model to bring the Gospel to thousands of unreached people groups, but this is not the only biblical or historical model for obeying Jesus' Great Commission. In his book, *The Marketspace: The Essential Relationships Between the Sending Church, Marketplace Worker, and Missionary Team*, Larry McCrary comments, "Although it may sound like it, I really do not have a lot against the modern missionary movement. I am all in when it comes to taking the gospel to the nations. I just don't believe that the only pathway is a full-time vocational missionary pathway."[4]

In the last few decades, tentmaking professionals in mission and more recently missional business (or similar models) have become more common and more popular. However, Christian mission has been equated with the marketplace since at least the days of the apostles. Paul argued for the resurrection of Jesus in the "agora" or marketplace of Athens (Acts 17:16–34) and mended tents in the marketplace of Corinth (Acts 18: 1–3). These models are well suited to an increasingly post-Christendom reality, where the mission-minded church is not necessarily wealthy (e.g., Ethiopia) and the "lost" are not necessarily poor (e.g., Japan). These models also more accurately reflect the ways in which the Gospel spread historically prior to the development of the Western mission agency.

A great deal of work has been done in the last decade to explore the area of vocation and mission with very encouraging results, including the recent Lausanne sponsored Global Workplace Forum. There are also significant conferences each year exploring Business as Mission or Missional Business, and initiatives like the online portal Scatter Global, seeking to encourage cross-cultural vocational mission. However, marketplace workers often find themselves working alone in a cross-cultural context. They have not been able to find a mission agency or supportive spiritual community in their context that understands their vocational world well enough to provide helpful resources in a marketplace-friendly way.

---

4. McCrary, *Marketspace*, loc. 72.

The church—where they grew up or had roots—does not see marketplace ministry as real missionary work; thus, the church has not supported them in any way. In *Working Abroad with Purpose*, Glenn Deckert states,

> Tentmakers need sustained prayer support throughout their time abroad just as donor-supported workers do.... Prayer support for us meant people who would not merely read about our intriguing experiences at that time, in a relatively unknown part of the world, but people who would pray for us systematically.[5]

In his book on tentmaking, Patrick Lai argues,

> Tentmakers are at the forefront of the greatest spiritual battle. Military troops in the frontlines of a military campaign need up to eight times their number in supporting roles. In the same way, tentmakers need a committed team to keep them adequately encouraged and supplied as they move God's kingdom forward. A solid sending church is needed for the tentmaker's well-being.[6]

God desires that we enter into mission together as supportive communities, as his people on his mission for his glory. Traditional mission agencies, sending churches and most missionaries understand the importance of this, but still many marketplace workers struggle without these supportive relationships.

Despite the fact that proponents of cross-cultural vocational mission will generally affirm the importance of the church in any expression of mission, both churches and marketplace mission workers struggle to develop strong, supportive relationships. It is easy for discussions about vocation and mission to become focused on the individual's vocation, leaving the church uncertain about the commitment to mission. Lai comments, "Many churches need help understanding what tentmaking is all about. Some churches may not perceive a tentmaker to even be a missionary."[7] The practical facts that vocational "missionaries" are less reliant on local churches for funding and that marketplace ministries are often valued because they do not have to "raise support" make this individualization of mission even more likely. There is a need to strengthen the relationship between local churches and individual marketplace mission workers.

5. Deckert, *Working Abroad*, loc. 577.
6. Lai, *Tentmaking*, loc. 3861.
7. Lai, *Tentmaking*, loc. 3870.

Larry McCrary's book on the marketspace focuses specifically on this "essential relationship." McCrary argues for the importance of partnerships for effective marketspace mission:

> I think there are five essential components that we must keep in mind as we encourage people who are already in this "marketspace ministry": the marketspace worker needs the blessing of a sending church; the marketspace worker needs a legitimate reason to be there; the marketspace worker, the sending church, and the missionary team need to be trained and equipped for their special roles; the marketspace worker needs a viable community to thrive in; the marketspace worker needs to seize opportunities with a strategic focus.[8]

How can we help marketplace workers develop a strong relationship with their church as one of the essential components of this partnership? McCrary states, "The church needs to learn to identify, network, encourage, and equip these marketspace workers and elevate their role in Great Commission work to the same level of validity as any commissioned missionary."[9]

Marketplace Mission Survey Findings

In 2016, the Evangelical Fellowship of Canada (EFC) and the Canadian Missions Research Forum facilitated the Canadian Evangelical Mission Engagement Study (CEMES), with survey responses from over 2,000 lay evangelicals and nearly 1,500 evangelical pastors—the largest survey ever done of Canadian evangelicals.[10] In one of the questions, pastors were asked whether they agreed with the statement: "Our local church would consider sending a professional or business owner to intentionally live and work abroad as a missionary." Twenty-eight percent of pastors indicated that they strongly agreed with this statement and another 40 percent moderately agreed. Only nine percent moderately disagreed, and another five percent strongly disagreed. Eighteen percent of pastors indicated that they did not know (Hiemstra 2017b, 28). These responses seem very encouraging for the development of cross-cultural marketplace mission in the Canadian context, but it is difficult to find many examples of churches actively and intentionally initiating, promoting, or supporting

---

8. McCrary, *Marketspace*, loc. 401.
9. McCrary, *Marketspace*, loc. 59.
10. Hiemstra, "Canadian Missions Study."

PART 4: PRESENT AND FUTURE OF WORKPLACE MISSION

professionals or business owners to live and work cross-culturally with a mission posture. In cooperation with the EFC, a follow-up survey was conducted with the 818 pastors who indicated a willingness to be contacted further. The survey sought to determine the actual engagement churches have with professionals and business owners who have an interest in working abroad cross-culturally in mission. This study calls these professionals or business owners with interest in cross-cultural mission as marketplace workers. Here are a few highlights of the research based on the responses of the 192 pastors who completed the survey.

Survey question number two (see Figure 1) is a repeat of the original CEMES survey question related to the marketplace, asking how pastors viewed marketplace mission. In the original survey, the pastors responded largely positively with 28 percent being strongly in favor and 40 percent being moderately positive. Nine percent moderately disagreed with the model and four percent strongly disagreed, with 18 percent saying that they did not know.

Figure 1. Openness of Pastors in Sending Marketplace Workers

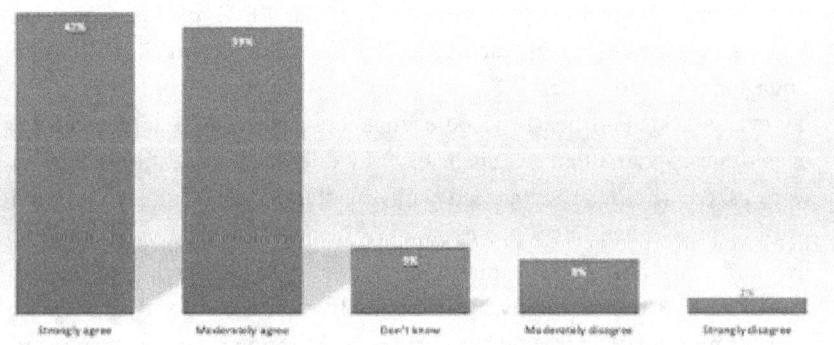

The new survey indicated an even stronger endorsement of the marketplace model. The increase in positive response from 68 percent to 79 percent is not totally unexpected as the 192 respondents had a likely positive bias towards marketplace mission, or at least the issue of marketplace mission, as indicated by their willingness to take the survey. However, it still suggests a strong endorsement of the marketplace mission model and is consistent with conversations with pastors who seem open to the marketplace model but struggle to implement it in their local church. Additional comments from the survey respondents illustrated this interest in marketplace mission and a desire to explore this area further. First, it is not a concept that is well-known to the majority of parishioners. Traditional vocational missionaries seem to be better known. Second, churches need to understand the changing landscape of the Christian mission and the post-Christian Canadian culture. Finding methods that work today through innovation and collaboration is much needed. Third, we need to continue to grow our understanding of God's mission in the world—to see it as infusing every area of our lives, including the time we spend doing our vocations.

The next question was intended to test this interest in marketplace mission by exploring actual practices. Survey question number three asked how many churches were involved in sending cross-cultural marketplace workers (see Figure 2).

Figure 2. Churches that Have Sent Cross-Cultural Marketplace Workers

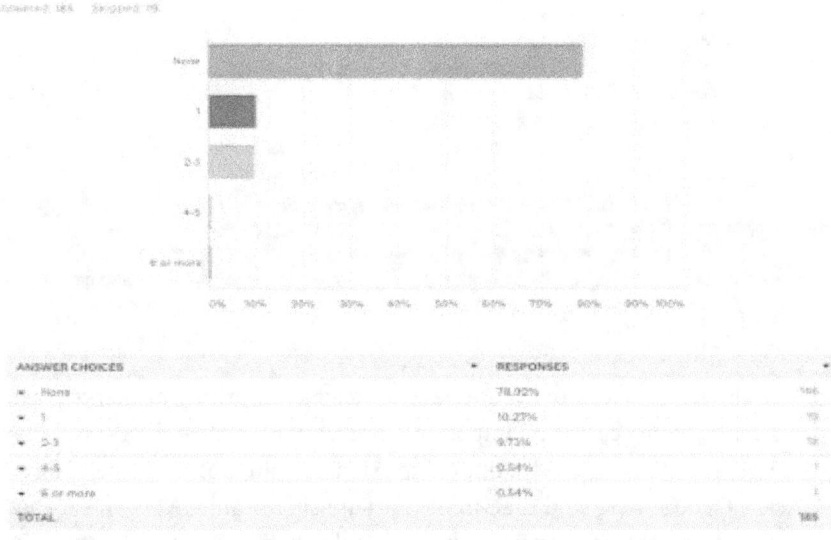

Workers had actually been sent by the pastors' churches in the last five years. However, the response appears to confirm the anecdotal evidence that interest in marketplace mission is not reflected directly in current

practice. While nearly 80 percent of pastors surveyed viewed marketplace mission positively, only 20 percent of those surveyed had actually sent anyone in the last five years.

The following questions were only answered by the 39 churches (20 percent of survey respondents) that had experience in sending marketplace workers, because these questions refer to actual practices in marketplace mission engagement.

Survey question number four asked where churches had sent marketplace workers for longer than one year (see Figure 3). In addition, the thirty-nine churches that responded had sent 73 workers in the last five years.

Figure 3. Location Where Marketplace Workers Have Been Sent

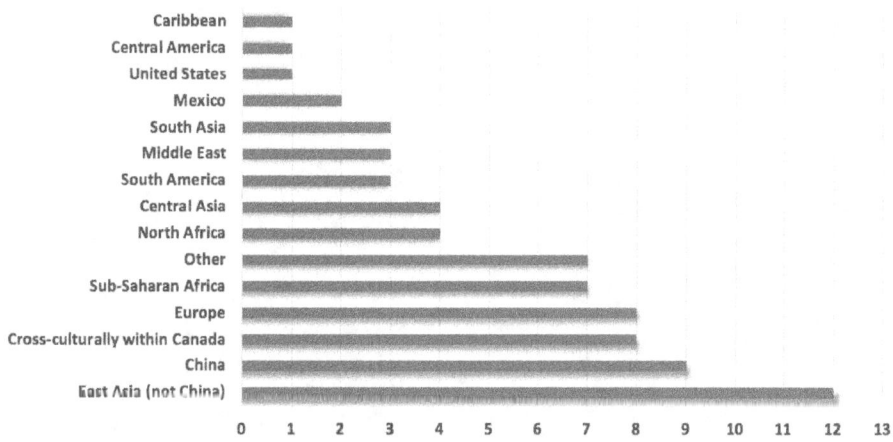

The strong focus on East Asia is somewhat surprising as marketplace mission is often seen as an important strategy for Creative Access Nations (CANs—contexts where traditional missionaries are not welcome). North Africa, Central Asia, and the Middle East are significant CAN contexts but were not as common destinations. This information is worth keeping in view for agencies and churches who are committed to strengthening Gospel witness in least-reached contexts and might consider promoting marketplace mission as one strategy to reach these contexts.

Question number 5 asked for information on the roles that marketplace mission workers have played (see Figure 4).

Figure 4. List of Cross-Cultural Marketplace Roles

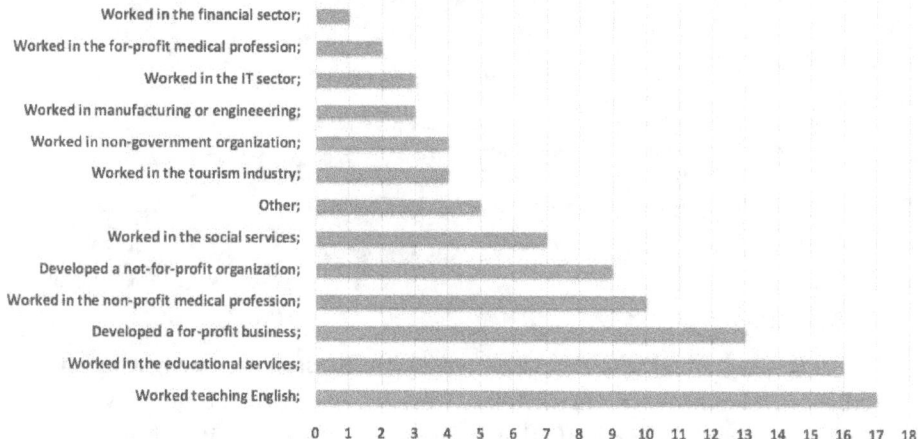

Teaching English and working in the educational services were the most common roles indicated, but there is some ambiguity in the question because some respondents may have selected both educational services and teaching English for the same person. It would have been clearer to have excluded teaching English from the educational services option. However, the results do indicate that teaching and education are still very important roles for global mission. Developing a for-profit business also ranked highly as did working in the non-profit medical profession. For some churches and agencies, it will be helpful to see how other churches are already engaged (e.g., educational services and developing for-profit businesses), and perhaps to consult with them in these areas of potential marketplace involvement. For other churches and agencies, the lack of engagement in some marketplace roles may present a strategic opportunity (e.g., the IT sector).

Survey question number 6 explored how churches are engaged with the marketplace workers whom they have sent (see Figure 5).

PART 4: PRESENT AND FUTURE OF WORKPLACE MISSION

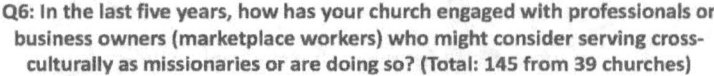

Figure 5. Church Engagement with Marketplace Workers

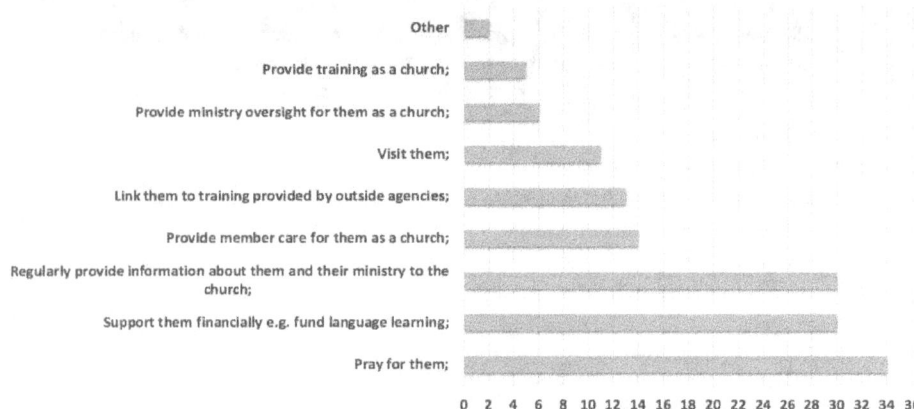

It is encouraging to note that prayer is the most common engagement that churches have with marketplace workers. At the same time, prayer is also an aspect of church life that is quite subjective and difficult to measure. One of the challenges for the marketplace worker is to intentionally nurture a prayer relationship with their church community through regular, appropriate communication. Churches that have missionaries on their financial budget, often have expectations around prayer communication. However, from conversations with marketplace workers, these expectations are rarely applied to marketplace workers.

The relatively high level of financial support was surprising. Most marketplace workers do not need financial support in the sense that traditional missionaries often do, and we would expect that this would translate into a lesser degree of financial engagement. It is encouraging that financial support is being actively practiced, but more work needs to be done here to clarify the actual degree of financial support. It would also be helpful to have a clearer idea of what specific areas of need are being funded for marketplace workers.

Training by the church is a relatively infrequent engagement, and training by an agency is also not particularly high on the list. This is interesting given that the responses to question number nine indicate that the pastor's two highest concerns for marketplace workers is the lack of cross-cultural and theological training. There is an opportunity here for marketplace workers to address these concerns about training in the relationship with their church.

While the previous three questions were asked only of those pastors whose churches have actually sent marketplace workers, the remaining questions were asked of all the 192 responding pastors. Question number nine explores how the church has supported the development of marketplace mission (see Figure 6).

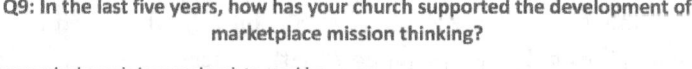

Figure 6. Church Support for Marketplace Mission Thinking

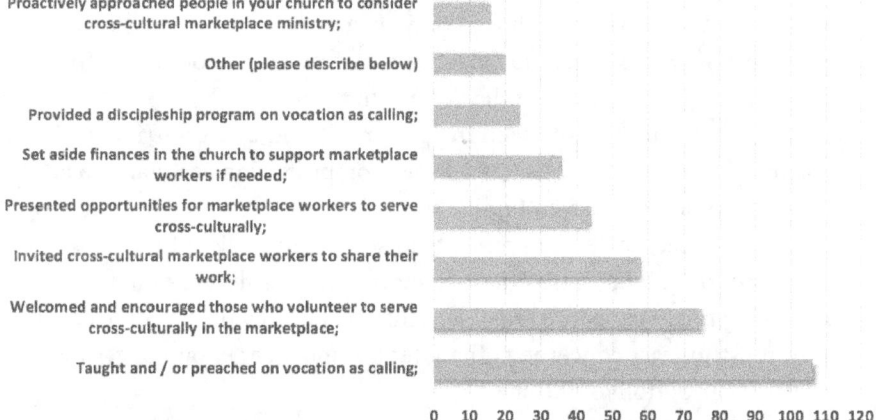

Clear biblical teaching on vocation and calling is one of the most important ways in which churches can contribute toward reducing the sacred/secular divide and encouraging the development of marketplace mission thinking, so it is encouraging that 65 percent (106 out of 164) of pastors who responded to this question indicated that they have taught or preached on this subject. One respondent described this as "gently laying some theological groundwork." Another respondent wrote, "As the Lead Pastor, I have done two sermon series on Marketplace Ministry but that has been focussed on people living out their vocation here in Canada as ministry, not cross culturally."

Pastors also indicated that they welcomed and encouraged those with an interest in marketplace mission and invited those actively serving to share with their congregation. However, since 80 percent of pastors

PART 4: PRESENT AND FUTURE OF WORKPLACE MISSION

report that their churches have not sent someone in this area of mission, this reality probably limits such interactions. Relatively few churches are actively discipling people in the area of vocation as calling or proactively approaching people to consider serving as marketplace workers. One pastor commented, "This is a brand new concept, so my missions committee is exploring ways to help people see that this is valid missions." Another pastor honestly wrote, "Never thought or talked about it." It was encouraging, however, to read from one pastor, "We are calling our people to discipleship in the workplace. Our hope is that some will catch a vision to work and live in hard places." For many smaller churches, exploring this area of ministry is a challenge: "As a small church with limited funds, we have made the choice not to support marketplace workers (as a philosophy of ministry). We have chosen only to support fulltime missionaries whose primary task is disciplemaking and evangelism. Because of this decision, we do not do any of the options in this list."

Question number 10 asked the pastors, "What concerns (if any) do you have with sending business owners or professionals (marketplace workers) to serve cross-culturally as missionaries?" This question has multiple choices, asking respondents to select from a list of possible answers and to rank them in order of concern. The results are noted in Figure 7, with the issues being rated in terms of how often they were selected from most to least concerned. The issues of most common concern are shown at the bottom of the chart.

Figure 7. Issues Affecting Marketplace Workers' Effectiveness

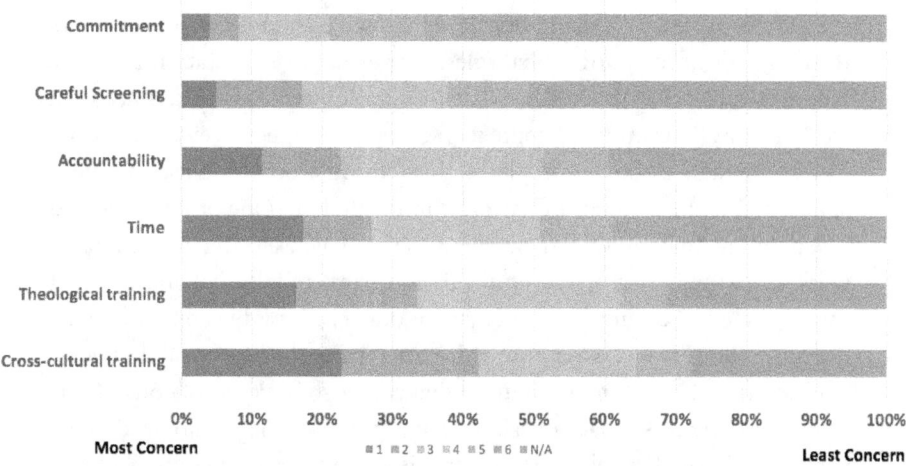

Concerns about training were the two most commonly identified concerns (as noted from the bottom of the chart), with cross-cultural training being the most common concern and theological training also being raised. This is not too surprising as marketplace workers often have not taken formal theological training before moving into cross-cultural ministry, and they often do not have the opportunity to take cross-cultural training before being deployed. It is encouraging that pastors recognize this need. There is a clear opportunity for traditional agencies and Bible training institutions to partner with churches in order to address these training needs. However, both the agency and the academy need to look for alternative delivery methods in order to make training accessible for marketplace workers. The need for cross-cultural training is also an opportunity for agencies and businesses in the "field" to consider how to deliver this training to marketplace workers as they are moving into cross-cultural vocational roles. In light of this, it was encouraging to have one pastor write, "We are transitioning to include a strong invitation and training and sending of marketplace workers. Right now, we're working on the training component as we identify those who are potential marketplace workers."

A lack of time was identified by pastors as their third most significant concern for cross-cultural marketplace workers. This is a concern often heard expressed by agency leaders in the cross-cultural context through statements like, "I would love to have marketplace workers on our team, but they are so busy with work that they have no time for ministry." Marketplace workers face a significant challenge for ministry engagement if they are expected to join traditional missionary team activities on top of the demands of their vocational roles. However, this expectation may be a failure to address the sacred/secular divide. Marketplace workers see their workplace as their ministry context and seek to be effective evangelists and disciple-makers in their workplace. This tension around the use of time is something that a number of pastors commented on. One pastor observed, "Overcoming the traditional beliefs of some who see full-time ministry workers as the best cross-cultural mission workers is a challenge. In fact, the opposite is the truth!" Another pastor unpacked this tension around the definition of a "real missionary." This pastor talks about a "small but vocal conservative element in our church" that can push back in not considering cross-cultural marketplace missionary as a real missionary who needs to be supported in the first place. However, the pastor sees some hope: "I think this small slice of the congregation could be educated out of that wrong kind of thinking, but it might take some time."

A third pastor articulates this tension as a matter of integrity, "[T]here may be a lack of integrity if a person has an ulterior motive for why they are in the marketplace in the first place. Our church would be very hesitant to send or support someone who was planning to do one thing (marketplace venture) as a guise for doing something else (evangelism). We would probably be more comfortable with someone either being in the marketplace and living out their faith naturally without calling it mission or being in an overt ministry role without the cover of another venture." The concern that the Gospel be kept central, was raised by another pastor, "In my experience, I have seen marketplace mission put a secondary emphasis on the sharing of the gospel. It seems that business takes the lead while God takes the back seat to the pursuit of sustainability, social concerns and profit. We would support someone to be a missionary who might also work in their location, as long as the central emphasis is on sharing the gospel."

Churches and mission agencies share a concern that marketplace workers are effective disciple-makers in their workplace, and this needs to be a clear focus for training and accountability for marketplace workers. However, this concern must celebrate the strategic importance value of disciple-making in the workplace, a context which traditional missionaries are often unable to influence.

Conclusion

The responses from the 192 pastors who participated in the Marketplace Mission survey—while not by any means a representative sample of Canadian evangelical pastors—do suggest three major inputs regarding marketplace mission and the Canadian church. These three inputs can serve as conversation starters in challenging the churches to consider this kind of mission.

Eighty Percent Positive View on Marketplace Mission

Although pastors acknowledge that this aspect of mission engagement is new and not well understood in their churches, and that these churches have some concerns, the pastors are also strongly supportive of the model in principle (as seen in the 80 percent of pastors who viewed marketplace mission positively). For some, this is an extension of the growing faith/work movement and a recognition that followers of Jesus must live out their faith in the workplace, not just on weekends at church. Others even see this as a practical response to the increasing restrictions on cross-cultural mission in some parts of the globe. Regardless of the motivation, there is a significant opportunity to explore and develop marketplace mission through Canadian churches.

Twenty Percent Church Involvement in Marketplace Mission

Only 20 percent of the pastors surveyed indicated that their church have been intentionally involved in marketplace mission in the last five years. Despite many pastors responding positively to the marketplace mission model, very few churches appear to be actually involved with this model. The disconnect between the level of interest (80 percent) and the level of engagement (20 percent) suggests that there is an important opportunity for mission agency and church leaders to work together on marketplace mission. Perhaps the most important outcome of this study is the opportunity to increase the practical engagement of the Canadian church in marketplace mission through intentional collaboration between the agency, church, and marketplace workers themselves. Such collaboration could increase the church engagement in marketplace mission from 20 to 40 or 50 percent, releasing vital new resources for global (including Canadian) mission, and perhaps in the process enriching the Canadian church's understanding of faith and work.

Concerns for Cross-cultural/Theological Training of Marketplace Workers

For the pastors surveyed, the two most common concerns about marketplace mission are cross-cultural and theological training of marketplace workers. Training was a greater concern than the issues of time or commitment, suggesting an opportunity for the church, agency, and academy to work closely together in training marketplace workers. Theological and cross-cultural knowledge and experience are available through the agency and academy, but traditional delivery methods do not work well for marketplace workers. Churches need to coordinate better with agency and academy leaders to provide accessible training opportunities, including in-service and online models that fit well with marketplace realities.

Field team leaders often express concerns about marketplace workers' lack of time and commitment to mission, concerns which are driven by an appropriate concern to see marketplace mission workers become effective disciple-makers. However, these concerns may reflect the failure of those field team leaders to understand the realities of effective disciple-making in the marketplace context. As agency and academy leaders work with the church to develop more accessible training models, they themselves also need to be more open to learning about disciple-making in the marketplace. While it is true that marketplace workers need a better understanding of the cross-cultural issues at play in their context, agency leaders need a better understanding of the marketplace cultural issues at play in their context. All parties will benefit from a well-developed theological foundation on these issues.

There are certainly other implications of this study that still need to be developed, looking at where and how Canadian marketplace workers are engaged in mission globally. A number of pastors commented on the potential for effective cross-cultural, marketplace workers to influence the work and witness of their congregations. One pastor commented, "My church members don't even know how to do mission in their present workplace let alone cross culturally." Another expressed the potential impact of marketplace workers, "Listening to marketplace workers has encouraged local marketplace people to think of their witness at home as well."

Thinking back to that dinner in downtown Tokyo, I hope that we could see many more stories like Phil's, whose church understood his calling to reach the Japanese through his vocation, committed themselves to pray for him and encouraged him in practical ways where there was a need. In a similar way, we hope that this research will result in an increasing number of Canadian churches intentionally supporting effective cross-cultural marketplace mission in Canada and around the globe.

Reflection Questions

1. What good Canadian examples have you seen of healthy partnerships between churches and marketplace mission workers? What made those partnerships healthy?

2. What factors make it difficult for churches to welcome and encourage their people to consider being involved with marketplace mission, either to go themselves or to stand with others who are going?

3. What can marketplace missionaries and partner agencies do to encourage and strengthen the Canadian church in this significant area of global mission engagement?

Bibliography

Bosch, David J. *Transforming Mission: Paradigm Shifts in Theology of Mission*. New York: Orbis, 2000.

Deckert, Glenn D. *Working Abroad with Purpose: The Way of a Tentmaker*. Eugene, OR: Wipf & Stock, 2019. Kindle.

Heimstra, Rick. "Canadian Evangelical Missions Engagement Study Methodology." Faith Today Publications, 2017.

Heimstra, Rick, and Karen Stiller. 2016. "Religious Affiliation and Attendance in Canada." 2016. http://www.intrust.org/Magazine/Issues/New-Year-2016/Religious-affiliation-and-attendance-in-Canada.

Lai, Patrick. *Tentmaking: The Life and Work of Business as Missions*. Downers Grove, IL: InterVarsity, 2005. Kindle.

PART 4: PRESENT AND FUTURE OF WORKPLACE MISSION

McCrary, Larry E. *The Marketspace: The Essential Relationships Between the Sending Church, Marketplace Worker, and Missionary Team.* Louisville: Upstream Collective, 2018. Kindle.

Scott, Andrew. *Scatter: Go Therefore and Take Your Job with You.* Chicago: Moody, 2016. Kindle.

Stevens, R. Paul. *The Other Six Days: Vocation, Work and Ministry in Biblical Perspective.* Grand Rapids: Eerdmans, 2000. Kindle.

Stroope, Michael W. *Transcending Mission: The Eclipse of a Modern Tradition.* Downers Grove, IL: InterVarsity, 2017.

Conclusion
Surfacing Significant Changes in our Understanding, Attitudes, and Actions toward Evangelical Mission

NARRY F. SANTOS

AS WE CONCLUDE THIS compendium, we need to surface the key themes from each chapter that speak to the past, present, and future of evangelical mission in Canada. To gain a sense of God's direction for the Canadian church in the future, we must seek to understand what he wants us to learn from our past and to discern what he is doing in the present. Additionally, the rapidly changing global and Canadian contexts prompt us not just to revisit our past and current understanding of mission but to also ask ourselves these new questions: "What is God doing in our midst right now? What does it mean to be a community of Christ followers where we are? Where is God leading us together as his people, in light of where the world is headed?" As Chan noted at the introduction of the book, "We are invited to prophetic evaluation of the past, but also to new imagination for the current uncertain present and the brave new future." She also raises the need for the Canadian church to find its way forward and as a guide to identify where we have fallen short in the past. In this final chapter, I will highlight the major ideas, concepts, and proposals in the previous chapters that help find our way forward and as a prophetic guide to reimagine the past.

Unprecedented Contemporary Changes

The way forward and the way to reimagine the past as a guide are prompted by unprecedented and disruptive changes[1] in the present. George recognizes that we now live "in a new world that is postcolonial, post-Western, post-Enlightenment and post-Christendom."[2] As a result, he observes that current Christianity is more global, more geographically dispersed, and more diverse than it has ever been in its history.[3] Thus, he calls upon missiologists to attend to these emerging contexts and dramatic societal transformations, along with the global church to develop mobile faith and fresh translation of the needs of mobile people that lead to cross-cultural diffusion and to Jesus being made incarnate among peoples of the world.

Martin also surfaces the current realities of pluralism (the co-existence of different worldviews and value systems in the same society) in the context of globalization, secularization,[4] and technological advance, as well as the reactionary push back of fundamentalism (the attempt to restore or create anew a taken-for-granted body of beliefs and values). However, he sees the twin realities of religious pluralism and fundamentalism as a multifaceted opportunity for the church to build bridges and to be God's practical presence in the middle of these polarized sides. Moreover, Lau details the multiculturalism story of Canada, affirming that diversity is a fact, and that inclusion is a choice. Thus, he argues for an intercultural ecclesiology, realizing that inclusion is not a choice but a biblical reality.

In light of these contemporary global changes and new Canadian realities (in addition to the COVID and post-COVID circumstances), we are faced with a glaring question: "How can the evangelical church consider change in these ever-changing contexts?" The previous chapters in this book present nuanced answers to the need for change in three areas of understanding, attitude, and action.

Changes in Understanding Mission

Changes in mission understanding involves the following: (1) the nature of God; (2) discernment from our triune God; (3) key paired concepts

1. Deymaz, *Disruption*; Grandberg-Michaelson, *Future Faith*.
2. For more details on post-Christendom, see Murray, *Post-Christendom*.
3. Tira and Yamamori, *Scattered and Gathered*.
4. Santos and Naylor, *Mission and Evangelism*.

(instead of dichotomized ideas); and (4) inclusive and collective mission. The first two changes relate to the new ways that we need to see God, while the last two changes deal with how we need to view mission differently. As a result of these changes in aptitude, we gain perspective in having more opportunities for creative mission rather than simply seeing the difficult mission challenges at hand.

Nature of God in Mission

First, our understanding of God in mission needs to keep expanding. Such understanding must include the *imago Dei, mission Dei, motus Dei*, and *patentia Dei*. Busuttil and van Weelden describes the image of God according to its three aspects; namely: (1) structural (who we are created to be, as we reflect the characteristics and attributes of God); (2) relational (how we are created to live in community, according to the model of our triune God); and (3) functional (what we are created to do as ambassadors, while we steward the earth's resources and serve as co-creators with God in the world). From the *imago Dei*, we need to proceed with the *mission Dei*, which gives the theological impetus to shift the focus of mission from human to divine agency, and which transitions God's people as full participants in fulfilling God's mission in a hungry and hurting world.

George extends the concept of the mission of God to the *motus Dei* (or move of God). God is a God on the move and is powerfully moving among the people on the move. He proposes that we reimagine mission theology kinetically, using the maxim "I move, therefore I am" (*moveo ergo sum*)." In response, Lee offers the balancing concept of the *patienta Dei* (patience or longsuffering of God). Lee asks, "In the mission of God, would tethering the movement of God with the patient or longsuffering character of God better prepare our mission-minded people for slow discipleship?" For Friedman, to grow in understanding the nature of God in mission is foundational for comprehending Greek philosophy in relation to Christianity (according to Clement of Alexandria) or for contextualizing Christianity in the African Traditional Religion (according to Mbiti) as *praeparatio evangelica* (or preparation for the Gospel). In other words, God uses philosophy and culture to prepare people for the good news of God. Thus, the church needs to rediscover who God is and to expand its understanding on the nature, character, and mission of God in relation to communicating and contextualizing the Gospel to different peoples and cultures.

Discernment from God's Spirit in Mission

Aside from expanding our understanding on God, we must also learn how to discern better the ways of God's Spirit in pointing us to Jesus. Martin asks, "How is God at work here to fulfill his promise to bless all nations through the seed of Abraham?" Draper also exhorts us to "discern where God's Spirit is already at work within a population or neighbourhood" and "to look to the work of God's Spirit to bring forth theological and spiritual reorientation," while Witt challenges churches in the city to become "more acutely aware of how God is at work in their midst."

To do this, we must direct the attention of diverse people to Christ, so that they can learn that "in Christ, Canadian Christians do not have to continue to adopt and have the mindset of their forebears towards immigrants and global Christians nor apply our secular multicultural conditioning to our ecclesiology" (Lau). In the context of reconciliation and the healing of memories, Böhm challenges those in conflict to "see our own life story, our own biography from God's perspective, to read the pages of our past together with God's Spirit," which leads to uncovering sinful ways and to setting paths toward God.

"Both/And" View of Mission

The third change in understanding mission is to view mission not as "either/or" but as "both/and"—seeing concepts of mission in pairs, not as disengaged and dichotomous ideas. Here is a sampling of major mission concepts that need to be discussed together: (1) witness and participation (which George considers as the new epistemological reconstruction of mission); (2) *motus Dei* as both displacement and rootedness (as Shu contends, since mission is not just being sent but also being tied down to a particular location with a particular people), along with the related pair of a community sharing love that spirals outward (centrifugally) as it moves out of itself and of a community sharing love that spirals inward (centripetally) as it gathers together; (3) LeBlanc's pair of truth-telling and integrity in engaging theologically, missionally, and ecclesially; (4) Friedman's proposal to understand both "Christian faith" (as universal reality) and "Christianity" (as the local manifestation of that faith in context); (5) Witt's endorsement of the two methodologies of partnership (through formal/structure practices of partnership building) and network (through informal/relational practices of network development), along with the fundamental relationship of unity and plurality (evident in the concept of "differentiated unity"); (6) reorientation of mission as both focused on the world and on God, which (as Draper argues) makes the people of God "fully open to the need of the world and yet have their eyes fixed always on God," along with the paired "cruciform weakness" (as expressed in the world) and "worshipful engagement" (as expressed before God); and (7) work as vocation and mission (a pair that Fuller observes has been falsely dichotomized to the point of marginalizing the majority of God's people).

Inclusive and Collective Mission

The fourth change in mission understanding is the intentional emphasis on inclusive and collective mission. A clear example of collaborative cross-denominational mission is the TrueCity network of churches in Hamilton, the slogan of which is "churches together for the good of the city." The network of churches agrees to bond together in cooperative engagement in the city through different arenas of mission. Such mission results in the thickening of the social and spiritual fabric of Hamilton, and in differentiated unity through partnership (characterized by genuine involvement, acceptance of responsibility, and willingness to accept liability). Additionally, in the context of cross-cultural marketplace ministry, Fuller highlights God's desire for the church, mission agencies, and workplace missionaries to enter mission together as supportive communities, as God's people in his mission for his glory.

Changes in Attitude toward Mission

So far, we have seen the four changes in understanding of evangelical mission (nature of God; discernment through God's Spirit; "both/and" perspective; and collective mission). This book has also observed major changes in our mission attitude. These changes in mission attitude involves the following: (1) posture of openness; (2) willingness to revisit the past and engage in prophetic evaluation; and (3) assurance of hope. These changes in attitude enable us to become better learners in life and ministry, encourage us to open our heart and try fresh mission approaches, and empower us to reignite our passion in fulfilling God's purposes.

Posture of Openness

The first change in mission attitude is the posture of openness, as expressed in developing relationships of trust and cooperative mission for missional engagement (which are "clear signs that God is at work among us"). This posture of openness is also evident in learning about discipleship in the workplace (as Busuttil and van Weelden advocate), and in inviting the Korean and Chinese churches to affirm women in ministry and leadership (as Pak and Chan request that women be restored to their proper place as full participants and ministry leaders in God's mission).

Other expressions of openness are found in listening and sharing of stories in the context of conflict (realizing that every conflict has a story, and that story is the language of experience[5]), and in making space for God's Spirit to speak and heal. Such posture of openness leads to breaking down gender walls, lessening the degree of cultural alienation, participating in contextualization, and building bridges between polarized sides and positions. An inspiring example of openness is described in the "healing of memories" approach that was developed in South Africa to bring healing and reconciliation in the post-apartheid relationships between victims and offenders.

Willingness to Revisit the Past in Prophetic Evaluation

In addition to the posture of openness, a significant change in mission attitude is the willingness to revisit the past and engage in prophetic evaluation. This willingness brings with it the needed humility in looking back and in learning hard lessons on mission. LeBlanc shares the value of looking back through the words of his grandfather when he and his father walked through the woods with him as a child:

> Always look over your shoulder at where you have been twice as much as you look ahead to where you are going on a new trail. That way, the landmarks behind you will be fixed in your mind the way they will appear to you on the return; you will be able to find your way back home.

In the context of engaging indigenous history thoughtfully, LeBlanc urges us to "always look over your shoulder twice as much as you look

---

5. Boomershine, *Story Journey*, 10.

ahead" in the two key areas of colonial mission glossing and church–state collusion. George calls for prophetic evaluation of the past through soul searching among Western Christians, in light of the collapse of the colonial enterprise and economic structures for foreign mission. Rossetto challenges us to rethink of our preference to tame God (rather than welcome his sovereignty and mystery) and review our "empire building cultures that accumulate power for the purpose of self-aggrandizement." Pak and Chan push for change regarding opening doors of opportunity for emerging young leaders. Boehm calls powerful groups to face their conflicted past—not to excuse it but to reckon with it through mutual confession and forgiveness. Draper calls for a prophetic critique of the evangelical church's adoption of "technique" (the human-powered enterprise characterized by human misuses of power and methodologies).

Moreover, engaging in prophetic evaluation involves the courage to "reinvent missiology for the coming generations[6]" (George), to "reimagine newer ways of Gospel engagement" (Lee), to "reinterpret ancestral traditions in a manner which will contribute to and integrate with present faith in Christ" (Friedman), to "renew the church by rediscovering the biblical vision of church as a diverse community" (Lau), to "reframe human powered understanding of mission" (Draper), and to "recalibrate our understanding of what God is calling us to do in the workplace" (Busuttil and van Weelden). Only when we are willing to revisit the past can we have the courage to engage it in prophetic evaluation.

Assurance of Hope

The third change in mission attitude is the assurance of hope, despite challenging and uncertain times. Rossetto sees this hope in Jesus who meets the church and still commits to make her whole. She explains this hope for the church, which is found in Jesus, through these words: "The hope for the church is that Jesus still comes out of his way to engage us in truth-telling and liberating conversations. Jesus tells us the truth of our past, we confess, and acknowledge him, and then we go tell others about him." Thus, we still have hope for the church as a "fellowship of those called out of the world to accept responsibility for the world" (Böhm). In Christ, the church finds its way toward an eschatological path "to its future which will

---

6. Sherwood, *Listening to Echo*; Wong, *Listening to Voices*; Powell et al., *Growing Young*; Allen, *InterGenerate*.

include communion" (Lau) of all churches from all nations. Martin spells out H.O.P.E. through this acronym: (1) Hospitality; (2) Openness (the antidote to polarization); (3) Practical presence; and (4) Eternal perspective. With H.O.P.E., the "locally engaged church can be a lifeline in chaos" and can optimistically see some "silver lining in our cultural crisis" (Martin).

Changes in Action toward Mission

Aside from the changes in mission attitude (posture of openness; willingness to revisit the past and engage in prophetic evaluation; and assurance of hope), this book also presents several mission changes in action. These changes in mission action involves the following: (1) bridge-building and integration; and (2) concrete acts of change. These changes in action reinforce our need for others, deepen our resolve to meet people where they hurt and need help, and create sustainable deeds of transformation in the Spirit's power.

Bridge-Building in Mission

The act of bridge-building seeks creative ways to connect people in the context of polar positions. To bridge the opposite camps of secularization and fundamentalism, Martin proposes the practical presence of counter-cultural Christ-followers. To bridge the extremes of assimilation and segregation of churches in the Canadian multicultural context, Lau proposes the intercultural church alternative. To bridge the universal reality of Christian faith and the localized manifestation of Christianity, Friedman proposes the creative innovation of critical contextualization. Such bridge-building proposals result in the integration of opposing positions. Through Clement of Alexandria's contextual approach to Greek philosophy in relation to Christianity, Friedman contends, "God integrated what was good in Greek philosophy toward his own ends." Through intercultural ecclesiology in the power of the Spirit, Lau sees the integration of voices missing in church and the integration in homily and ecclesial leadership.

Concrete Acts in Mission Change

Finally, several chapter contributors recommend their own set of action change in mission. To develop a relevant evangelical missiology, George recommends these three steps: (1) learn from lessons in the past; (2) assess contemporary realities of the world; and (3) develop a robust evangelical missiology for the future. To start out fresh again in mission, LeBlanc argues for navigating home to Jesus through three steps: (1) developing a right relationship with God and other spiritual powers; (2) developing right relationships with others; and (3) developing right relationships with the rest of creation. To realign the church concept of power to that of Jesus, Rossetto presents the following steps of alignment in the church: (1) keeping weekly rhythms of Sabbath centered on worship of God and sharing in community through hospitality[7]; (2) engaging in truth-telling and reconciliation processes; (3) providing church budgets that seek to protect the vulnerable; and (4) living and proclaiming the good news of God in Christ. To develop intercultural competence,[8] Lau proposes that we learn to speak each other's language by intentionally seeking to increase our intercultural awareness, repenting of our prejudice, and starting to integrate voices that are missing from our churches.

To forge ongoing partnerships, Witt presents the straightforward four-fold "task of establishing strong relationships, shared purposes, joint plans, and shared resources," resulting in the "connective tissue" of optimal collaborative alliance. To engage in collaborative mission for the city, he also specifies the following arenas of mission: volunteering in neighborhood schools; welcoming refugees[9]; engaging art communities; caring for creation; getting involved in youth ministry and indigenous reconciliation. To practice the "healing of memory" approach in church, Boehm employs Robert Schreiter's four practices: (1) healing (of wounds, rebuilding trust, and restoring relationships); (2) truth-telling (as testimony of what really happened in the past and as common effort to reconstruct public truth); (3) pursuit of justice (not as punitive but as restorative justice); and (4) forgiveness (aimed toward the wrongdoers, not on their actions).

In conclusion, evangelical mission has had a seasoned history in Canada but is currently at a crossroad in its development for relevance in

---

7. Cook et al., *Beyond Hospitality*.
8. Rah, *Many Colors*.
9. Santos and Naylor, *Mission amid Global Crises*.

the next decades. The significant changes in understanding, attitudes, and actions toward evangelical mission that were surfaced in this closing chapter can serve as catalysts to clarify how relevant our future influence will be to our communities and country. May we experience God's power (his "gift when expended in love expands to invite others to experience power of creative flourishing and worship of the living God") and his people's catholicity (the "totality of the interconnected reality of the global expression of the church and to the fulness God intends for this totality to become part of the new creation). May we be able to keep engaging in the prophetic evaluation of our evangelical past and to keep reimagining God's mission for an uncertain present and a brave new future.

Bibliography

Allen, Holly Catterton, ed. *InterGenerate: Transforming Churches through Intergenerational Ministry*. Abilene, TX: Abilene Christian University Press, 2018.

Boomershine, *Story Journey: An Invitation to the Gospel as Storytelling*. Nashville: Abingdon, 1998.

Cook, Charles, et al., eds. *Beyond Hospitality: Migration, Multiculturalism, and the Church*. Toronto: Tyndale Academic Press, 2020.

DeYmaz, Mark. *Disruption:Repurposing the Church to Redeem the Community*. Nashville: Thomas Nelson, 2017.

Grandberg-Michaelson, Wesley. *Future Faith: Ten Challenges Reshaping Christianity in the 21st Century*. Philadelphia: Fortress, 2018.

Murray, Stuart. *Post-Christendom: Church and Mission in a Strange New World*. Milton Keynes, UK: Paternoster, 2005.

Powell, Kara, et al. *Growing Young: 6 Essential Strategies to Help Young People Discover and Love your Church*. Grand Rapids: Baker, 2016.

Rah, Soong-Chan. *Many Colors: Cultural Intelligence for a Changing Church*. Chicago: Moody, 2010.

Santos, Narry F., and Mark Naylor. *Mission and Evangelism in a Secularizing World: Academy, Agency, and Assembly Perspectives from Canada*. Eugene, OR: Pickwick, 2019.

———. *Mission amid Global Crises: Academy, Agency, and Assembly Perspectives from Canada*. Eugene, OR: Pickwick, 2020.

Sherwood, Tom. *Listening to the Echo: Young Adults Talk about Religion, Spirituality, God, gods, and their World*. Victoria, BC: Friesen, 2016.

Tira, Sadiri Joy, and Tetsunao Yamamori, eds. *Scattered and Gathered: A Global Compendium of Diapora Missiology*. UK: Langham Global, 2020.

Wong, Enoch. *Listening to Their Voices: An Exploration of Faith Journeys of Canadian-born Chinese Christians*. Canada: CCCOWE, 2018.

List of Contributors

Manuel Böhm, Peace and Reconciliation Network of the World Evangelical Alliance, and ordained pastor in the Evangelical Free Churches in Germany.

Laurie George Busuttil, Associate Professor and Chair of Business at Redeemer University College.

Marilyn Draper, Assistant Professor of Practical Theology at the seminary of Tyndale University, church planter, and ordained minister with Canadian Baptists of Ontario and Quebec (CBOQ).

Matthew Friedman, Professor of Intercultural Studies and Global Ministry Program Director at Kingswood University.

Jonathan Fuller, OMF International Director for the Americas, and DMin student at Tyndale University.

Sam George, Global Catalyst of Diasporas for the Lausanne Movement and Director of Global Diaspora Institute at the Billy Graham Center of Wheaton College.

Sherman Lau, Manager of Agency Collaboration at Mission Central (formerly Missions Fest Vancouver), and DIS (Doctor of Intercultural Studies) student at Western Seminary.

LIST OF CONTRIBUTORS

Terry LeBlanc, Mi'kmaq/Acadian, founding chair and Director of NAIITS: An Indigenous Learning Community (NAIITS) (formerly North American Institute for Indigenous Theological Studies).

Shu-Ling Lee, Downtown Markham Campus Pastor and Discipleship Pastor at Richmond Hill Christian Community Church.

Glenn Martin, Managing Editor of *Glocal Conversations* Journal with the University of the Nations.

Lisa Hanmi Pak, Global Strategist of Finishing the Task, former Regional Director for Ontario and Nunavut at the Canadian Bible Society, and DMin student at Tyndale University.

Claudia Rossetto, instructor at Columbia Bible College, and chaplain at Evergreen Baptist Housing.

Susan J. Van Weelden, Dean of the Social Sciences Division at Redeemer University College.

Dave Witt, Missional Network Developer for International Teams Canada, and DPT (Doctor of Practical Theology) student at McMaster Divinity College.

www.ingramcontent.com/pod-product-compliance
Lightning Source LLC
Chambersburg PA
CBHW070329230426
43663CB00011B/2258